EX LIBRIS

TONY BENN

A Blaze of Autumn Sunshine

The Last Diaries

Selected and edited by Ruth Winstone

HUTCHINSON
LONDON

Published by Hutchinson 2013

3 5 7 9 10 8 6 4 2

Copyright © Tony Benn 2013

Tony Benn has asserted his right under the Copyright, Designs
and Patents Act, 1988, to be identified as the author of this work

This book is a work of non-fiction

First published in Great Britain in 2013 by
Hutchinson
Random House, 20 Vauxhall Bridge Road,
London SW1V 2SA
www.randomhouse.co.uk

Addresses for companies within The Random House Group Limited can
be found at: www.randomhouse.co.uk/offices.htm

The Random House Group Limited Reg. No. 954009

A CIP catalogue record for this book
is available from the British Library

ISBN 9780091943875

The Random House Group Limited supports the Forest Stewardship
Council® (FSC®), the leading international forest-certification
organisation. Our books carrying the FSC label are printed on FSC®-
certified paper. FSC is the only forest-certification scheme supported by
the leading environmental organisations, including Greenpeace. Our
paper procurement policy can be found at:
www.randomhouse.co.uk/environment

Typeset by SX Composing DTP, Rayleigh, Essex
Printed and bound by CPI Group (UK) Ltd, Croydon, CR0 4YY

Contents

	Editor's note	vii
	Illustrations	ix
	Who's who	x
	Abbreviations	xiii
	Foreword	xiv
1	May–October 2007: Brown's honeymoon	1
2	October–December 2007: The calm before the storm	56
3	January–May 2008: The end of New Labour	82
4	May–August 2008: Crisis of capitalism	124
5	August–December 2008: Labour in crisis	158
6	January–July 2009: Brown's nemesis	203
7	2009–13: Life after diaries	278
	Index	295

Editor's note

This, the last volume of Tony Benn's *Diaries*, opens in May 2007 with Kofi Annan inviting him to join Jimmy Carter, Richard Branson, Desmond Tutu, Peter Gabriel, Mary Robinson and other international 'Elders' at a gathering in South Africa. In July 2009 the dictated diary ceases, as Tony Benn having just had an operation muses on an uncertain future with the words 'That's all there is, for my diary, unless something sensational happens tonight.'

Because these years are so full of personal reflections by Tony in his eighties – on ageing, on failing health, on widowerhood – as well as a record of dramatic and unexpected political and social developments, I have kept the editing to a minimum, retaining, I hope, the personality of the diarist as he dictated, sometimes falteringly. I have also left uncut a greater proportion than usual of the original text, to give the reader a fuller picture of Tony Benn's life as he approaches the 'autumn sunshine'.

The latter part of the book is a reconstruction by him of the period July 2009 to the present, with his insights of a personal and political nature on these extraordinary times.

As ever the book could not have been completed without the work of Alison McPherson, who has transcribed millions of words with great empathy, the copy-editing of Mandy Greenfield on whom

I relied so much this time, and the editorial advice of Emma Mitchell of Hutchinson. Georgina Manley stepped in to assist at the early stages of the editing during my mother's illness and death in 2012, and Lucy Quinn and Laura Rohde helped to research, correct and edit the account of the latter years 2009–2013 which Tony Benn had to reconstruct from memory.

It has been a great privilege to be associated with the *Diaries* over the course of twenty-seven years, and to count myself one of Tony's closest friends.

Ruth Winstone

June 2013

Illustrations

1   On the set of *Will and Testament* at Ealing Studios
2   Filming at the House of Commons
3   Tony through the lens at Ealing Studios
4   On the set of a recreation of Tony's office
5   Headlines on set for the film *Will and Testament*
6   On location for *Will and Testament* with Michael Miles and
      Mervyn Gerrard
7   Tolpuddle Martyrs plate
8   Make Tea Not War mug
9   40th anniversary of the Welfare State plate
10 Durham Miners Gala plate
11 Vial of Tony's blood
12 With Ruth Winstone and Tony Whittome
13 Tony handling a racing pigeon
14 On tour with his editor Ruth Winstone
15 At University of Lincoln
16 With Billy Bragg and friends at the Tolpuddle celebration
17 With his brother David
18 With family and friends in the empty family home
19 With his children Joshua, Melissa, Hilary and Stephen
20 With his only daughter Melissa

Who's who

Caroline Wedgwood Benn (Pixie) (wife of Tony Benn) d. 2000

Children
Stephen Benn (m. Nita Clarke)
Hilary Benn (m. Sally Clark)
Melissa Benn (Lissie) (m. Paul Gordon)
Joshua Benn (Josh)

Grandchildren
Michael (m. Penny Brough)
James (m. Dr Blake Pritchard)
William
Jonathan (m. Zohreh Khairoldin)
Caroline
Emily
Daniel
Hannah
Sarah

Other Family
BENN, David	Brother, b. 1928
BENN, Piers	Son of David and June Benn
NESTOR, Frances	Daughter of David and June Benn
NESTOR, Michael	Husband of Frances Nestor
NESTOR, Michael	(Little Michael) Son of Frances and Michael Nestor

Friends and colleagues

BAILEY, Roy	Retired professor, folk singer
BICKERSTAFFE, Rodney	Former General Secretary of UNISON, President of War on Want
BRAGG, Billy	Musician and political activist
BURROWS, Saffron	Actress, political activist
BUTLER, David	Political historian
BYRNE, Tony	Builder
CAMPBELL, Barbara	Helped care for Caroline during her illness and continued to help TB
CARTER, Peter	Architect, close friend of Caroline and the family (known as PC)
CORSTON, Baroness	(Jean Corston) Chairman of the Parliamentary Labour Party; former MP for Bristol East
GABRIEL, Peter	Musician and activist
GERMAN, Lindsey	Leading campaigner of the Stop the War Movement and coalition of Resistance
GRICE, John	TB's driver
HERBERT, Grahame	Architect, designer of the 'Seat Case'
KAPLINSKY, Natasha	Television presenter
McDONNELL, John	Labour MP for Hayes and Harlington
MILIBAND, David	Labour Minister for Education and Skills; Secretary of State for the Environment and Rural Affairs; Foreign Secretary
MILIBAND, Edward	Leader of the Labour Party
MILIBAND, Marion	Socialist writer, mother of David and Edward, widow of Ralph Miliband
MITCHELL, Emma	Publicity director and associate editorial director, Hutchinson, Random House
MULLIN, Chris	MP for Sunderland South 1987–2010; Minister in Departments of Environment, International Development and Foreign Office
REES, John	Leading campaigner of the Stop the War Movement and Coalition of Resistance
SHALLICE, Jane	Former deputy head, Holland Park School
SILVERTON, Kate	Journalist and presenter
SIMPSON, Alan	Labour MP for Nottingham South 1992–2010
WHITTOME, Tony	Editorial director, Hutchinson, Random House
WILLSMER, Basil	Long-time family friend; Essex builder. Died 2009
WINSTONE, Ruth	Editor of the Benn Diaries since 1985; senior clark, House of Commons; close friend

Political figures

ANNAN, Kofi	Secretary General of the UN
BLAIR, Tony	Prime Minister 1997–2007, Labour MP for Sedgefield
BROWN, Gordon	Prime Minister 2007–2010, Chancellor of the Exchequer 1997–2007
CAMERON, David	Conservative Prime Minister 2010–
CAMPBELL, Alastair	Prime Minister's Official Spokesman 1997–2003
CLEGG, Nick	Liberal Democrat Deputy Prime Minister, 2010 –
HAYES, Billy	General Secretary, Communication Workers' Union
MAJOR, John	Conservative Prime Minister 1990–1997
MANDELSON, Lord	(Peter Mandelson) Former Labour MP, Cabinet Minister and EU Commissioner
REID, John	Secretary of State for Scotland, Northern Ireland, Health, Defence, Home Secretary
SHORT, Clare	Secretary of State for International Development
STRAW, Jack	Home Secretary; Foreign Secretary; Leader of the House of Lords 1997–2007; Lord Chancellor
THATCHER, Baroness	Conservative Prime Minister 1979–1990
WOODLEY, Tony	General Secretary, TGWU (part of UNITE)

Abbreviations

AIPAC	American–Israeli Public Affairs Committee
ARP	Air Raid Precautions
BNP	British National Party
CAP	Common Agricultural Policy
CBI	Confederation of British Industry
CIA	Central Intelligence Agency
CND	Campaign for Nuclear Disarmament
CWU	Communication Workers' Union
Defra	Department for the Environment, Food and Rural Affairs
DFID	Department for International Development
FBU	Fire Brigades' Union
GMB	General Municipal and Boilermakers (Union)
LAP	Labour Action for Peace
LSE	London School of Economics
NEC	National Executive Committee
NFU	National Farmers' Union
NUM	National Union of Mineworkers
PCS	Public and Commercial Services Union
PKK	Kurdish Workers' Party
SWP	Socialist Workers' Party
TGWU	Transport and General Workers' Union (now part of UNITE the Union)
TUC	Trades Union Congress
UKIP	United Kingdom Independence Party
UN	United Nations
UNISON	The public service union
UNRRA	United Nations Relief and Rehabilitation Administration
WBAI	American listener-supported radio station based in New York

Foreword

Concluding his penultimate diaries, Tony Benn wrote in July 2007:

> When my dad was my age, in 1958, just before he died, I took my
> eldest two boys to parliament to be with their grandfather. In a
> broadcast describing his political and family life for the BBC, my
> dad ended with these words, 'So you will understand that I live
> in a blaze of autumn sunshine.' I too am enjoying that autumn
> sunshine now with my grandchildren, and although I may never
> publish another volume of diaries, if I ever did, I think the best
> possible title would be just that: A Blaze of Autumn Sunshine.

Tony has had the good fortune to see *A Blaze of Autumn Sunshine* in print,
but it is a book of two halves which needs some explanation. From
June 2007, when the previous volume ended as the premiership moved
from Blair to Brown, until July 2009, Benn continued his life-long habit
of recording events in his own life, in parliament, in Britain and on
the international stage. These included his participation in the early
formation of the 'Elders', his presidency of the Stop the War movement
and his patronage of a number of campaigning groups at home. He
also maintained a busy schedule of meetings and lectures. The two
years were dominated by the banking collapses which precipitated a
wider international debt crisis affecting the Western world.

In July 2009, Tony Benn suffered a health collapse and, at the age of eighty-four, after sixty-nine years of writing, typing or dictating almost every day, he stopped keeping his diary altogether although, once recovered, he continued to maintain a formidable programme of public engagements. Further highly significant changes and dramatic events occurred both in Tony Benn's own life and in the world at large between July 2009 and the present year, 2013, and these are recalled in the latter part of the book.

Chapter One

May–October 2007:
Brown's honeymoon

Friday 11 May 2007

While I was snoozing, Kofi Annan rang. He said he very much hoped I would be able to come to Africa at the end of May. I had previously had a phone call from Richard Branson about a meeting of the 'Elders' in South Africa, but with no other details. Mandela's going, Carter's going, Mary Robinson's going, and also somebody called Hernando de Soto Polar, a right-wing economist. Oh, Desmond Tutu is also going to be there, so it is very tempting.

To the Victoria and Albert Museum, where I gave lecture on slavery. Huge attendance! It's a maze going round all the stuff that had been stolen from our colonies!

Three young women drove me home, in a tiny little French car.

So, there we are – that's the first day of my new diary: *A Blaze of Autumn Sunshine.*

Monday 14 May

Up at six, after a good eight hours in bed.

Ruth Winstone suggested that Josh should come to South Africa with me.

I decided to write to Gordon Brown enclosing a draft legislation, which I introduced twenty years ago, that would transfer all the royal prerogatives to the House of Commons. Among the sponsors in 1987 was Dawn Primarolo, who is of course Brown's Financial Secretary to the Treasury. I also sent a copy to Ed Miliband, and referred in my letter to Gordon to the fact that Ed had worked in *my* office as a young student twenty years ago.

Josh is very happy to come to South Africa.

Tuesday 15 May
I did receive, in the course of the day, a formal invitation from Richard Branson and Peter Gabriel to go the founding meeting of the Elders' conference. I must say, it's a wonderful opportunity to meet Carter and Mandela, Tutu and Mary Robinson, and King Hussein of Jordan. I'm getting quite excited about it.

In the evening, I went by taxi to the Soho Hotel to see a film called *Taking Liberties*. Michael Mansfield and Shami Chakrabarti were there. It was a wonderful film, amusing in the way it was presented, but terrifying – it was the Blair legacy. It made my blood run cold watching how all our civil liberties have been eroded.

Wednesday 16 May
There was a rattle on the basement door, and I opened it up and there was Saffron Burrows! So I gave her a huge hug, and then another hug, and then a kiss and another hug, and she gave me a hug. She said she was going to the Cannes Film Festival and would be back next week, and hoped to see me before I went to South Africa, so I hope that will be done. She's so sweet, I must say!

Thursday 17 May
A mass of papers were emailed through about the Elders – I thought my printer was going to run out. This organisation has been planned for years, so the idea that I thought of it first is an illusion. I'm only an adviser, I'm not one of the Elders themselves, but I wouldn't be sorry if they let me in on the discussions.

Of course what I also realise is that it's a very high-level group and it has a top-down perspective on the world, whereas my contribution

– in so far as it's of any value – will be more historical, philosophical, religious and visionary, and I don't know how easily it's going to fit in. They've sent briefings on Darfur, on Zimbabwe and all sorts of other things.

In the evening, I finished picking twelve items for *With Great Pleasure*, which is going to be broadcast on 13 June on Radio 4.

My God, I have a heavy programme! Whoo! I just hope my health stands up. I've got to go and have my pacemaker checked next week, and if the hospital veto the trip, then it's off.

Saturday 19 May
Jimmy Carter, in a BBC broadcast today, described Blair as 'abominable'. Of course, yesterday or the day before Blair was in Washington, receiving a warm tribute from Bush – so humiliating for everybody! I think he's overdone it. I think he's turning people off, and now he has no patronage, no authority; I think it's the beginning of the end of Blairites – he won't find many of them soon.

Up at 5.45, was collected at 7.30 and taken to Burford. I arrived there early, talked to a few people, and then there was the interment of Alan Hicks's ashes in the churchyard. Alan Hicks was a factory worker, went into the army, was captured, was used as slave labour (working in Germany for IG Farben, who made the equipment used in the Holocaust), then came back, became active in the Workers' Educational Association. He is a keen member of CND; at the heart of the Levellers' movement when it started again in 1975; he ended up with a BA from Oxford Brookes. His wife, Hazel, was at the church. It was a lovely family event – I said a word or two.

I was freezing cold. There were rain showers in Burford and I hadn't taken a coat, or hat. I was also very hungry, so when I got back I had a huge meal, turned on all the heaters and tried to have a bit of a sleep for half an hour.

Oh, Kofi Annan rang this afternoon and said, 'Is everything all right for Africa?' so I had a lovely talk to him.

Sunday 20 May
Not a word in *The Sunday Times* about the fact that Jimmy Carter said yesterday that Blair's support for Bush was abominable.

Monday 21 May
Bad, troubled night.

It's a nightmarish time for the next few days: hospital, a lecture, then a broadcast tomorrow; on Wednesday up to Southport to speak to the prison officers, plus a lecture (on 'Living after seventy' – I want to make it thoughtful, but I haven't had time to think about it yet). On Friday I'm off to South Africa . . .

Josh and I are planning the trip. He rang round a number of insurance companies to see if he could get me insurance, but when he told them I had chronic leukaemia and that I had a pacemaker, they said 'uninsurable'. Age Concern wouldn't insure me! In the end he found an insurance company that would give me year-long insurance for £1,800 or something, but wouldn't cover me if I had a heart attack or died of cancer. So I am now uninsurable! It was what you might call a reminder, by means of market forces, that I am legally almost dead.

Tuesday 22 May
Took a 148 bus to the House of Commons and was so early that I had time to have a cup of tea on the Terrace, before going over to St Thomas's for my pacemaker check. They adjusted it a little bit. The registrar said there was a bit of a risk, with high blood pressure and high cholesterol, of a stroke. We discussed medicines like warfarin, but they didn't want to give it to me before I went to Africa.

Friday 25 May, visit to the 'Elders', South Africa
We were greeted at Heathrow airport by a young Virgin official called Nyree, who took Josh and me to the Clubhouse in Terminal 3. The cabin was called Upper Class: it had beds, and Josh and I were next to each other. He was immensely helpful, sorting me out, and then the air hostesses starting coming round with everything you could want. One young woman, absolutely immaculate, said, 'I'm your therapist', so I said, 'Thank you very much, but I'm fine.' By eleven o'clock I was sound asleep. The fact that I had a proper bed meant there was no strain from the travelling at all.

Saturday 26 May

Arrived at Johannesburg, and met again by someone from Virgin. Taken to a little, federal airport, and caught a flight, in a twin-engined jet, which landed at an airstrip where we had to get out and wait. Then another little plane came in, this time with a single engine, and flew us to the airstrip at the game reserve – Richard Branson's land – which is called Ulusaba.

Discovered, when we arrived there, that Nelson Mandela had left that morning and that I'd only missed him by a matter of hours – that's a pity.

First we sat in a round-table arrangement, and Archbishop Tutu led a discussion about the Elders' project: whether they should go to Darfur, intervene in Zimbabwe, and so on – all sorts of issues. I said something about nuclear power – I forget what it was now. Mary Robinson, the former President of Ireland, was there; and Jimmy Carter, former President of the United States.

Then we were driven to Rocky Lodge, up a huge hill, and had dinner (with an African woman singing in the background). I sat with Richard Branson and Peter Gabriel (who lives round the corner from me in London), and with Carter and Tutu. After dinner we just talked about things generally. It really was a fantastic day, and to think it started about midnight in London and ended here, in Africa!

Sunday 27 May

Up at about quarter-past five and went on a game drive, in a little open-topped jeep. We saw lots of animals: impalas (look like little deer), antelopes, hippos submerged in water, a beautiful lioness – would be about five years old – sitting watching wildebeest, which looked so thin. The lion began approaching them and they began to scatter. Spectacular!

Then we got back, and at eight o'clock there was a service led by Desmond Tutu in the hotel. He conducted it in a very informal way, with lots of jokes, and took the Bible round for people to read from. Carter read one bit. Then we had bread and wine, and an African woman sang a song, (the same woman who had sung at the dinner last night). Afterwards, everybody hugged – it was quite happy-clappy (except Desmond Tutu is much more serious than that).

At breakfast I sat next to a Professor Kiang from Beijing University. It was very interesting, talking about China and capitalism. He himself is a Buddhist. Seventy per cent of the wealth in China is now owned by 4 per cent of the people – it's a real capitalist country. But, he said, socialism is coming back, through young people. They are now beginning to complain about the inequalities.

At 10 a.m., we had Kofi Annan address us on a video link. He said the Elders may be attacked for what they do, and that we've got to contact the real players, who are not necessarily the most important people; that we've got to make the case for the Elders, and to choose members very carefully. I intervened a few times and said that we're looking for self-government for the world. I talked a little bit about the history of Zimbabwe, and said we must be prepared to speak to everybody.

We had a report by Ray Chambers, who is one of the (very wealthy) founders. He was talking about the need for a strategic plan. A woman told us that McKinsey were advising us.

We had a long presentation on Darfur by Gayle Smith, who had worked in Africa for twenty years and was an adviser to Clinton. She said it's partly a tribal conflict, partly a conflict between central power and local power, partly a conflict between the farmers who find their farms being eroded by the nomads, and partly because the central government is so awful.

The question of China and its interest in oil came up. Then Zimbabwe. Obviously the Elders want to get rid of Mugabe. That came out quite clearly in the video we saw yesterday.

We then came to Burma, and Desmond Tutu raised the question of Aung San Suu Kyi, and burst into tears. He obviously knew her very well. We came on to the Nigerian elections, and a young Nigerian man spoke. He stressed the importance of African leadership, that African institutions should be taking the lead, which I agree with of course.

The Middle East: Carter, who has played an active part there, intervening all the time, said that we must talk to Hamas. It is a scandal that since Hamas was freely elected in Gaza in 2006 (his own Carter Centre verifying that the elections were free and fair) the Middle East Quartet – the UN, the US, the EU and Russia – had refused to recognise the elections. The Elders must intervene.

Then we had lunch, and I was put at the Elders' table. Actually, it wasn't just Elders. I sat opposite Richard Branson.

About six o'clock we went over, in the Land Rovers, to have dinner in the bush. We drove for ages and then came to an area where all the trees had lights in them and there were masses of tables with heaters over them. There were African drummers and dancers – a tremendous noise – and it was a sort of glorified global barbecue!

I had a word with Scilla Elworthy, whom I have met before, a very nice woman, and she discussed with me the appointment of new Elders and gave me a little handbook of all the potential Elders and, to my delight, I was listed there. I was pleased about that.

After dinner, Josh and I came back and went to bed.

Monday 28 May
Josh went off on the game drive this morning, and he saw leopards and rhinos. I stayed back because I had to pack, and I wanted to prepare my final points.

Had breakfast at 8.45 with Jimmy Carter and Mary Robinson. I mentioned to Carter how my officials at the Energy Department had been very suspicious of his strict attitude to proliferation, and that I was very much on his side. I told him about materials supplied to Israel without my knowledge, and about the way in which our plutonium had gone to the Pentagon for their nuclear-weapons programme, and so on.

Just before the session began at 9.30 I said to Desmond Tutu, 'If there's a chance of allowing me to say something, I'd like to.' He said my request was registered.

Then, at 9.35, Jean Oelwang (Branson's organiser) and Richard described the project's plans. I'm not an Elder, though I'm on the list of possible Elders; among the other names was Oprah Winfrey, the American interviewer, who has a worldwide reputation now; and possibly Bill Clinton and Al Gore.

A discussion took place as to when the Elders could be officially announced – should it be on Human Rights Day on 10 December, or earlier, on Nelson Mandela's birthday, 18 July? If the latter, it could be in Johannesburg.

Then Carter made his contribution about the importance of the Middle East and healthcare.

Before that, Graça Machel (Nelson Mandela's wife) said, 'Whatever you do, don't oversell it', and I agree strongly with that. I said the Elders are about hope and that's enough. It will arouse great excitement, but don't be too detailed to begin with.

We went back to issues again: Israel, Zimbabwe, Darfur, Burma, Nigeria, Iran, and so on.

I took my opportunity. 'If I may say something about the things that have moved me over the years: in Rhodesia, during the war, an eighteen-year-old pilot said to an African who was sweeping the path, "Voetsek!", which is a very rude word for *Get out of the way!* The African stood up and quoted Rousseau: "Man is born free, and everywhere he is in chains." Tom Paine said, "My country is the world; my religion is to do good." And Reinhold Niebuhr – I know President Carter is interested in Niebuhr – said: "Man's capacity for evil makes democracy necessary, and man's capacity for good makes democracy possible." '

Shortly afterwards Desmond Tutu said, 'Tony, you wanted to say something?' I replied, 'Archbishop, I've said it already.' He said, 'You are restored!' Such a lovely guy.

Mary Robinson said that whatever we do, we mustn't mention that we're going to intervene in Zimbabwe because it would make it worse.

'Leave Zimbabwe entirely to Kofi Annan,' said Tutu.

Then a brief discussion of Darfur again, and Burma, and it was decided to invite Aung San Suu Kyi.

I said I thought we should consider including Mordechai Vanunu, and Tutu said, 'We can't take up every civil-liberties case.' I said, 'It's not quite that – it is a question of his campaign on Israel's nuclear weapons.' Anyway it was brushed to one side.

Professor Kiang, whom I've got to like very much indeed, suggested that the Elders might meet in China.

Carter said that we've been working with Sam Nunn and Henry Kissinger on nuclear proliferation (I thought: God, is the old American Establishment being brought in!). And then, believe it or not, Richard Branson said, 'I think I'll have a word with Gordon

Brown – I think I can persuade him to abandon Trident.' Whoof!

Tutu called on me again, and I said, 'Well, it is really the old question of war and peace. During the war we realised we could rebuild society by planning for peace, instead of killing Germans, and that's how the Welfare State came about.' Tutu said, 'Tony, it is for that contribution that you were asked', which was very nice of him. He said, 'You bring such passion to it.'

There was a brief discussion about members. There are three vacancies and it was agreed that two of them should be women. It was finally agreed that the Elders would meet on 17 July in Johannesburg, on the eve of Nelson Mandela's eighty-ninth birthday.

We had a collection for the staff, said our goodbyes and headed home.

Tuesday 29 May

We landed at Heathrow airport just after seven. Met by someone from Virgin, cleared customs and everything, and were given a limousine home.

It was really a very remarkable event. My impressions (I'll put them down now) were, first of all, about Josh – I mean, he was fantastic! I couldn't have done it without him, and I now realise my limitations. Virgin helped, but even so, I couldn't have done it on my own.

But what I felt, on balance, was that it was as if I had been invited to attend a drafting committee for the Sermon on the Mount, under Archbishop Tutu, and another drafting committee on the Declaration of Independence, with Jimmy Carter.

There were a couple of funny things. I did feel that a lot of rich white men, living in a very wealthy game reserve, discussing poverty, was a bit odd – but there you are. They have the resources and, as Josh says, 'He who pays the piper calls the tune.' I think what will emerge from the Elders is really a sort of global House of Lords, with all their political feelings. I was almost certainly the only socialist there, although I suppose Mandela had been a socialist. But they let me take part, and of course I would be very honoured if I was made an Elder, but the main thing is actually having been there.

So, that's it – that's my Africa diary.

Wednesday 30 May
Taxi with Ruth to Paddington, and caught the 1.52 to Malvern. I left my anorak on the train and it had the lovely woolly cap Ruth gave me, in one pocket, and the red neck-scarf that Stephen gave me in the other, and I was really sorry about that, but I'll try and get it back.

Malvern was just like the railway station in *Brief Encounter* – fantastic! Anyway, from there we changed trains for Hereford and went to the Swan Hotel.

Thursday 31 May
Hay-on-Wye. Up at 5.45, had tea, breakfast and then went to give my lecture to 1,254 people.

A few photographs were taken by *The Guardian*, and then I gave a *Guardian* podcast. In the afternoon, to the live Sky TV feed: Mariella Frostrup was interviewing someone called David Crystal (who is a great expert on language) and Harry Hill (who was a doctor and is now a comedian). I was asked to pick two books that I hadn't read and would like to, so I chose *Life of Pi* by Yann Martel and *Small Island* by Andrea Levy. Ruth had briefed me on them, of course.

Then we were driven to Hereford, caught the train to Newport, and from there missed the London train by two minutes. As we waited in Newport, lots of people came up – for example, a lawyer who'd written to me years ago about Chomsky and Niebuhr. Then an older man, who said his wife had been to some of my lectures . . . quite a few encounters like that.

Tomorrow Hilary and I are doing a joint interview with *The Observer*, and I've agreed to do an interview with Chomsky over a satellite link, at Loughborough University.

Friday 1 June
The Observer interview was at 9.30, and Hilary and I talked about our family influences and then moved on to how politics really worked. At the end we discussed Iraq.

Took the train to Loughborough and was met by Will Learmonth, a very imaginative twenty-six-year-old who had arranged this link-up with Noam Chomsky. I sat in a chair in Loughborough and Chomsky sat in a chair in New York, and we could hear each other quite clearly. In the course of the hour I had about one-third of the time, because he spoke at great length. I didn't disagree with him, but I added dimensions that he'd left out and made points that I wanted to make. As we approached the hour, I had to chip in to thank him very much and call it off. He treated me as a distinguished professor might treat an intelligent student who keeps interrupting. But I think it was worthwhile. I think it was a great success actually. I think either Al Jazeera or Channel 4 will take it.

It's been a killing programme for eight days really – an incredible week. I'm absolutely whacked!

Sunday 3 June
I had nine or ten hours' sleep.

Thursday 7 June
I prepared for *Question Time*, which I'm doing in Truro tonight. I hate doing it at short notice, because I don't have time to do all my research. They pay £150, and since it takes about twenty-four hours' preparation and travel, it's only just about the rate of the minimum wage! So I might mention that to David Dimbleby.

Well, I worked at home, and then was picked up and taken to the station to catch the 2.05 train to Truro, which arrived at 6.44 – that's four and three-quarter hours, but it was a lovely journey through the West Country. A beautiful day, through Taunton, Exeter, St Austell and Plymouth. On the train I met Julia Goldsworthy, the Liberal Democrat MP for Falmouth and Camborne, a bright, young, not particularly radical Liberal.

On the panel: Melanie Phillips (journalist and author), Francis Maude (Chairman of the Conservative Party) and Boris Berezovsky (one of the Russian oligarchs; he was allowed by Yeltsin to buy state assets for a song, became a multi-multimillionaire and used the money to fund Yeltsin's election victory, then Putin's election victory; he fell out with Putin, successfully applied for asylum in the UK, and has recently called for a coup to oust Putin.)* So that was the panel!

* Berezovsky committed suicide in his Ascot home in 2013.

I had rightly guessed all the questions: on the new Cold War, on the Olympic logo, on terror laws, on Britishness and on the environment, and I did quite well.

Came back on the 10.44 sleeper.

Friday 8 June
Arrived at Paddington about 5.30 a.m. There was to have been a BBC car, but it didn't turn up, and so I caught a cab home and went to bed for two hours, I was so tired.

Saturday 9 June
I have bad backache and I'm exhausted. I wonder whether it's psychological?

I caught the bus to Central Hall Westminster, for the Compass conference. Compass is a sort of left-wing, soft-left Fabian Society group that has attracted the attention of a lot of people in the centre of the Party, though not the so-called hard-left or the Stop the War Coalition. It indicates that there is, within the Party, an unease about New Labour.

So I went along, wondering what it was about. There were 1,000 people there, and I attended two fringes.

I went first to the Demos fringe meeting, in a little room in Central Hall. Demos is made up of the old *Marxism Today* ex-communists, who were very right-wing and opened the way for Blair and all that. It was an absolutely packed meeting. The other speaker was Salma Yaqoob, who is a psychotherapist in Birmingham, a councillor for the Respect Party. I like Salma very much indeed, and we had a bit of a talk. There were the two of us, and one other guy from, I think, Demos speaking, and it was just an open discussion. I argued that you had to make the UN democratic.

It was very good, and from there I went to the *Labour Left Briefing* fringe; John McDonnell was there and made a fine speech; he was ready to listen, and not hard-left at all.

I had taken a little stool with me, because I simply can't stand any more. I found, at the very first meeting, that there weren't enough chairs, so I sat on my stool, fell over and banged my arm on the radiator. I used my stool again later when I had to wait for the 148 bus on Victoria Street to Notting Hill Gate.

I've had some stuff from the Labour Party – no mention of 'New Labour' now, just the Labour Party. I think that phrase will sink with Blair. You never know. Parliament is the buckle between the people and the law, and the Labour Party is the buckle between progressive people and their representatives in Parliament. Both those buckles seem to be strengthening a bit. I mean, with the Tories calling for a written constitution, which I've already provided, and with the Tories and the Labour Party wanting to deal with the royal prerogatives, which I had also dealt with in a draft bill, I feel that those little acorns that I planted years ago are beginning to appear as . . . as oak trees.

Monday 11 June
I'm not sleeping, but I relaxed a bit yesterday.

Went to see Dr Pettifer for blood tests, and she said my blood pressure was now normal, which is good news. Later on I did a radio interview on ageing.

Tuesday 12 June
Jonathan was here from ten till two in the afternoon – we had a lovely talk! He has had very good results from university. He just wanted to talk about his work, how he's getting on. He told me that someone had asked him, 'What class are you?' And he said, 'I'm a member of the thinking class', which I thought was a smashing answer!

Friday 15 June
Blow me down, an email came through today saying that, in Johannesburg, the Elders were launched by Mandela, Carter, Tutu and Kofi Annan. I had no notification of it at all, and Josh's instinct was correct – I wasn't the right person for it. I'm glad I had a view of it. They are very, very rich . . . Richard Branson, a billionaire, and Peter Gabriel, a great pop star. They've apparently raised £18 million to keep it going for three years.

I went through the legal report on *The Diaries*. The lawyer, Roger Field, had removed a lot of abuse that I'd put in, and I realised – reading it all – that I'm an angry old man. I have been very abusive, and despite all I say about not making personal attacks, my diary is full of them: 'he's an awful man', 'I loathe him', 'he's pompous', 'he's arrogant'. So the libel lawyer has done me a good turn in making the diary . . . well, much kinder.

Sunday 17 June
Baddish back, took some ibuprofen. Felt a bit gloomy and depressed all day.

Cleared my emails and spoke to Lissie, Josh and Steve.

Today is the fifty-eighth anniversary of my wedding . . . fifty-eighth anniversary – I can't believe I married Caroline nearly sixty years ago. As I've put in my diary before, what is so strange is that my life was divided: divided first between the time before I was married and the time after I married. Now, it's divided between the time before I was married, the time after I married, and the time since Caroline died. It's strange . . . very strange.

Anyway, it's a boring entry, this Sunday, but that's what life's sometimes like.

Monday 18 June
At about twenty to eight I took a cab to the Serpentine Gallery, because I'd been asked to Tina Brown's party. (Tina had come to see me, last year, I think, when she was writing a book on Diana. I don't know why she wanted my contribution, but anyway.) I had read that the party was going to be a big celebrity affair, so I had some doubts about going . . . When I arrived there was a battery of photographers outside. At the moment I turned up there was a model parading as she went in, so I managed to jump in without turning to face the cameras.

It was crammed with just the sort of people I don't like. Three gossip columnists came up and asked why I was there. Who else was there? William Rees-Mogg, the former Editor of *The Times*, and Melvyn Bragg . . . just tons of celebrities. I hope there aren't any photographs of me in the papers tomorrow – it's the last thing I want to be seen doing!

Wednesday 20 June
Up at 5.25 and caught the Oxford Tube at 7.15 for Jimmy Carter's

honorary doctorate ceremony. Michael Carmichael was in Oxford. I'd only met him once before, an American, very active in Democrats Abroad. He's campaigned for . . . ooh, every Democratic candidate since the Sixties, I would think. He's working with Dennis Kucinich.

Just before eleven we went to All Souls and were met by Fraser Campbell, who had invited me, then to the Sheldonian Theatre for the Encaenia (the annual awarding of honorary degrees). Outside were a lot of animal-rights protesters shouting.

I hadn't been in the Sheldonian for about sixty-five years – I think the last time was when I got an MA that my mum bought me!

Chris Patten is the Chancellor, now that Roy Jenkins is dead. There was a huge ceremony, and Carter came in, in a red robe, looking very distinguished. The tribute to him was read in Latin, and Patten awarded him the degree in Latin (although all the English was printed alongside). I found it a bit boring actually. It reminded me of the House of Commons, although at least we do speak in English . . . institutions love all that ceremonial stuff.

Outside, when it was all over, I thought I'd go and have a word with the animal-rights protesters. I walked up and down and shook hands with quite a few of them, and asked if they knew about Safer Medicines, and of course they did, and I think some of them remembered the fact that, a couple of years ago, I chaired a meeting on animal experimentation in Oxford.

Then we went over to All Souls for lunch. By this time it was quite sunny (there were a few drips of rain earlier) – all of the academics and honorary graduates standing in the Quadrangle in their bright robes in the sunshine.

Anyway, I saw William Waldegrave, John Redwood and Lord Butler. At lunch, to my amazement, I had been put on Carter's right. He remembered being together at the Elders' conference in South Africa. He said that there's no doubt whatsoever that the 2000 election had been fixed in Florida, and Bush didn't win. He talked about his relations with Jim Callaghan, and how he liked him, but didn't get on so well with Thatcher.

I asked him whether he would be prepared to endorse any Democratic candidate this time, and he said: no, except for Al Gore, who I don't think is going to stand. I wondered whether he might agree to endorse Dennis Kucinich, but he said: no, though he knows him and talks to him from time to time.

I then asked him about Michael Moore, who is making the film *Sicko*. I think he'd met Moore. He certainly said he'd met Hugo Chávez. And then we talked about how authoritarian tendencies develop even in progressive groups.

I asked about the Elders. I said I thought that perhaps their main function was to open up channels of communication. They couldn't be an alternative government. But 'What have they achieved?' he asked. I agreed that's the problem, and we've got to try to lubricate the process of diplomacy. I put to him the idea that people who have held high office and were free had 'graduated' to becoming citizens of the world.

I asked about Gorbachev, and he said that Mandela thinks he let his country down.

We're only six months apart in age. I entered politics in 1950, and he didn't get in till '63; but Carter went to the top of the most powerful country in the world. As we left, Rosalynn Carter, his wife, made a special point of leaning over to shake me by the hand across the table. 'How very nice to see you again,' I said (we had met in South Africa).

If it weren't for Carter, I wouldn't have dreamed of going to Oxford for the Encaenia. I am glad I did – it was such an enjoyable day.

Thursday 21 June
Gordon Brown has offered Paddy Ashdown the job of Secretary of State for Northern Ireland in his government. Well, first of all, there already is a Secretary of State for Northern Ireland, Peter Hain, and to hear your job being offered to somebody else is a bit much. Secondly, Paddy Ashdown is a Liberal. It's all very well Brown saying he wants a government of all the talents, but for heaven's sake, if you vote Labour, you expect a Labour government, and Brown has a huge majority! I mean, if we had lost the election and it was a hung parliament, it would be a different matter, but what sort of sense does it make of democracy if you vote for one party and are governed by somebody from another party? It's a complete mockery! Of course, what it's done is to infuriate the Liberals. Menzies Campbell, the

Liberal Leader – who had been talking to Brown (which I think was a funny thing to do anyway), then said he wouldn't cooperate – discovers that Brown has offered a Cabinet job to one of his leading figures. So I think if that's Gordon Brown, then he has no political sense at all – he's in deep, deep trouble.

I think that's pretty well the end of . . . oh no, it isn't quite the end!

The last EU Summit that Blair will attend is taking place. They're trying desperately to get through this European constitution (which was defeated in France and Holland, at the last referenda), by calling it treaty *amendments*. The Poles are hostile to it, and said today that one of their objections was that Poland had fewer votes than Germany – Germany having killed so many Poles during the War. Well, that has infuriated the Germans and everybody else!

Saturday 23 June

In the early hours Blair, predictably, agreed to the modified European constitution, on the grounds that all his points had been met – *his* points, I might add! – about a charter of rights, voting, foreign policy and so on. And then Gordon Brown said, 'Oh, we're not having a referendum – all our points have been met.' All of *his* points have been met! So all this talk about consulting people is ridiculous, and the Tory Party has, quite properly, come out in favour of a referendum. I shall give full support for that campaign. If Brown wants, and Blair wants, the European treaty, well, they should vote for the bloody thing, not tell us that because they're satisfied we can't have a view. Fundamentally undemocratic! It makes me really angry.

So anyway, that's the next stage . . . a decision on our relations with Europe. I shall throw myself into that, because democracy is being snuffed out. The idea that we'll have a President of Europe we haven't elected, a Foreign Minister for Europe we haven't elected . . . Britain's been reduced to a local authority!

So, that's the end of Saturday 23 June, which of course is the anniversary of my brother Mike's death in 1944 – sixty-three years ago. He'd have been eighty-five, bless his heart, nearly eighty-six, probably a retired bishop, and if he'd lived, of course, he would have inherited the peerage, so my life would have been wholly different.

What a wonderful guy he was . . . I spoke to Dave, as I always do on these matters.

Sunday 24 June

Up at half-past six, took a cab to Paddington and got the train to Castle Cary, where I was met by the trade unionist Geoff Martin, who drove me to Glastonbury. He told me that a hundred-year-old Spanish Civil War veteran had come to the festival and been carried in on a stretcher. Whether he'd made a speech or not, I don't know.

Glastonbury's always fantastic. It had been pelting with rain, and the mud was up to my ankles. I'm so glad I took my wellington boots.

The thing about Glastonbury is that 175,000 people turn up and they're all themselves . . . it's really the re-creation of the old folk-festival atmosphere, so I love going, and I had three meetings to do.

The first one was 'Another World is Possible', and it was Frances O'Grady, Deputy General Secretary of the TUC, who took the chair. I hadn't prepared any notes, but I'd been thinking about it, and I must say it went down extremely well.

In the second speech at the Left Field I was alone on the platform, talking about weapons of mass destruction. After that I wandered around a bit, and met Kate Silverton of the BBC. She also conducted a little interview with me, which Dave told me he saw on BBC News 24. She asked me, 'What do you think Brown will do?' and I said, 'Well, the important thing is: what are *we* going to do?' The whole atmosphere there is exciting. It's a sort of permanent rallying cry of the people.

I was picked up and driven halfway across the muddy fields to the Green Tent – a little tent, only about eighty people there, including Michael Eavis, who owns Glastonbury. I had a brief word with him, and I spoke there and had questions and answers. One woman shrieked that Blair should be put on trial for war crimes, and I said, 'I'm not in favour of war-crimes tribunals – I'm in favour of truth and reconciliation.' So she shrieked at me and stamped out. Anyway, that was the only nasty thing in the whole day, and it wasn't particularly nasty.

Old friends from Appledore Shipyard were there, and tons of

people came up and said: I met you here, I met you there, years ago, did this and that; and it was very agreeable. I loved it!

Then I was driven from the Green Field to Castle Cary. A pack of people was there, including two girls with hoses and brooms wiping mud off people's wellington boots before they boarded the train, which was nice.

Back to Paddington, taxi home.

Josh rang. He thought that this deal over Europe would almost certainly mean that Blair would become the first President of Europe, in which case he'd be the unelected President of Europe, still senior to Brown, who would be the unelected Prime Minister of a country where there was no referendum on the proposal. Josh is very shrewd, politically.

Wednesday 27 June

Tony Blair's last Prime Minister's Questions: I found it a bit revolting. He's as competent as ever – the lawyer with his brief – but it was less controversial because everybody paid tribute to him; and at the end, as he left the House, everybody stood and clapped and gave him a standing ovation, which I've never seen before in Parliament. But still, that's that.

Just as that finished, Lissie turned up, bless her heart. We went out to Marks & Spencer, bought lunch and came back and watched the TV. You saw Blair going to Buckingham Palace and resigning, with a scene outside Number 10 Downing Street as he left. You saw Brown thanking the Treasury and going to Buckingham Palace, staying for a long time and coming back. Then Brown went back to Downing Street – no cheering crowds, just himself and Sarah, his wife. He said that he'd do his utmost and he would be resolute, and then he went in.

Brown talks about a government of all the talents. He tried of course to get Paddy Ashdown, the former Liberal Leader, to be Northern Ireland Secretary, and later today he apparently had a talk with Shirley Williams.

Then I thought I ought to go to the House of Commons for the Campaign Group, of which I am still a member. The first item was a report from Pete Firmin of the Communication Workers' Union, on the industrial action at Royal Mail. I was told that TNT and these other private contractors, who are only interested of course in central areas, are still requiring the Royal Mail to deliver their stuff, even though they're their competitors, and of course they pay lower wages, so they're trying to cut the wages of the Royal Mail staff in order to bring them down to the level of these private contractors, who don't have to meet requirements to deliver in Orkney and Shetland and down in Cornwall. It's an absolute outrage!

I said I thought the Government had decided to destroy the Royal Mail, and that I feel very strongly they should get their case across to the public as far as possible, using leaflets and publicity.

There was quite a bit of speculation about Brown calling an early election.

Then the question came up as to what will happen to the left. Somebody said, and I think they may well be right, that Gordon Brown may discipline left MPs who vote against the Government.

If the economy goes wrong in a big way, I can imagine a screaming British National Pary, which is anti-Europe and has a certain appeal with the anti-immigration lot; and a left that is as divided as the German left in the 1930s.

But Brown is entitled to a fresh start of his own, and nobody should go off at half-cock. These are my personal thoughts anyway.

I'm very depressed – what Churchill called his 'black dog'. Politically depressed.

So that's the end of Wednesday 27 June 2007, a day I have longed for. Blair's gone up to Sedgefield and announced that he's going to resign his seat. There will be a by-election. There are all sorts of uncertainties about the Cabinet, and at this moment I have no idea whether Hilary will be in the new Cabinet or not, because there could be a clean sweep. God knows what will happen if Brown fills the vacancies with right-wingers.

Thursday 28 June
Had a reasonably late lie-in.

The reshuffle is in progress: no mention of Hilary . . . no mention of Hilary . . . and then he rang to say he'd been given Defra. He also said that Gordon Brown had given him a letter for me, thanking me for the information I'd sent him on transferring the royal prerogatives to Parliament. So a manuscript letter from Gordon, the day he became Prime Minister, is one for the archive.

Friday 29 June
Up at five. To the sorting offices to support the pickets.

Sunday 1 July
The smoking ban came into force in England today, so I feel a hunted man . . .

Had a flat battery in the car, and had to call the AA.

I managed to get to Hilary's house by taxi, where the whole family was gathered. Hilary was very happy with Defra, and he has got from Brown an agreement that he handles the international aspects of the environment, although no doubt Edward Miliband, who has been given Energy and Climate Change, will want to take charge.

While I was there I had a phone call from an FM station in Dublin, because I'd said I'd be available at eleven and I'd totally forgotten about it! Anyway, they rang on my mobile and I had half an hour with them about Blair's mission in the Middle East and about Brown's Cabinet, and so on and so on.

I rang Marion Miliband and had a long talk to her about David and Edward. She's obviously very pleased about it, as I would be.

Monday 2 July
Hilary was making a statement in the House of Commons today on the floods. He was very calm and competent, and received a warm welcome for his appointment.

Kate Silverton turned up about half-past eleven and said she was ravenous, so we went to the Pizza Express. Frederico arranged for us to have a table in the window. Then, after that, we went and had coffee at All Bar One, just across the way. Kate was really wanting to talk about her plans for her career to get beyond being a newsreader – to make programmes. She's interested in religion and diversity and the Middle East. She's a very scholarly woman and I hope I encouraged her a bit.

I filed this today – the handwritten letter from Gordon Brown:

Dear Tony,

I was so grateful to you for sending me your paper on the royal prerogative. I have asked Hilary to show you our new proposals. I hope you agree that, 30 years later than you wanted, action is being taken. Well done!
Gordon

Tuesday 3 July
My granddaughter Carrie came over at 9.30 and stayed for six hours, replying to sixty-three letters. She was brilliant – rapid, accurate and efficient. She was such fun to talk to. She's nearly nineteen, going to take a year off before she goes to college. I really enjoyed having her here.

At 3.30 I turned on the *Parliament* programme and watched Brown make a major constitutional statement. It was very thoughtful – it must have been worked on for ages. Jack Straw is now the Lord Chancellor within the Ministry of Justice, sitting in the House of Commons, so that's a fairly big change. He made a whole series of proposals that would give Parliament greater power, involve greater public consultation, and remove the royal prerogative and transfer it to the House of Commons. After it was over, I wrote Gordon a personal note:

Dear Gordon,

Many congratulations on your statement in the House today, which I watched throughout on TV. It was by far the most comprehensive analysis of constitutional relations in my lifetime and could have a profound influence on our whole political future. Your readiness to encourage a debate in a consensual way was equally important. This is a debate in which I hope to take part.
Yours, Tony

I posted that off and sent a copy to Hilary.
It is really very important now that Blair's gone, and necessary

to take a constructive approach to the new government. Although Brown is a neo-liberal in economic matters, and personally I have a lot of reservations, at the heart of it all is the fact that this is the beginning of the dismantling – with the consent of the new Prime Minister – of those centralised powers that Blair used in order to dominate the whole political situation.

I did a few office jobs.

There was a strange man outside the basement door this afternoon. I saw him there and thought he might have been from the roofing firm (who are fixing the leaking roof). He said, 'I'm waiting because the rain is pouring down.' So I said, 'Would you like a cup of tea?' 'No.' 'Would you like a chair?' 'No, I'm all right.' And then he disappeared. Afterwards I did wonder whether he'd been casing the joint!

Wednesday 4 July

Alan Johnston, the BBC man who was abducted and kidnapped in Gaza, was released today, partly through the influence of Hamas, which I think has done a bit of good for them – hope so.

I wrote an article for the *Guardian* on Brown's constitutional reforms, announced yesterday. It's the first time I've said anything good about a Labour government for a long time. (I also added points about the West Lothian question and about the EU referendum and about the House of Lords.) I think it will be useful, having done it.

Sanjiv Shah, my doctor friend in New York, rang me up to say he had watched Michael Moore's film *Sicko*, and at the part where I said 'Why is there always money for war but not for health?' apparently the audience applauded! That film will be seen by millions and millions of people. Good!

I didn't do very much in the afternoon. When you have a free day, you very often just do nothing.

In the evening I watched a programme on BBC about Cherie. Fiona Bruce interviewed her about her life at Number 10, and it was a terrible mistake on her part to have agreed to it. They simply looked up every nasty thing that had ever been said about Cherie and gave her an opportunity to reply – exactly what that awful man whose name I've forgotten [Piers Morgan] is always doing. It just isn't worth it, because all you do is remind people of horrible things, and your denials are very unconvincing.

So, it's now about quarter-past ten. I'll do a little bit more work, and go to bed.

Saturday 7 July
Rose very early to go to the post office because there was a Special Delivery letter that required a signature. I was going to go in the car, but when I went to the car, the battery was flat again, so I had to walk – took me about half an hour. The letter was from a nutter, enclosing three letters to send to the head of the CIA, Stella Rimington at MI5 and the Queen (I think), so it was a complete waste of time.

Saffron phoned from Los Angeles and we had a bit of a talk. She says that this contract for an American television series in which she plays a progressive lawyer in a public-service legal firm, would meet her financial requirements for many years.

Sunday 8 July
The Sunday Times had the front page and three inside pages on an interview with Alastair Campbell about his *Diaries*, so Blair is back on the front page again. Poor old Brown can't survive with continual coverage of Blair!

I drove to the annual Marxism conference, where I made a speech about how to achieve a left government, which is an interesting theme, pointing out the difficulties of cooperation, and so on.

Went back to do *The Writing on the Wall* show with Roy Bailey at the Marxism conference. Home by nine.

Monday 9 July
Up early, for BBC Radio on Alastair Campbell's *Diaries*, which of course I haven't read because I haven't seen them.

Campbell's *Diaries* had arrived by lunchtime, so I've got them by me now. They are a formidable piece of work: to have kept two and a half million words in manuscript and have them all transcribed. It is the work of a very loyal and devoted press officer to Blair, a man of enormous influence who was in on everything; a man who was never elected to Parliament or came through the professional Civil Service. He was what could be called a 'favourite', in America. On the question of the war, he was unrepentant that it was absolutely right to go to war and that Blair didn't lie. But it's a serious piece of work, which will tell us more about the Blair years than we'll ever learn from anybody else.

I realised that Tony Blair is no longer an MP. He 'took the Chiltern Hundreds' last week and so he's not an MP, he's not Prime Minister, and by Thursday of next week there'll be a new MP for Sedgefield, and Blair will be history. Except that, of course, Alastair Campbell's *Diary* has dominated the papers today.

Wednesday 11 July
Ruth and I discussed the possibility of another book, called 'Letters to my Grandchildren', about the sort of world the grandchildren – and their generation – are likely to inherit, and in which hopefully I can pass on a little bit of wisdom.

The Campaign Group was interesting – we heard from an Iraqi who described the oil law that is being pushed through by the Iraqi Government, under heavy pressure from the Americans, which would in effect mean that foreign companies could acquire and control and sell Iraqi oil and export the profits back to America. It's an outrage!

Afterwards I went up to the Smoking Room, and there were two Tories, Richard Shepherd (an independent and libertarian right-wing MP) and Sir Michael Spicer (who's also an independent right-wing MP). So I had a talk to them and they were extremely friendly. At one point Spicer asked me if I missed the Commons. I said, 'No, I miss my constituency.' He didn't quite understand that.

I remember my dad saying that the trouble with the House of Lords is that there is so much goodwill, and the House of Commons is just the same.

John Hutton, the new Minister for Business and Enterprise, said that Labour is the natural party of business. Digby Jones, businessman and former Director General of the CBI, has been brought in. Blair, of course, had brought in Shaun Woodward, the former Tory MP, and Brown is hoping to get Liberals into the government.

Thursday 12 July

Up early. Josh arrived about eight, and the roofing company came and cleared the gutters, which he'd organised, bless his heart.

I've been thinking about three new books. 'Confessions of a Socialist', the political lessons that I've learned; and what encouraged me to think the way I do. That would be fun to do, and it's a good title. The second one: instead of 'Letters to my Grandchildren', 'Discussions with my Grandchildren' or 'Listening to my Grandchildren', asking each of them about life and what they've learned and how they'd like the world to develop. The third one, 'The Daddy from the Daddy Shop', would be a children's book.

I've got a tremendously clear diary; very few engagements – I've been refusing most. I realise I've come to a point where I can't go dashing round the country all the time.

I have to be up at five to go to the picket line for the postmen, and then I am off to Durham and I won't be back till Saturday night. Tolpuddle on Sunday night, and on Monday, I am at Fox Primary School. Oh God, it's a heavy period!

Friday 13 July

At Durham I got a cab to the Royal County Hotel, Room 209, and then wandered and talked to a few people before dinner. I sat next to Paul Kenny, who's the General Secretary of the GMB and really quite a progressive guy. It was a tremendous evening – Mike Elliott did one of his comedy turns . . . it was just so friendly and supportive.

I went to bed absolutely exhausted! So that was the end of Friday 13 July.

Saturday 14 July

I didn't wake up till about seven o'clock. A lovely hot day! Went onto the hotel balcony and masses of old friends came up. I saw my banner – the one with my portrait on from Blackhall Colliery – being carried down the hill, so I left the hotel and joined the crowd, and walked in under my banner onto the racecourse.

There were five speakers: Ian Lavery, the President of the NUM; Frances O'Grady, the Deputy General Secretary of the TUC; Tony Woodley; Paul Kenny; and Dennis Skinner. I just sat on the platform, and people came up throughout the whole two hours, and I signed cards and forms, and so on.

After that I travelled back with Bob Crow and his wife and Frances O'Grady and a couple of friends, on the 3.41 train to London. We moved to the first-class coach – I didn't have to pay the first-class supplement, which was very nice. We just sat and talked most of the way.

Then, at 10.30 tonight – in about an hour's time – it's *Straight Talk* on BBC News 24, with Andrew Neil, and they're going to send me a DVD, but I might try and watch it anyway.

So that's the end of Saturday 14 July. Sunday morning I've got to be up at the crack of dawn to go to the Tolpuddle Festival.

It's a killing programme, and I keep saying to myself that I can't go on like this, but I just do go on doing it!

Sunday 15 July
Up at 5.30 and caught the 148 bus to Waterloo, and the train to Moreton in Dorset for the Tolpuddle festival. Alison Shepherd, who is the TUC President this year, was also travelling there.

Rain showers and I got wet, but it was the wonderful warmth and friendship, just like Durham – it sort of penetrates you, keeps you going. Lots of trade union leaders were there, and Billy Bragg. I walked to the churchyard with them and laid a wreath.

I did an interview with the BBC *Politics Show* and it was absolutely horrible! The reporter said, 'Our theme is that, now everybody's rich, they don't care any more about trade unions.' They asked me about that, and I've got a recording of the interview if it comes out. I said, 'Well, of course we are rich, but we're wasting the money on the war, we're wasting the money on Trident, we're wasting the money on ID cards.' People around were all cheering, but he said, 'Nobody's interested any more.' It was just typical BBC – designed to demoralise.

Anyway, I went on the march (a long march) through Tolpuddle and made a speech.

Then, coming back on the train, an extraordinary thing happened. On the next seat ahead of me there was a woman of about sixty sitting – a very plump, jolly-looking black woman – and all of a sudden she started screaming, and I really mean *screaming*. It was so loud it was frightening. Then she collapsed under the seat. The person who was with her said, 'Don't worry, she's got diabetes.' This was at Southampton station, and a very nice man came along and it turned out – absolutely unbelievable – to be one Peter Butler, Professor of Medicine at the University of California, Los Angeles, who specialises in diabetes. He found her pills and treated her and she recovered.

I thanked him very much and he said, 'Oh, you're Tony Benn!' It turned out that he was an Englishman, who said he'd left the country because of Mrs Thatcher; that, as a young man, he was politically active. He said he supported Barack Obama . . . Coincidences make such memorable occasions.

Monday 16 July
I was so tired; I had a very late lie-in.

Josh arrived, and we went over to Fox Primary School. He was there – oh gosh, in the early Sixties – and he was thrilled to go back. There are sixty-six nationalities there now!

We went into the Assembly Room, and there was wonderful singing and dancing that lasted for forty minutes. Perfect – they knew all the music and they were so good. Then, after that, the school leavers were brought to the very front and put on benches, and they asked me all sorts of questions: 'What's the most interesting thing you've done?' . . . oh, very sensible questions (their homework project had been research on me). I talked about peace and the importance of encouragement, and all the rest of it. They seemed to quite like it.

Anyway, it was enjoyable and warm, and when we came home Josh and I had a long talk.

I am going to bed early, because I have to go for a blood test in the morning and I couldn't have any food or drink after ten o'clock. I've had my last cup of tea, so there's nothing to stay up for now.

Four Russian diplomats have been expelled from London because the Russians will not extradite to us the man we said murdered Alexander Litvinenko.

Tuesday 17 July
Up at seven. No breakfast. I went for my blood test at the surgery, and I took with me a bun with marmalade and a thermos of tea and

a banana – ludicrous! I was only about five minutes away from home. It wasn't the food I'd been missing, but the tea.

Office jobs all morning, had a bite to eat, a snooze, went and did some shopping for 'healthy' food.

Prepared for my interview tomorrow on the fiftieth anniversary of the foundation of the BBC Radio 4 *Today* programme.

The gap between rich and poor in Britain is the widest that it's been for forty years; also in the news, according to a hair-raising account on Channel 4, there are 10,000 doctors who've not yet found employment after graduating, because of some ghastly muck-up in the Ministry of Health.

I rang to find out if Blake, James's girlfriend (who is a young doctor), has got a job, and she has, so that's all right.

It's now nearly midnight, and I've got a very busy day tomorrow, so I'm going to slip to bed.

Wednesday 18 July
The BBC came at 8.30 to do the *Today* interview. And after that I caught the Oxford Tube. I had a cup of tea first of all, and then I went to the Oxford Union and sat in the garden. It's so funny – it was a lovely day, and I was reflecting that I met Caroline there fifty-nine years ago. Somehow, the passage of time . . . thinking about her and about me. Time plays funny tricks on you. But I was very relaxed and contented. It was nice, in a way.

I walked over to Mansfield College for a seminar with some American teachers. I talked about the Special Relationship. We had a wonderful discussion! Then I walked back to the Oxford Union, because I was due to talk to the 'Oxbridge' Group. This is organised for school students from private schools in America who come over to Oxford every summer by Dr Richard Grayson, of New College. I don't suppose they'd ever heard the arguments I put forward about the war and peace and the UN, but, at the end, they gave me a huge standing ovation, which I must say was surprising.

I might mention that Kate McCann, whose little baby Madeleine disappeared two months ago, has now been interviewed by the police and is thought to be a 'suspect' by the Portuguese police. She and Gerry McCann, having been built up to be absolute god-like figures, are now being treated as 'suspects'; the British press is in a terrible state, because if it were to turn out that the police (the Portuguese police) could establish that they had some responsibility – they obviously didn't kill the girl – then all the press hysteria about this would subside, and I don't know what people will do.

Saturday 21 July

Rainwater has come into the house again. There was a pool in the kitchen, and when I pulled a drawer out, the drawer broke. Oh boy, that's all I need! There's water on the carpet. I'm afraid the roof still leaks.

Hilary phoned on his way to Worcester, where the flooding is horrific; and again this evening, saying he'd been attending 'Cobra' – that's the top-security emergency committee, chaired by Gordon Brown – this afternoon.

Forgot to mention that Saffron Burrows told me she saw *Sicko* last night, and that when I came on I was the 'star' of the whole show. And she also said the cinema audience cheered – I've heard that from a few people now.

Tuesday 24 July

The floods absolutely dominate the news. Went out to the bank to pay my income tax, and I also bought some tobacco and nicotine pills and patches. I explained to the pharmacist that I'm not intending to give up smoking, but that I use them on long journeys when I'm not allowed a puff.

To the Communication Workers' Union lobby at the Commons about the destruction of the Postal Service. I made a speech strongly supporting them. I said it is a public service, and people use it and love the postmen. I finished up by saying that I've been on all the picket lines, and I will be there when the next day of action takes place – the great thing about the picket line is that I can smoke. Everybody laughed.

Friday 27 July

Busy office morning, then, in the afternoon, I was picked up and taken to Iranian Television studios for a discussion with a rather dour

Scot, who was a Muslim and a Professor of Islamic History. I had to bow to him on his knowledge of history, but he said that Islam was a revolutionary doctrine and that he didn't like democracy . . . He compared Islam and sharia law to a very severe Jacobean position in Scotland, where all the laws were made from above and people accepted it. We had a bit of an argument about that.

Saturday 28 July
My first trip out today was to the Oxfam shop, where I took a box full of coins – five-pence pieces and coppers. I would guess there was £30 or £40 worth of coins there.

Sunday 29 July
I had a long discussion with Hilary about New Labour. I wasn't argumentative, but I put all the points, and he said, 'Oh, Dad, you know, we've kept the economy going, increased investment, raised the living standards of the poor, more pensioners being helped', and so on. He is completely committed to the government of which he's a part.

He rented a house in Italy for two weeks' holiday; most of his children are there, and he feels he ought to go. But I did put to him, as clearly as I possibly could, that if he wasn't here when there was a crisis, it would utterly destroy his reputation. And there will be a lot of anger about the floods, and people will look for somebody to blame, and they can't go on holiday, but they'll see he's on holiday. I hope I persuaded him, but he's still hoping he can go at the end of the week.

I mentioned that I'd seen Lord Butler in Oxford in June, and that I sent him the copy of my diary entry on the occasion when the Cabinet considered the question of a referendum on the Common Market, in 1975. He wrote me a long letter back describing how he vividly remembered the events of the week or two leading up to the referendum on the Common Market in 1975 when Harold Wilson told the Cabinet that unless he achieved some key concessions at the Dublin Council, he would advise the Cabinet to recommend a 'no' vote. He then put it the other way round in a speech to the Society of London Labour Mayors, and told them if he got these concessions, he would advise a 'yes' vote. When the Cabinet realised what he had done, he was already on the way to the Dublin Council. Harold Wilson told Lord Butler that, if any Cabinet Minister got in touch with him (he was Duty Private Secretary) he was to reply that the Prime Minister's speech to the London Mayors was in line with the Cabinet minutes: 'So it was in logic, but perhaps not in spirit.' Furthermore, Lord Butler believed that Harold had squared the concessions with Helmut Schmidt at Chequers over the weekend before the first Cabinet meeting. Great days! as Robin Butler signed off to me.

It was a two-page manuscript letter, quite a historic thing.

I was a little worried about what he might think of my referring during the Iraq war period to Lord Button – a composite of Lord Butler and Lord Hutton.

Tuesday 31 July

Woke up at 2.30 choking. So I rushed to the bathroom, and I thought: Well, this is the moment when it happens, you know . . . the end. I coughed and coughed and coughed and finally got rid of it, and went back to bed, but couldn't sleep for about an hour, so I had a cup of tea and smoked my pipe. It was frightening.

I had an email from Jimmy Carter, a very friendly one. I'd sent him one, congratulating him on the Elders.

Wednesday 1 August

I had my hair cut this morning. There was a young girl of twenty, from Morocco, making tea – talking to me – and I thought she must be training to be a hairdresser. Not at all! She's going to university to study accountancy. She'd been in France, she spoke Arabic, French, Spanish and English. And these are the people who are going to get to the top. I think this was a case of what Professor Toynbee called the 'stimulus of transmarine migration'.

Friday 3 August, Stansgate

There's been a foot-and-mouth outbreak in Guildford, and Hilary will have to come back from holiday. Oh! He's been away for . . . well, I think, twenty-four or perhaps forty-eight hours – it's really rough!

We spent a late night talking, after a beautiful hot, hot day. Stansgate was absolutely lovely.

Sunday 5 August

Hilary was on the Peter Sissons show this morning, doing very well, on foot-and-mouth; and he was on News 24 – competent and relaxed, and so on.

I had this dream that I was wrong about everything, and I had to go today to South Africa to see Nelson Mandela. I did wonder if the message of all this was whether perhaps the sensible thing to do would be to retire and just enjoy the family. I've got enough money to manage. I don't need a lot of money. Josh said, 'No, Dad, you've got to explain things and encourage people, but don't dash around the country so much.' So that's what I think I'm going to do.

Friday 10 August

The world financial market is on what they call a roller coaster. Yesterday the European Central Bank put €93 billion in. Today the American Federal Reserve put $38 billion in. It's all rather worrying, but it's something I've been expecting for a long time, and now all the commentators say they've been expecting it too.

Sunday 12 August

Heathrow by 5.45, three hours early for my flight to Edinburgh. Then the plane was on the runway for two hours, because some passengers hadn't turned up, but their bags were on the plane.

There was a gay couple in the plane, an Indian from Goa and his Scottish partner. They couldn't have a civil partnership in Australia because John Howard is opposed, so they were coming back to Scotland for a ceremony presided over by the Bishop of Edinburgh, Richard Holloway.

Got a taxi to St Cuthbert's, where Roy Bailey was waiting. A boy called Daniel Gillius, aged eleven, had sent me an email in April saying he'd like to meet me and have a talk, and there he was with his father, and Daniel sat down and asked me a lot of questions – a very serious little boy. I signed some *Diaries* and talked to people.

After the concert I went and had a cup of tea with Ann Henderson, and caught the seven o'clock train from Edinburgh – home about ten past midnight.

Monday 13 August

This afternoon, I watched *Speaking Personally*, in which my dad, aged eighty-one, took part many years ago. To see it now, at my own age – eighty-two – gave me a new perspective. I enjoyed it very much.

Then I drove up Ladbroke Grove and went to Westbourne Studios, to Film-makers Against the War. The first film was an absolutely horrible film, about a man who'd been tortured. His penis had been cut with a razor by masked men, to force him to say things, and he was utterly shattered by it. Then there was one on Afghanistan, which I introduced, and then there was another one on the rights of women in Afghanistan, which had been partly funded by DFID. That was interesting.

Friday 17 August

Late start, wasting time most of the day. My capacity to waste time is unlimited.

Lunch and then, from 2.00 to 3.15, Lindsey German and Judith Orr, Editor of the *Socialist Review*, came and did an interview with me.

I rang Steve, and I rang Lissie, and I rang Josh, and I rang Dave. I moved the telephones upstairs, which I'd meant to do for a long time.

I wrote a letter to Paul Stephenson in Bristol about becoming a Freeman of the City and also to get him an honour.

Went to bed about 11.15.

Sunday 19 August

Stephen drove Lissie and me to the Albert Hall, and Lissie and I went to the Simón Bolívar Youth Orchestra concert in the Albert Hall, part of the BBC Proms. The Albert Hall was absolutely packed. I'd been invited by the Venezuelan Ambassador, Alfredo Toro Hardy, and his wife. Ken Livingstone was there, so I had a bit of a talk to him, and his wife or partner.

It began with Shostakovich Symphony No. 1 which I must say I found terribly boring. It took fifty minutes, and then there was the interval, and then we had a few drinks, and then, after that, there were extracts from *West Side Story*, which I didn't recognise, finishing up with tumultuous applause! All the orchestra had put on jackets with the Venezuelan flag, and people went absolutely berserk. It was lovely, a tremendous success!

In about half an hour I'm going to watch a programme called *The Muslim Jesus*, which I'm interested in.

Monday 20 August
Baby Jeremy, my brother who was stillborn, would have been seventy-two today, and I rang Dave – we always do that on the anniversary.

Thursday 23 August
Stephen phoned this morning and said, of all things, that Emily has been shortlisted for the selection conference of Prospective Parliamentary Candidate for East Worthing and Shoreham. It's unbelievable! She's still only seventeen, and if there were a by-election now she wouldn't be eligible! Of course, if she's selected, she'll have Nita to advise her, and Stephen, and Hilary, and myself, and maybe even Tony Blair to go and help her. It's really something!

Rang Natasha Kaplinsky to tell her that she was referred to in the diary, and she answered the phone herself, to my surprise.

Then I rang Saffron, thinking she'd be filming, and she rang me back. She had a day off, and she's reviewing *Sicko* for the *Guardian*, which is wonderful.

Tuesday 28 August
Had a talk to Dave in the morning, then we all said our goodbyes. I must mention one of Josh's jokes – he is full of jokes. A man went to a psychotherapist, absolutely naked, except in cling film, and the psychiatrist looked at him and said, 'I can clearly see your nuts.'

In the evening, I was invited to go on *Newsnight* with Gavin Esler, whom I like very much, about President Bush's speech. Bush made a speech in which he said that he'd given instructions to the armed forces to deal with the murderous attacks by the Iranians, so it does look as if there's going to be a bombing of Iran. I was on with an American – and with somebody who was, in effect, the ambassador in Britain for the al-Maliki government in Iraq; and Labour MP Mike Gapes.

I had a word with the Iraqi afterwards and he said, 'The last thing we want is Iraq to be the battleground between America and Iran.' So it was interesting. I felt I held my own.

Wednesday 29 August
Well, it was quite a memorable day today.

I caught the bus to Parliament Square for the unveiling of the Nelson Mandela statue; Mandela and his wife Graça Machel were there. Parliament Square was closed to traffic – absolutely packed with people!

I made a note of everyone I saw: Benjamin Zephaniah was in the chair next but one to me, and he introduced the gospel choir at the beginning. He said he'd been in touch with Melissa about visiting Queens Park School (her children's school).

Saw Simon Fletcher and Joy Johnson, who both worked for Ken Livingstone of course.

Had a brief word with Jesse Jackson. He's been over for this conference on black rights and economic opportunity. I don't really like Jesse Jackson . . . I don't know why.

Saw Rodney Bickerstaffe.

Then, just in front of me, were Menzies Campbell, the Liberal Leader, and next to him David Cameron. I said to Cameron, 'We've never met,' and I added, 'I gather you enjoyed *Arguments for Democracy*?' 'Yes, I did,' he said, 'I never got on to reading *Arguments for Socialism*!' I said, 'I wish we could have had a debate – we need more serious debates about these things.'

Ed Miliband was there – he came up and had a brief word – and so was David Miliband. I saw Dawn Primarolo. I saw Peter Hain and his parents; he, of course, escaped from South Africa. Saw Diane Abbott, David Lammy, Barbara Follett who had also escaped from South Africa, Ken Gill. I had a word with Derek Simpson, from Amicus, who said he wasn't in favour of a referendum on the European constitution.

When I went near the statue one or two people took some photographs, and then Richard Attenborough, who'd been responsible for it all, came up to me and said, 'You must come with me to the Banqueting House' (which was where the reception was), so I got in a car. It was very nice of him. I've hardly ever spoken to him, but he's a real luvvie. He's eighty-three I think, now. I remember him as a young actor in the war. Couldn't have been nicer!

It was a wonderful reception – speeches by Gordon Brown, Richard Attenborough and Mandela himself (shaky on his legs, but clear as a bell) and then gospel singing and banners. Had to have a snooze when I got home.

Thursday 30 August
Absolutely hideous cramp at a quarter to three; it lasted half an hour and I was forced out of bed. The pain was really quite acute. I didn't think I could stand that amount of pain. Anyway, I had a sip of tea and a pipe, and by about quarter-past three it had gone. But I woke up very early.

My first engagement today was at the Royal Geographical Society.

I came home by cab and then, at one o'clock, Jean Oelwang, the Managing Director of Virgin Unite, came to see me. She had been at the Ulusaba conference in Africa. She's got a team of about fifteen people, as the head of Virgin's political/charitable activities, a woman of forty-one, of German and Dutch extraction; she went into industry and then worked for Cable & Wireless, went and did mobile-phone development in Africa and Australia and met Richard Branson in Australia, and he appointed her Managing Director of this outfit, which must spend millions and millions of pounds. I didn't quite know why she'd come to see me.

We walked over to Pizza Express and then came back, and she wanted my advice on the Elders, so I talked a lot and she wrote everything down, and she seemed to quite enjoy it. She's not at all political. She said, 'We're trying to change capitalism to make it socially responsible', which is quite impossible, but at any rate, she was interested in the points I made, which were that the Elders should really be an independent resource, available to think and discuss problems and make contact across great divides.

Friday 31 August
Keith Vaz, who was the former European Minister under Blair and supports the European constitutional treaty, has now come out in favour of a referendum. He says this has got to be settled for a

generation. Now previously all the people who have come out for a referendum have been against Europe. So that's a very important development – the build-up of support for the referendum is getting stronger anyway.

Later in the day the phone rang to say that the *PM* programme, which reaches three and a half million listeners, wondered whether I would have a discussion with David Steel about a referendum. So I said yes, of course, and a car was sent round straight away.

I had prepared very carefully what I wanted to say: how important the treaty was, the changes it made; that it was the same really as the constitution; that people wanted a referendum; and that you couldn't say opposition to it was 'anti-Europe' when the Dutch and the French had voted against. On the whole I did reasonably well. Steel said, 'Oh, a referendum is expensive!' 'Well,' I said, 'would you have preferred a Scottish Parliament without a referendum?' 'Oh, that's different!' 'Well, do you think Scotland could leave the UK without a referendum?' 'Oh no, that's different!' On the whole I won the argument.

Then by Tube to the TUC for Ken Gill's eightieth birthday. All the old lefties were there. When Ken was speaking, his grandchildren – little children of two and three – were just climbing round the rostrum where he was standing.

Sunday 2 September
World news . . . I haven't even read the papers actually! There's a bit of a break in the Special Relationship, and I think we will withdraw our troops from Basra – although the warnings of an attack on Iran get stronger and stronger. I saw a little video of Hillary Clinton on YouTube, saying no option would be taken off the table to prevent Iran getting nuclear power and weapons, and so it's a very frightening situation.

Monday 3 September
I couldn't get on to my emails, so I got on to Josh, and he took long-distance control of my machine and discovered that my email account had been cancelled by Orange. The background to it is this: my original email address was 'fsnet' and Orange bought 'fsnet'

and it was renamed 'pop.wanadoo', and then, quite without giving anyone any opportunity to do anything about it, at least that I was aware of, they wiped from their system every 'fsnet' person they had – Josh thinks about 200,000. Orange's customer office said it can't do anything about it, it's all over, and wouldn't talk to Josh about it.

Josh finally got on to a man called Olaf Swantee, who is, believe it or not, the Chief Executive for Orange Europe. Someone at Orange knew my name and when they heard I was furious, they got really worried. I think other people had also complained. So, blow me down, Olaf Swantee rang me at home to apologise, and apparently reconnection is going to take place. It shows what a brilliant guy Josh is – he's absolutely brilliant!

Had lunch. Afterwards I got a car to Al Jazeera for a four-and-a-half-minute interview on the British withdrawal of troops from Basra to the airport. It is the beginning of a staged retreat, but of course it was presented as a redeployment and all that. But I was very candid about it, and they seemed quite pleased.

Tuesday 4 September
At his press conference today, Gordon Brown praised Mrs Thatcher, and said that she was a conviction politician who'd made many changes that needed to be made. Michael Ancram, former Chairman of the Conservative Party, attacked David Cameron for having abandoned Thatcherism. So this is the sort of elaborate game being played . . . But there might be an election in the autumn. Brown didn't rule it out.

There's no email service yet, so I'm still sort of paralysed.

Wednesday 5 September
My brother Michael was born eighty-six years ago today. I'll ring Dave, as I always do, or he might ring me first.

Tony Byrne was at work all day on the kitchen. No water, so we had to go and buy ten litres from Tescos. Ruth and I had coffee at Starbucks, sitting in the street. I quite enjoyed that.

Friday 7 September
To Oxford, and I walked up to Wycliffe Hall Theological College. Got there a bit early, and sat in the garden and smoked.

The conference was called by the Society for the Study of Christian Ethics. The actual subject: the 'Ideology of Managerialism in Church, Politics and Society'.

Of course, Wycliffe Hall is in a great row with the university because Dr Richard Turnbull, the Principal (who wasn't present), is a very unreconstructed evangelist – and doesn't think women should be ordained. And Oxford University is threatening, or considering, whether Wycliffe Hall can still be accredited as a theological college, so I felt I was going into an absolute lions' den.

Sunday 9 September
I rang John Rees because I heard that George Galloway had attacked the Respect party at some conference, so I thought it would be useful to know what was going on. John said that George was very much a loner, but that he was in contact with some fundamentalist Muslims in his constituency; that on a left–right basis he was on the right, not the left. John felt that George's life was best expressed through the media – he has his own weekly Talksport programme.

The capacity for the left sectarians to split and split and split again means that, possibly, Respect will come to an end. You can't build a political party around a personality.

I am now quite determined to write 'Confessions of a Socialist'. When Brown became Leader, he issued a new document called 'Extending and renewing party democracy', which in effect means disenfranchising constituency parties and trade unions. Clause IV was dropped by Blair. I left Parliament because I wanted to devote more time to politics, and my worry is that politics is having less and less to do with the Party. Political life will move outside the Party and I will certainly join anyone who is campaigning against privatisation, against the war, against student fees, for pensioners to get a good deal, for civil liberties, for trade-union rights, for comprehensive education. I don't want to see the Tories win – I think Cameron is totally inadequate and his policies right-wing – but from now on all my work will be done outside Parliament.

The changes will destroy the Labour Party as a party, and membership of the Party as an instrument of social change. It just becomes the fan club of the rank-and-file for the leadership when elections come, and it will have a huge effect on the future of the Labour Party. Of course, if they do succeed in getting state funding for political parties, then political leaders won't need their party any more.

So it's another example of the vehicles being used to undermine democracy in Britain, along with Europe, the IMF and NATO, and so on. I've got to think it all out, because I would like to make sense of all this, and I think some of the thoughts I've just dictated, in a random way, will go into my next book.

As well as being devoted to politics, my thoughts increasingly incline, very simply, towards being the best grandfather that I can be.

Tuesday 11 September
My email has started again, which is wonderful, all due to Josh sorting out my computer so that I can always get onto broadband, which I've had difficulty in doing.

Wednesday 12 September
I had a phone call from Emily. She has been adopted as the Labour Prospective Parliamentary Candidate for East Worthing and Shoreham in Sussex. She won 75 per cent of the vote, defeating two other candidates, who were both over fifty, one of whom is a doctor. It's phenomenal! She's a very determined and competent young woman, and so there you are – that's another relative standing for Parliament. She'll have a really good campaign there, and it might have an impact. So I rang all the members of the family and told them, and I rang Ruth, woke her up, and told her.

I was selected as a candidate in October, I think, 1950 – that was fifty-seven years ago; and then in 1999 Hilary got elected; and eight years later Emily gets adopted, the youngest candidate in the history of British democracy. So it's an exciting day. I don't quite know how to put it – I'm just over the moon!

Thursday 13 September
Gordon Brown went to the front of Number 10 and welcomed Mrs Thatcher: she was there with him for two hours and, after his warm tribute to her the other day, he confirmed his Thatcherism, although

the BBC is saying he's doing it simply to embarrass David Cameron. Actually I think it's embarrassing the left more.

The front doorbell rang and it was Sister Antoinette. She is a Nigerian nun from the convent next door. She came to see me when she first arrived two years ago, and went back to Nigeria in January, and now she's head of a school. Had a bit of a talk to her, and I gave her £200 towards a new computer for the school.

Friday 14 September
Ruth typed for me an article for the *Guardian* on the proposed changes to the Labour Party Conference, which would make it impossible for any resolutions to come forward; all that would be left for the Conference to do would be to present issues to the National Policy Forum, and then the manifesto would be put to the Party on a 'take it or leave it' basis.

Political news at the moment is that Northern Rock, which is a big bank handing out mortgages, has in effect collapsed – well, not quite collapsed, but it is in such a serious liquidity crisis that the Bank of England has had to give it money. People have been queuing up at the branches to withdraw their money in case the bank collapses, which put me in mind of what my mum told me when she was in America in the 1930s during the recession. People were queuing up at the banks then, too – and there was no money to give them. I mean, it's a terribly serious business, and it could have repercussions in . . . well, it began in America, but in Britain, in Europe, maybe even in China. You wonder whether the socialist case might come back again by default. I don't want it to happen like that, because then the BNP is more likely to benefit than anybody else, but at the same time once people get really, really frightened, you don't know what's going to happen. I do think neo-liberalism will be seen for what it is: legalised gambling.

I read an article in the *Weekly Worker* about the row between the Socialist Workers' Party (SWP), and John Rees on the one hand, and George Galloway on the other, over the body of Respect. My guess is – I may be wrong – that this is going to lead to the break-up of Respect, comparable to the break-up of the Scottish Socialist Party. You cannot build a political party on the personality of one man, however charismatic   and both Galloway and Sheridan are charismatic.

Saturday 15 September

I got up at six to go to Dudley for the Women Chainmakers' Festival in the Black Country Living Museum. I must say, it was a very enjoyable day.

The chainmakers' strike of 1910 is one of the great stories in the women's – indeed, trade-union – movement.

Ken Purchase, the MP for Wolverhampton, was there, with his wife; and Billy Bragg was there. He goes to all these things: I see him all the time.

They had recreated a village – a school, a chapel – rebuilt them brick by brick, and there were people dressed in the clothing of the time. I'm a bit ambivalent about heritage museums, because I feel that we don't make anything any more, but we do make museums to show what we used to make! But still, the atmosphere was very good and, as I say, we wandered round, and I had a couple of sandwiches and a cup of tea.

There were a number of speakers. Sylvia Heal spoke, and somebody from the Women's Trade Union Movement spoke, because it was a TUC event, and then I spoke, for about eight minutes. It was intended as a fifteen-minute speech, but I spoke more quickly than I realised.

There were 5,000 people there, so a really big event.

Today over a billion pounds' worth of savings have been withdrawn from Northern Rock, and if it spreads to other banks, which it might do, then we are in for really big trouble. Capitalism is just a casino. It all depends on confidence.

Monday 17 September

Ended up having a lovely family day yesterday. Josh was here till late – he's very intellectual. He sorted out a computer problem and we had a good talk about electronic voting, looking at it from a political point of view.

Most of this morning was spent on the phone: it's Carrie birthday. I also rang Frances Easton, one of my party members from Bristol, who is ninety.

I heard on the six o'clock news that the Chancellor of the Exchequer has guaranteed all the savings of everyone who had money in Northern Rock. It's absolutely unparalleled! It indicates how frightened the Government must be that this will spread to other building societies (like Alliance & Leicester, for example, which apparently is also suffering a bit of speculation). In one fell swoop, market forces and globalisation have been deeply undermined. I think it will have a profound effect on the Conference.

Tuesday 18 September

We are moving towards the Conference period and I've begun preparing my diary of fringe events. The more I think of it, the more it seems that Conference has been gutted. There seems to be utter contempt for the trade-union delegates on the National Executive and inevitably the unions will distance themselves, if not disaffiliate completely, like the Fire Brigades' Union. Better to do that and campaign hard for what they believe in than take on the role of tame rabbits within the Party. The Labour Party is no longer a campaigning organisation, and that's something to think about.

You can see why people get frustrated and angry. I heard Brown being described as 'ten times worse than Blair' today. (That is an error of judgement, of course – Blair had nothing to do with the Labour Party. Brown is a right-wing monetarist member, of the Callaghan variety, but he does have to be treated differently from Blair.)

The prospect of an early election seems remote, but if it's left too long, if the world economy gets even worse, if the Labour Party faces the same problems it had in 1978/9 . . . you never know, there may be a change. Not that Cameron is any good. But sometimes it's a question of 'expect the unexpected'.

Wednesday 19 September

This morning, very early, I rang a man called Tony Littlewood, who today is lying in intensive care in a hospital in Sydney, Australia. He has Guillain–Barré syndrome, which is what I had in 1981. His son got on to me through Hilary, to say that his father had the disease and would I ring him? Tony can't speak, but I rang the intensive-care unit and the nurse who is looking after him put the phone next to his ear and he could hear me, so I did a friendly little monologue, telling him what had happened to me, how frightening it was, how I had recovered; I hope it did cheer him up. I rang his son, who seemed pleased.

There was a tap at the door later in the day and in came a motorbike courier with *More Time for Politics*, the book. I couldn't believe my luck that I've finally got it in my hands, because we only signed the contract about six months ago, and there it is! Ruth has done a brilliant job.

Thursday 20 September

All day trying to find out if the book can be sold at Conference; there's no bookshop there this year – can you imagine a socialist party without a bookshop! But Alastair Campbell has got permission to do a fringe meeting at Conference, and sign and sell his books at the Party stand. So I tried to get through to the Labour Party. It was 'Press 1, press 2, press 3; I'm afraid this number is not available', etc. No resolutions and no books – that's the Labour Party!

Friday 21 September

I'm staying in a no-smoking room, but I had a word with the proprietor and he said, 'I'm sure we'll understand in your case', and so I took that to be permission.

The left at the Conference fringe are now useless, because they're all splitting up.

There were rumours in the papers that there might be an early election, and I can see the argument for it: Brown is doing very well, Campbell is muddled, Cameron is completely out of his depth, so if Brown did go to the electorate now, I think he'd win a handsome majority.

The Government has guaranteed every deposit in any bank up to £100,000, which is an enormous responsibility to take on, and if the world crisis develops, then the Government would be responsible for guaranteeing the savings of billions and billions and billions of pounds' worth of savings. So intervention is coming in, to save the system, but it's not dealing with the real problem.

Sunday 23 September

I didn't have breakfast in the hotel because there was someone downstairs I wanted to avoid. So I walked over to the Bournemouth International Hotel and had breakfast there.

I had a short interview with Adam Boulton and I did the best I could. He did ask about the *Diaries*, in a very general way, but I didn't want to talk about them; people want to know 'Will my son be sent to Afghanistan?' or 'Will there be a war with Iran?' 'Will my hospital be privatised?' 'Can granny get a hip operation?' 'What about my grandchildren going to college?'

Then I came back and sat outside the conference centre. As Tony Woodley (head of the TGWU) went by, I asked, 'Where are you going?' and he said, 'I'm going to the demonstration.' I said, 'What's the point of going to a demonstration when today you're voting to see that that demonstration can't put its problem on the agenda?' He said, 'I'll talk to you later', but I think he felt a bit guilty about it.

I checked and there is no bookshop at Conference. It is not the Labour Conference any more – it's a rally.

Into the Conference at three o'clock, and listened to Ed Miliband presenting the case for abandoning resolutions, with great charm. He made a good start (about his dad speaking at the Conference).

The changes were carried unanimously. Somehow to see a party abandoning its claim to put forward proposals was really quite frightening to me.

Later dear old Alan Simpson said, 'You must come and have a meal', so we had dinner in an Italian restaurant in the basement of the Wessex Hotel. Somebody came over from another table, or sent the waiter over, at the end and said, 'Your bill is paid.' So I went over to thank him; his name is Mervyn Wilson and I found out later that he was at college with my editor, Ruth!

Monday 24 September

Went and bought the *Daily Mail* to see what they are making of it all. I ate a banana and one or two other things. I also bought *The Sun* because they had a huge piece about the European referendum, which I think will put heavy pressure on Brown.

I heard that Emily was likely to speak, so I went down to the Conference and I just heard the end of the morning conference. Quentin Davies, the former Tory MP, made a very long speech denouncing Cameron up and down. Well, I'm all for people being converted to us, but a turncoat is not somebody who appeals to me very much. I think if he'd said, 'Look, I was a Conservative. I've joined Labour, I believe in this, positively', but it was negative campaigning of a horrible kind; and Shaun Woodward (another turncoat) presented a report on Northern Ireland and he sounded like the Managing Director of a corporation.

Anyway, Emily wasn't called – disappointing.

I watched Gordon Brown's speech. I dozed off in parts of it. It was based on his experience, his life, his commitment, his family, his damage to his eye, and the NHS. It had integrity and authenticity, and undoubtedly it was an election speech – I mean, it launched the election campaign.

Thinking about it, just after Brown's speech, I took a new view of the Conference. Yesterday, I said I think it's a waste of time coming, but I now see it in a new light. I see the Labour Conference now as part of our culture, like Parliament and the Church.

We gather once a year and meet a lot of old mates. We have no decisions of any kind to reach. I quite like it, because I meet old friends, everyone is very friendly. But it is nothing whatsoever to do with democracy, any more than religion has anything to do with the teachings of Jesus. Anyway, after Brown spoke, I went to the Euro-Safeguards meeting in the Bournemouth International Hotel. I go every year. It's the same people – Austin Mitchell, John Mills and all the old anti-European faithfuls. I made a speech, as I always do. I'm not a nationalist, but I do think that you've got to develop a completely new form of Europe, by cooperation.

Did a couple of fringe meetings, then walked to the Campaign for Labour Party Democracy meeting. A man came up – I didn't know who the hell he was – Lord Hunt, who now works for Jack Straw as Minister of Justice. Billy Bragg was there, whom I like very much. I said, 'I hope you'll allow me to call myself one of your Blokes.' I spoke there, then slipped out again.

At the *Guardian* party, just as I was leaving, Gordon Brown was arriving and, blow me down, his wife Sarah came up to me and said, 'Thank you so much for writing "The Daddy Shop".' That was a reference to a story I sent her for a book of children's stories she put together.

I hadn't spoken to her before. I also saw Lauren Booth, Cherie's half-sister, so I gave her a big hug, and there were endless photographs – all day, photographs, photographs, photographs!

Now, it's about half-past midnight. I'm much too tired to do a diary, but I felt I had to get something down.

Tuesday 25 September
The Times and the *Independent* had articles about Emily.

I had breakfast in the hotel. Chris Mullin and Jeremy Corbyn were there, and I gave them both copies of the *Diaries*.

Then I went to Conference. I happened to see on the television monitor Wendy Alexander, the new Leader of the Scottish Labour Party, who is the sister of Douglas Alexander, and I realised she sounded like a completely phoney Blairite. There was nothing authentic about it. It was cheap snubs, attacks on the Tories, and I thought: If that's the Labour leadership, then I tell you, Alex Salmond will do very well.

I went to the Conference and sat in the Purbeck Hall, watching David Miliband speaking on the war, saying that peace can never provide a military solution – that's kind of obvious. They haven't even won the war, let alone the peace.

At 3.15 photographs with Emily and Hilary and Stephen. I did a little TV interview with Emily for Southern Television.

The rain kept coming and going, but when I could get outside to smoke my pipe, I did. I heard Emily was going to make a speech, so I rushed in and it was a tremendous success. She began by saying, 'Emily Benn, Prospective Parliamentary Candidate for West Worthing and Shoreham. I'm seventeen, and I must say this to the Prime Minister: Don't call the election till I'm eighteen!' The whole Conference laughed, and then she added, '. . . next Wednesday' and they laughed again. It was a very good, powerful Blairite speech.

I had a word with Tony Woodley: he was worried about having voted to end the Conference resolutions. I think what happened was that Brown phoned all the General Secretaries personally on the matter and said, 'I do need your support.'

Emily and Stephen heard me speak at the Labour Representation Committee, where I tried to talk about the future, and say that we had to look ahead. 'You know I'm always talking about the Chartists and the Suffragettes. Well, look ahead – we've got to have the world run by global Chartists. The UN has got to be represented in proportion to the population of the world.' It probably seemed as mad to them as the Chartists sounded. I have to develop the point more fully.

I saw Alastair Campbell and Philip Gould, on the train. Alastair said, 'Oh, we don't want the election now. We'll get a much bigger majority later.' Philip Gould said he was doubtful about an election. I said, 'Well, you've been able to deal with Northern Rock, but if Chase Manhattan Bank and Lloyds go down, you're in trouble, and I think it would be much better to have the election over by then.' Philip Gould said, 'I think that's a very persuasive argument.'

I cannot tell you how glad I was to be home after Conference! A lot of thinking to be done about it, because it was a momentous Conference in ways that people don't quite understand . . .

Wednesday 26 September
I wrote an article for *Tribune* about the Conference: without attacking Brown, I linked the situation with Ramsay MacDonald because, after all, Brown has now got Mrs Thatcher on his side; he's got Norman Tebbit, of all people, on his side; he had Quentin Davies, who made a horrible speech.

I rang Natasha Kaplinsky. She told me that she had had an offer from Channel 5 to do a programme for a great deal more money, but she didn't want to leave the BBC. I'm hoping she's going to come at the end of the week for a chat.

Thursday 27 September
I did something very funny – I thought so anyway. At the Conference the Fawcett Society was handing out T-shirts saying, 'This is what a feminist looks like.' I bought one and at home, and with great difficulty, I squeezed it over the huge bust of myself by Ian Walters, which is in the front room. Then I covered the head with a scarf. I had

an interview with Margarette Driscoll from *The Sunday Times* about my *Diaries*. I said, 'Would you like to see this?' She said, 'Well, I wanted to ask about it . . .' So I pulled the scarf off and she laughed. As she left I gave her a hug; I said, 'I don't see why I should only be allowed to hug Natasha Kaplinsky.' She may make absolute fun of me!

Friday 28 September
I will watch the seven o'clock news, all about the crackdown in Burma, and if the police do crack down on those who try to march down Whitehall next month, that will be the parallel – Rangoon and Whitehall. I'm almost tempted to run the risk of being arrested myself, but then I'm in a foolish mood at the moment.

Saturday 29 September
I heard later that some Buddhist monks are coming on the march on 8 October, but of course, if I am arrested under the Terrorism Bill, I'll never be allowed to go to the United States again, and that would cut me off from Cincinnati and prevent me going and doing a lot of things I'd like to do, but maybe Hillary Clinton would give me a pardon – I don't know.

Anyway, I drafted a letter to the Home Secretary, Jacqui Smith, saying what we were planning to do and hoping she'd help, and enclosing a postcard I'm issuing to people who want to march. Then I copied that to Jack Straw, to Commissioner Ian Blair at the Metropolitan Police, and Number 10.

At 3.30 Natasha came looking very glamorous, and she talked about the move from the BBC to Channel 5. Channel 5 has offered her seven times the salary of the BBC and there was no security at the BBC. So it will certainly give Channel 5 a huge boost, and she's going to read news bulletins and have programmes of her own. I had prepared seven pages of a memorandum for her about the kind of interviews she could do – exploratory interviews. She said her mother had said it would be nice to have Tony Benn as her son-in-law, so that was a sort of platonic joke.

After Natasha had gone I decided to deliver my letters myself. So I went to Number 10, drove up to the gate and the policemen talked to me. Then on to the House of Commons, with the letter for Jack Straw, and the policeman there said, 'I'll see that gets through.'

Sunday 30 September

My granddaughter Carrie came to clear the logjam in my mail. She also taught me how to use Google for maps. I paid her fifty quid.

After she'd gone, Josh arrived and he put me onto Google Earth, which allowed me to get close-ups of Stansgate from the air, and Bideford, where Ruth's house is, and Holland Park Avenue.

Tuesday 2 October

Wrote letters all morning tackling the Stop the War march ban: to Sir Ian Blair, the Metropolitan Commissioner, asking to see him; to the Speaker, asking him whether he had ordered the ban; to the Lord Speaker, Hélène Hayman, to ask if she'd been responsible; to Malcolm Rifkind (my MP); to William Hague, asking if he could raise a point of order on the ban; to Menzies Campbell, the same; to Ian Paisley, Alex Salmond and Adam Price, all MPs.

Wednesday 3 October

Problems with the cordless phone, which is interrupted by the wi-fi that Josh has installed.

I have been thinking for some time whether to try my luck in standing as Labour candidate for North Kensington, so I drafted a letter to the local Labour Party saying I would be available.

In the afternoon, Cameron made his speech, daring Brown to call an election – quite clever; of course their policy is to cut inheritance tax, no ID cards, an EU referendum, which is quite attractive and simple.

If North Kensington Labour Party don't select me, it won't worry me; if I am selected and the National Executive vetoes it, it won't worry me; if I fight the seat and lose, it won't worry me. The real worry will be if I win, with four more years of really hard work; but in a constituency where I live, I won't be travelling around the country, and I'll be very conscientious about surgeries. I'd make a few speeches in the House, and I'd get a bit more coverage as an MP. After all, I'm eighty-two. Mr Gladstone was Prime Minister at eighty-four. Davy

Logan, from Liverpool, whom I knew, was an MP at ninety-two. So it's not a ridiculous thing to do.

Thursday 4 October

I wanted to get to Waterstone's early because Bill Clinton was signing his book. So I rang Waterstone's headquarters and said, 'I'm on my way for that', and when I got there, I found the shop was closed and a queue about a mile long with people waiting to see Clinton. I managed to get through the security, and there was a huge crowd of twenty-five photographers, and as I walked to where Bill Clinton was to do the signing, they all photographed me, and I had my book in my hand, so that was rather fun.

Then Stephen turned up, bless his heart – he has a way of getting through everything!

Then Bill Clinton arrived, and stood there in front of a mass of photographers. So I waited till he was just about to go and sign, and I rushed across to where he was and I said, 'Bill, Tony Benn – you very kindly gave me your book when you were last here, so here's my book, *More Times for Politics*, and there's a nice picture of you and my son,' and I reminded him of our mutual friend, Saffron Burrows. He said, 'I had dinner with Susie Burrows (her mother) last night, and we rang Saffron in California', and so on.

Then I said, 'I'm thinking of standing for Parliament again,' and he said, 'What a good idea!' Well, I had slipped into my pocket a mini tape-recorder, and I haven't heard it yet, but I think I've got a record of him saying, 'What a good idea!' That was a wicked thing to do, but still! I really wanted to make a note of that before I forgot.

Josh turned up later, worried about the prospect of my fighting North Kensington. 'You've got to be cautious,' he said. 'There might not be an election for three years – you'd be the Prospective Parliamentary Candidate for three years, and then you might win and have five years in Parliament. You'll be ninety – you've got to be serious, Dad.' So it persuaded me to draft a letter much more cautiously.

I think what I have to do is send a very short note to Lee Jameson, the Secretary, saying if there is an immediate election and you are stuck for a candidate, I would be available for the selection conference, but on the basis of campaigning in the election for all the things I believe in, and making it clear that I'd vote for them in the House if I was elected. That, I hope, might make them unlikely to select me. The interesting thing is, the opinion polls today show that Labour has dropped from an 11 per cent lead to 4 per cent – some people think 1 per cent – lead, so I should think Gordon Brown will not now call an election, and that does wipe out the possibility of my being a candidate.

It's now twenty to ten, and I haven't had any food today.

Friday 5 October
Ruth and I planned various things – gosh, endless phone calls! It was really an extremely desperate morning, and my office is a complete mess.

Sam Gurney, a thirty-three-year-old TUC official, came to see me because he's put his name in for Kensington, but said he didn't want to compete against me for the candidature. He's backed by all sorts of trade-union people and he's got a good background, and I wouldn't want to stand against him. So I showed him my statement, and he said, 'Well, I agree with it.' So I said, 'In that case, I'll withdraw', but we'll have to see how it all works out.

Saturday 6 October
At eleven o'clock I was picked up by Adam, the driver, and driven to Cheltenham Literary Festival. When I got there, who was there but Emma Mitchell, from Hutchinson, bless her heart!

The first meeting was with Oona King, former East London MP, and James Naughtie. I had read Oona King's *Diary,* and it was fine. She comes across as a gushy Blairite, with a huge smile, and you feel she wants to hug you. The *Diary* is interesting, about the difficulties as a part-Jewish, part-black MP, how her husband didn't like politics, threatened to leave her, how she couldn't have children . . . it's a tragic personal story. Then we went over to Cheltenham Racecourse Assembly Rooms, where there was scope for 2,500 people, and it was packed. Chaired by Libby Purves, whom I've always liked. It was 'Is Politics an Honourable Profession?' and on the panel were: Matthew Parris, a cynical ex-Tory MP; Ian Hislop, who's a funny man, also very cynical; and Douglas Hurd, former Foreign Secretary, who's very cool and 'Whitehall'. They were so contemptuous of politicians that I didn't like them at all, and they didn't like me, either.

I think the recession that is coming along is going to affect the sale of books a bit.

That was the end of Saturday 6 October.

Sunday 7 October

I got up latish, and the Sunday papers were full of the postponement of the election. I forgot to mention that yesterday. It became clear that Brown, in the light of very unfavourable polls – particularly in marginal constituencies where the Tories are now in the lead – announced yesterday that he'd decided there wouldn't be an election until perhaps 2009.

That greatly affects my own position over Kensington, so I rang Lee Jameson, the Secretary of the Party, and said, 'I had, as you know, said I'd be available, to prevent the National Executive from imposing a candidate, but now there's plenty of time, there will be a normal selection conference, and I don't think I want my name to go forward.'

The Assistant Police Commissioner rang me about the demonstration. I said, 'I understand the difficulty, but we are entitled to march, and we want to uphold the sessional order, which I've voted for for fifty years, every year.' I also said I sympathised with the police and mentioned the miners' strike, when the Mets were sent into strike areas. I thought that would be helpful.

He said, 'Well, we can let you walk on the pavement on the left, down Whitehall.' I said, 'No, that's not good enough.' There will be a thousand-odd people there. We don't want any trouble, we want to be agreeable, but I am quite clear about what I'm going to do.

Monday 8 October

A very busy day, the day of the demonstration in Trafalgar Square and the banned march.

When we got to Trafalgar Square, I began a whole series of television and radio interviews: Sky TV, BBC Radio, LBC, Al Jazeera, Russian television, French television, German television, Canadian television, CNN . . . So I did the best I could throughout the day. Then, just as I was going onto the platform at Trafalgar Square, I was told that the police had lifted the ban. Of course, the crowd was far bigger than it would have been if there hadn't been a ban! So I climbed up onto the platform. Speakers included Brian Eno; Kate Hudson; Lindsey German; Jeremy Corbyn of course; I think John McDonnell spoke. I was asked to make a very brief speech. I might add that there was a complete media blackout on the meeting, but that is the BBC and ITV and they do not want to cover any alternative views. It's utterly disgraceful, but there you are – that's them!

So, as I say, I heard the ban had been lifted. After I had spoken I had a pain in my chest; I thought: this is a warning. So I sat down quietly on my portable seat. I wore my medals. I did it to intimidate the police, and actually I think it's not a bad idea . . . a bit boastful, it sounded, but I did.

Marched all the way down to Parliament Square – most of the crowds were at Parliament Square, and apparently they broke down the barriers.

Walked into the Commons – Gordon Brown had made his statement on the war, which I had missed, but Hilary, by coincidence, was making his statement on blue tongue disease and foot-and-mouth. Gordon Brown stayed for his statement. I never remember Blair ever supporting one of his colleagues. Hilary answered questions – a terribly difficult job.

I had a brilliant idea, just before I went to bed: a free vote in the House of Commons as to whether or not to have a referendum. That gets Brown off the hook completely, you know, underlines what he said about consulting Parliament – and does mean nobody could ever criticise him for whatever he did, for or against, because Parliament will have decided. I bet he won't do it.

There was one thing I forgot: just as I walked across the pavement, to my house, a young cyclist came whistling down the road and nearly knocked me over – if he had, he'd probably have broken my hip – and then turned round and shouted at me! Cyclists are a menace.

Chapter Two

October–December 2007:
The calm before the storm

Wednesday 10 October 2007

Apparently today David Cameron absolutely hammered Gordon Brown at Prime Minister's Questions, and Brown is on the back foot over delaying the election, and over the charge that he copied the Tory policy on inheritance tax in the Spending Review.

This is the difficulty I'm in at the moment: I desperately don't want Cameron to become Prime Minister, but Gordon Brown doesn't listen to anybody! He told the postmen to go back to work, which annoyed me. He won't have a referendum on the European treaty. Also, he stopped the Conference from having any discussions.

New Labour has now been in power for twelve years, and people just want a change. Cameron is younger than Brown, and that's a factor. Brown, although he's a safe pair of hands, is very boring – and doesn't listen.

I desperately want to help the Government, but they've got to help me a bit too . . . So I'm going to get on to Ed Miliband and see whether I could talk to him. The trouble is, people don't think this government listens to anybody, which is true, I'm afraid. I'm certainly not going to attack Brown, under any circumstances, because I do have a responsibility to the Labour Party, but I'm a bit miserable and I'm a bit low.

Thursday 11 October
The Sun did not print my article on a free vote on a referendum.

Rodney Bickerstaffe rang me this morning and said that he and Ken Gill had been much chuffed by the idea of my standing for Kensington, so I had to tell him that I wasn't.

Friday 12 October
Just before I went to bed, I heard the postal strike had been settled in negotiations between the Communication Workers and Royal Mail.

Also, the courts have today announced that the strikes next week are illegal. The way working people are treated is an absolute disgrace!

Saturday 13 October
Caroline's eighty-first birthday, and I think of her all the time . . . and how she'd be observing us from wherever she is.

I met Emma, we got on the train, went to Manchester and I had a bit of a doze on the train. Met by Emma's parents, Jean and Tony Mitchell, and we drove to their house in Burnley, a very nice house and when we got there, Stanley (Tony's father) and Simon (his son) and his wife Heather and little baby girl Ellie were there. It was a family scene.

What was really interesting about it – talking to them and seeing their house, which was absolutely perfect – it was sort of an Ideal Home Exhibition house, beautifully kept, beautifully clean, beautifully tidy, beautiful furniture. Tony, Emma's father, failed the 11-plus, went on to get a Higher National Certificate and a Higher National Diploma (HND), became a tool-maker and then a draughtsman, and now is a salesman in a firm that deals with packaging, in its widest sense – not just individual packaging, but all the mechanical processes that prepare for packaging. His wife, Jean, has worked all her life in a chemist's shop, and among their interests is opera, and this evening, they're in a Gilbert and Sullivan opera.

Also, I had a talk to Tony, Emma's father; he's a member of the Swedenborg Church founded by an eighteenth century Swedish engineer and philosopher, Emanuel Swedenborg. Tomorrow he's giving a sermon in church.

Anyway, the rest of the family arrived. Stanley, Emma's grandfather arrived absolutely immaculately dressed, in slacks, and couldn't have been a tidier pensioner of eighty-seven. And then Simon, Heather and little Ellie, who was just very cute.

So that was it. It was an example really of the pride of the English working class – very well read, very cultured, with a religious connection, highly skilled artisans, a thing that's almost gone now. It's almost as old as the sort of landed aristocracy who ran everything. I found it very interesting, and I liked them very much.

Anyway, we went over to the Mechanics' Institute: Roy Bailey, *The Writing on the Wall*, a massive standing ovation! I mean, it was difficult to get off the stage.

Monday 15 October
I got up at five, and just before six I turned up at the local post office, thinking they'd be on strike over planned closures, but they weren't, so I left the little 'Support the Post Office' stickers.

Tuesday 16 October
Had a very late lie-in, about eight and a half hours' sleep, and then, oh, I did office jobs – phone calls, emails, letters, and so on. Had a bite to eat.

To the Commons for a meeting of the Campaign Group. Simeon Andrews and John McDonnell and Jeremy Corbyn all thought the moment had come to be quite honest with each other, and the honest truth is this: very few Labour MPs turn up at the Campaign Group, and a lot of members are not paying their subs of £30 a month, which is quite a lot actually.

Also, Diane Abbott, who is an officer of the group and I don't think has turned up for two years, but did turn up today and made a very angry intervention about the extent to which the Labour Representation Committee, which John McDonnell is involved in, was taking over the Campaign Group – ridiculous!

The big four (union leaders) are doing nothing whatever to support the left.

Truthfully, there isn't a left in Britain at the moment. The fringe left – that's the Socialist Workers' Party, Respect, Socialist Alternatives, the Scottish Socialist Party, Socialist Labour Party – are completely defunct, built around individuals like Arthur Scargill, Tommy Sheridan and George Galloway, so they are a complete flop, and they're ideologically pure and divisive in character.

The big four still believe that a quiet word with the Prime Minister will give them what they want – i.e. a little titbit to keep their members quiet. Prentis is a right-wing leader, and Simpson is a disappointment, and Woodley is weak; Paul Kenny is better than the others. So what is the function? The trade unions are not very political now, because their power has been broken.

So what can we do? We agreed that the main thing was to concentrate on the issues, and try and make the Labour Representation Committee as broad as the Fabian Society, so that people who weren't members of the Labour Party could join it, which I think is an excellent idea. The only thing you'd have to ensure was that you excluded people who stood against the Labour Party, so the SNP would be excluded.

It was a useful talk, but it was a sort of moment of truth: this idea that there is a left which will come to power and change things just isn't on the agenda.

I had a phone call from a man in Sheffield who said his wife thought we were related. I said, 'What's your surname?' and he said, 'Rutherford' and told me that Margaret Rutherford used to visit his family, and so on, so there obviously is a connection.

Friday 19 October
Lissie came for lunch, which was lovely, and she had the page proofs of her new novel, *One of Us*. She was so happy. She's going to send me a copy so that I can read it. She's a well-known, well-respected writer.

Saturday 20 October
Tony Byrne looked in, and he said that the Thomas Crapper loo on the ground floor of the house was leaking, so it had to be removed. I was sorry, because I am rather fond of it.

There's going to be a three-line whip forcing Labour MPs to vote against a referendum, which is an absolute disgrace.

What's the other news? Oh, Blair, I heard him yesterday morning on the radio, and there was a picture of him in the paper today, in evening dress, at a Catholic conference in New York. He was saying that Iran was a terrorist centre and was as big a threat as Hitler was in the 1930s. When I hear his voice, it makes my blood turn cold.

Monday 22 October

At ten o'clock this morning, Alfredo Toro Hardy, the Venezuelan Ambassador, came to say goodbye. He's been here for seven years, done a brilliant job in bringing alive the Chávez case and the Venezuelan case. I had an hour's talk to him. He's being moved to be the Venezuelan Ambassador in Spain, and he'll have his embassy in Madrid. He asked me to come and stay with him and give a lecture there.

He was a history academic, and one of his pupils was Hugo Chávez, so when Chávez came to power, he sought out Alfredo.

I am in a bit of a state at the moment, and engagements are too pressing. I can't go on dashing round the country as I have done this last week and next week. I just can't go on doing it.

Tuesday 23 October

To the House of Commons, where I met Stephen, and we went over to the Abbey for the memorial service for Lord Weatherill – Bernard Weatherill ('Jack'), who had been the Speaker of the House of Commons after George Thomas, until he retired in 1993. Went to the Lords and became chairman of the cross-bench peers. The whole Establishment turned out in the Abbey, except that there were no Labour people there apart from Michael Martin, the current Speaker. Lord Hunt – David Hunt, a former Tory MP – gave the address. I couldn't hear a word he said, but Stephen told me that Hunt mentioned the Zircon debate, which I had brought about, and which Jack had considered one of the most memorable debates of his career.

Afterwards I went up to speak to Lady Weatherill, in a wheelchair. She said that Jack had actually written a letter asking me to speak at his memorial service, but had made a mistake in the letter and rewritten it, but never posted it. That was nice to know. The service was full of hymns and prayers, which, if you take them literally, nobody could believe, but they are a part of the culture of our society.

The papers are full of obesity and crime and football . . . So it's very difficult to find out what's going on in the world, although the threat to Iran remains, and the Turkish Parliament has voted to authorise the Turkish Government to invade northern Iraq, Kurdistan, to destroy the Kurdish rebels there, and that's frightened Bush, because he thinks it might escalate out of control.

Wednesday 24 October
At 4.30 I was driven to the Odeon in Leicester Square for the London Film Festival Premiere of *Sicko*, the Michael Moore film. Moore wasn't able to be there, and I was asked 'Well, would you like to say something?'. I got onto the stage – a very warm reception – and I talked about how the Health Service in Britain came to be developed, and what a scandal it was that the richest country in the world didn't look after the nation's health, and that was all right. Then I sat in the seat and watched the film. It's a very clever film, because he uses individual instances to make his point, and he doesn't play a leading part himself – he's just an observer of it all. Then I went upstairs. There was another film premiere with Halle Berry on next, so a whole new group of people went in, and I was driven home.

Thursday 25 October
I spent the evening preparing to do *Newsnight* with Chris Huhne, a Liberal MP since 2005, about Lloyd George, because apparently there's going to be a statue put up to Lloyd George in Parliament Square, and John Pilger and one or two others have objected to it because of the fact that, when Lloyd George was Prime Minister, he bombed Iraq, which is true. On the other hand, looking back over it all, you have to see Lloyd George's life in the round, and he was a remarkable man: war leader in the First World War; very radical in the early days, with the People's Budget and the battle with the Lords; then the corrupt sale of honours; and visiting Hitler and

recommending a negotiated peace during the war. You just have to take him as a whole.

I'm now dictating this later. It was quite an agreeable discussion. The Lloyd George statue has been unveiled. It gave me an opportunity to say I'd met Lloyd George. Chris Huhne was doing it to help his campaign for the Liberal leadership.

Sunday 28 October

I think I may have forgotten to mention that yesterday, before I went to bed, I finished reading *The Confessions of a Capitalist* by my Uncle Ernest, Sir Ernest Benn. It was really his autobiography, in terms of his business, describing in elementary terms how small businessmen work, how they get a profit, where the value comes from, about the customers, the workers, and so on; he hated all government intervention, thought the Post Office was a disaster and so was the telephone service, objected to high taxation. It was a small businessman's view. In 1925, I think he had two motor cars and earned £10,000 a year, which was a lot of money, and 2,000 people worked for him. It's pure Mrs Thatcher.

Anyway, I was so tired I stayed in bed all morning. Every time I tried to get up, I went back to bed. I was exhausted! I wonder whether my heart is the trouble again. I have a sort of suspicion it may be.

Monday 29 October

I felt much, much better today! I woke up at 5.30, quite cheerful. I think it was all the hours I spent in bed last night.

Mary Fletcher's granddaughter phoned. Now Mary Fletcher – Mary Auld that was – was the nurse I had a crush on when I was training in Rhodesia in 1944 and 1945, and she will be ninety on 31 December, and the granddaughter said that her grandmother was worried she hadn't heard from me for a time.

Then I had a phone call from Doris Heffer's sister, to say that Doris has had dementia for two months, and she's had to leave her house, with all the books and everything that she and Eric collected. She's not on the phone any more. She's gone to a nursing home. I'm going to write to her.

Thursday 1 November
News today . . . The Metropolitan Police were fined £175,000 and £235,000 costs for a failure of health and safety in the shooting of Jean Charles de Menezes, the Brazilian electrician who was shot in the head five times in a train because the police thought he was a terrorist.

The New York stock market has fallen substantially and there's anxiety about that.

I wonder if my exhaustion and dizziness could be something to do with a worsening heart problem. I hope it isn't, but there you are.

Friday 2 November
Went for my flu jab and had a blood test.

I had lunch. Most of the afternoon I spent in preparing for the Putney Debates, which are taking place in Putney church tonight.

I drove there, and found I was discussing them with Geoffrey Robertson, QC, a great human-rights lawyer who's written a book on the Putney Debates; Tristram Hunt, the historian, who, in the course of the discussion, said he was strongly in favour of the monarchy (I think he must be New Labour); my dear friend Shami Chakrabarti from Liberty; and Billy Bragg. It was a bit discursive. I didn't feel we focused on the things that mattered.

Afterwards they took me over to a meal in a Spanish restaurant, just opposite the church, which I didn't like very much. There was massive noise, I couldn't hear anybody and I didn't like the food! Anyway, I left at about a quarter to twelve and got home about midnight, and went to bed about one.

Saturday 3 November
I was very tired this morning.

At 9.30 a cab came to pick me up to take me to the BBC to record an interview for Broadcasting House on Dr Anthony Clare, the Irish psychiatrist, who died last week, and who had interviewed me for his programme *In the Psychiatrist's Chair*, in 1995.

Went shopping, got two bottles of milk, some Sweet William pears, which I like, and some fruit cake.

I began reading Michael Horovitz's new book, *A New Waste Land*, which is a tour de force, a denunciation of New Labour in all its forms. I'm reviewing it for *Time Out*.

Sunday 4 November
Emily had a whole page, 'A Day in the Life of Emily Benn', in *The Sunday Times*, a very professional job.

I was picked up in a cab and taken to BBC Western House to do a twenty-minute interview on *The Diaries*. At Western House a driver got out of his cab and said, 'I'm from Somalia and I greatly admire you, and I did so enjoy what your mother said, "The great thing about your last journey is you don't have to pack."' What an extraordinary thing!

Tuesday 6 November
I went off to the Commons for the Speaker's party for the new session. The Queen's Speech contained very little really: longer detention for suspected terrorists; a house-building programme; quicker planning consents for building; and the environment.

I saw the Serjeant at Arms, General Sir Peter Peterkin, who I think is retiring, and Angus Sinclair, the Speaker's Secretary, who writes me nice letters.

I heard when I got home that Basil Willsmer died this morning at 10.10 in Broomfield Hospital – such a lovely man! I've known him for thirty years. He did all the building work at Stansgate . . . designed the grave for Caroline. He had cancer.

Then I caught a cab to the Friends' Meeting House, with an immensely aggressive cabbie who said you've got to drive 'all these al-Qaeda and Bangladeshis and Muslims' out of London. I attended the memorial meeting for Jim Addington – eighty-two, just my age – who had been in the RAF, as I had been, was originally a Conservative, but shifted to a progressive position. He wrote for the *Morning Star*, was in Labour Action for Peace, CND, the Campaign for UN Renewal, the Stop the War Coalition. There were 100 or more people there, mainly older people.

Wednesday 7 November
I took a couple of Crampex tablets last night and woke up with the

most ghastly pain in one ankle. I don't know whether it was caused by the tablets or whether it was the arthritis, but I could hardly walk.

Friday 9 November
I was waiting for John Rees and Lindsey German to come and have a meal with me. The phone rang and it was John and he said, 'We're at Pizza Express', so I walked to it and found fourteen people there. The entire leadership of the Stop the War movement. They had organised the dinner in my honour because of the work I'd done stopping the Metropolitan Police from banning our march on 8 October. It was awfully sweet of them. They gave me a little ceramic medal. It was just lovely!

Sunday 11 November
Had ten hours in bed and really needed it, and was very tired even when I woke up.

Tuesday 13 November
Went to Tesco's and spent £31, but I did get a mass of food for it – it's very cheap.

Thursday 15 November
There was a bit in the *Guardian* about David Miliband calling for the European Union to be ready to exercise hard power (i.e. military power), turning the EU into a . . . well, a military unit really – very dangerous.

Had a letter from a woman who was a midwife at Queen Charlotte's Hospital when Hilary was born on 26 November 1953. Her name is Lady Marion Brett. She described it and said how wonderful Caroline had been, and asked if I had any recollections of the day. So I went back to my bedside diary and I had a full account:

2.45 a.m. contractions; 3.45 examination at Queen Charlotte's; 7 a.m. Labour Ward; 9 a.m. Delivery Room; first stage, five hours; second stage, eight minutes; afterbirth, fifteen minutes. Sister Blake, with Dr Diamond watching, delivered Hilary at 9.40 a.m., eight pounds fifteen ounces. 11.15, I heard him crying on the telephone – huge rejoicing. Caroline is a model patient. I visited the hospital at 3.30 and 7 p.m.

I replied and said, 'I realise this is a record of your day's work rather than mine, but I feel sure Hilary will be interested, and I'm forwarding your letter and this letter to him.' So that was a nice little family item.

The other thing was that I had an email yesterday from a woman in Minnesota referring me to her blog, in which she said she would like to have my babies. So I sent her an email back, saying what a charming letter, 'There are many socialists, we're not alone' etc.; and she then sent a further email back saying, 'Thank you very much indeed – I hope I didn't give offence.'

The only political news of importance today, is that the Government is trying to get the right to detain people without trial up from twenty-eight days to fifty-eight days. Admiral Lord West, who was a former head of the navy, first of all yesterday said it wasn't necessary and then, having seen Gordon Brown, who said it was necessary, he changed his mind.

And of course the world economy is very uncertain. The loan to Northern Rock from the Treasury has gone up to £25 billion. Apparently Richard Branson is now thinking of buying it. Of course, if he buys it and the guarantee remains, people are bound to bank with him. But if you give £25 billion to a bank, you'd think that would be the grounds for nationalising it. We're a very long way from going along those lines, but that argument will come up again if further banks collapse, which I fear is likely, because there are a lot of warning signs.

I got my car back from the garage – £1,075 in repairs. Ruth said the time had come to think of giving up my car, and certainly the insurance, the tax, the parking permit and the congestion charge, not to mention the petrol and the repairs, are terribly expensive for the use I make of it.

Sunday 18 November
The Blair Years by David Aaronovitch was on TV, and I think it really was a disgracefully biased programme! It was all Blair, Blair, Blair, and

whether Brown was disloyal to him. Everyone (except Ian Gibson) was pro-Blair: Lord Birt, Alan Milburn, Peter Mandelson, Charles Clarke, Alastair Campbell. It made Brown out to be an absolute swine and Blair a courageous man. In so far as the media have turned on Gordon Brown, probably the attacks will have a bad effect on him.

Monday 19 November
Alistair Darling, the Chancellor, made a speech about Northern Rock, and the Government is in a real mess about it. It is being compared to Black Wednesday, and Alistair Darling to Lamont, who was the Chancellor at the time of Black Wednesday. I think New Labour has to be defeated. My fear is that we are just moving now to a Liberal/Tory nineteenth-century situation, with no substance; it's comparable to the Democrat/Republican split, where the test is how much money you can raise, how clever your PR is; how you escape from that is the real question.

Tuesday 20 November
Alistair Darling made a statement to the House: details of twenty-five million people receiving child benefit were downloaded onto a computer disk, sent via TNT – not the Royal Mail – to the National Audit Office and lost; another couple of disks were sent – by Royal Mail registered post – and got through. It is an absolutely major crisis of confidence. I think it's not impossible that this, plus Northern Rock, could see the downfall of the New Labour Government.

Wednesday 21 November
My emails have built up, because I realise I haven't been handling them properly. What I tend to do is just print them off and treat them as letters to be looked at, but actually people expect an immediate reply to emails.

I came home, in the pelting rain, and had to catch up with various emails. It's now ten past nine, and I've got to have a meal and go to bed and be up in the morning at six o'clock for Basil Willsmer's funeral, and then, after that, for the Thanksgiving party; and then I've got to be up again the day after at five o'clock in order to do this News 24 paper review.

Thursday 22 November

My precious darling Pixie died seven years ago today, at ten past ten in the evening. The *Morning Star* printed the little notice that I put in every year.

Josh collected me at 7.45, and drove me to Burnham, Essex, for Basil Willsmer's funeral. It was really very moving, and the order of service had a beautiful picture of Basil on the front, and on the back a photo of Basil with his little granddaughter sitting on the bench at Stansgate.

A friend of Basil's, who was a superintendent in the police force, gave a wonderful address, and referred to the fact that Basil valued his friendship with the Benn family and his connection with Stansgate. So we sat and talked to all the family, and I gave Heather a big hug and, oh, it was lovely. I was very moved by it. They used in the service the poem 'Do not stand at my grave and weep', which I read at Caroline's graveside and which I sent to Basil's widow, Heather. It was very moving.

Thanksgiving dinner at Hilary's house.

Friday 23 November

Up at five o'clock. Went and did the review of the papers for BBC News 24. I brought up the item on QinetiQ, the defence-research establishment sold off by the Ministry of Defence: four civil servants who'd been involved in negotiating it ended up with £107 million.

It was a cold, clear day. I came home and was very, very tired. I had a word with Ruth, and then I had two hours' sleep.

I had an extraordinary dream that this was the time to die, here and now, and I lay wondering if I was going to die, and how long it would be before my body was discovered. I think it's a combination of yesterday being Caroline's anniversary and the political situation, which is awful.

In the afternoon John Rees and Lindsey German came to talk about the possibility of setting up a People's Assembly to discuss a whole range of issues, which I'm in favour of. If I could bring the Stop the War Coalition and the Labour Representation Committee together, it could provide a platform for a whole range of progressive ideas.

Sunday 25 November
Up at six.

The news is that John Howard, the right-wing Prime Minister of Australia, has been beaten by Kevin Rudd, the Labour Leader. He doesn't sound very radical, but Rudd has said he'll withdraw from Iraq and sign up to Kyoto, so that's a good sign.

Monday 26 November
I went to get a new Commons pass. The new one is one of these touch-passes. Unfortunately it said on it 'Ex-Member' and not 'Freedom of the House', so I went to the Serjeant at Arm's office and they said they'd put it right.

The Diaries (*More Time for Politics*) are in the shortlist for the Channel 4 Political Biography of the Year. 14,000 copies have been sold so far. Alastair Campbell is there too. I just conceivably might beat Campbell.

Tuesday 27 November
The conference headed up by Bush and Ehud Olmert, the Israeli Prime Minister, with Mahmoud Abbas, the Palestinian President, has been launched with a deadline of a year – it's the old Road Map back. As Hamas, which is the elected government of Palestine, hadn't been invited, the likelihood of anything coming of it is absolutely zero, I think, but still, any talks are better than no talks. And of course Tony Blair hovering about in the background of the Quartet, with his awful smile – I must say, it does really drive me mad just to see him there. But still, I must control my feelings.

Wednesday 28 November
To the Palestinian lobby at the House of Commons. I met a mayor from the West Bank, who said he was surrounded on three sides by the wall. They think the talks are a complete fraud without Hamas.

Thursday 29 November
I collected Lissie this morning for Christmas shopping. She devoted hours to it! It's just so sweet of her – I mean, because time is the most valuable thing. We went to Waterstone's and bought lots of books

and videos, and to Gap. After lunch she walked over to see Ruth Fainlight, the poet, who was a friend of Mum's and mine and hers, and Alan Sillitoe, the author, who live together round the corner. He has got cancer.

In the evening, after I'd had a bite to eat, I was driven and taken to the BBC to do a programme called *The Late Edition* for BBC4. It has an audience of 150,000 people, with a guy called Marcus Brigstocke, who's a comedian, and I got ten or eleven minutes discussing *The Diaries*, and it came across quite well – I'm pleased.

Friday 30 November
James Benn, who's sixty-three, my first cousin once removed, the son of Glanville, came this morning for an hour. I signed a *Diary*, and he asked me to sign another *Diary* for him. We had a lovely talk. He said his wife, Claire, is very interested in textiles and the design of textiles. Couldn't have been nicer!

I was picked up and taken to GMTV for an interview with Steve Richards, on *The Diaries*. Vincent Cable was there – I'd never spoken to him before. He said he once worked with John Smith, advising him, as a member of the Labour Party, but left the Party because of Militant.

Later I got a taxi to St James's, Piccadilly to take part in a Rhythm of Dissent event, organised by the Stop the War Coalition. Julie Christie and Prunella Scales were both there. I spoke very briefly, and then I came home.

Saturday 1 December
At the moment, Ruth is transferring all the names and addresses from my old Psion Organiser onto my new computer, which is a wonderful thing to do because, otherwise, my whole Christmas-card system is totally paralysed.

Sunday 2 December
I got up at 5.55 to watch the interview with Steve Richards about my *Diaries*. It was eleven minutes, very fair, and I did get a tribute in to Ruth, which I was pleased about.

To the 'Christmas without Cruelty' fair at Kensington Town Hall;

the whole place had been taken over by all the different groups – the vegans, the fruitarians, Animal Aid, Safer Medicines. I wandered around before being taken into the lecture hall, which was packed, and I gave a talk, starting with my interest in Anti-Vivisection as a child, and then about Hilary turning me to vegetarianism, and then the case against drug-testing on animals and the debate in Oxford which Safer Medicines organised. I ended up by saying how progress takes a long time, and so on.

A British teacher in the Sudan has been sentenced to fifteen days in prison for allowing a child to call a teddy bear Muhammad.

Monday 3 December
Before I went to sleep I watched the last of the Tony Blair programmes about God. The man is such a menace! Really, I found it difficult to watch, but I felt I ought to.

Josh rang to say he was talking to a policeman who was present in Parliament Square during the Stop the War/CND protest when we read the names of people who have been killed in the Iraq war. This superintendent apparently said that I was within a hair's breadth of being arrested. I'd like to have a look at the police report – I think it's very interesting, because I did actually go and speak to a superintendent just before we read the names, and I said, 'Play this soft because it's not in any way aggressive – it's just getting this across.' Obviously I was near the line.

Had to go and do a little bit of shopping in Tesco's. Said to the young man behind the checkout, 'Where are you from?' and he said Kenya. He is studying psychological counselling.' I said I had been in Kenya, and he said, 'You were there as part of the colonial administration, I suppose.' So I said, 'Yes, but opposed it.' I told him I knew Jomo Kenyatta and supported the Mau Mau, and he said, 'Oh, my father was a member of Mau Mau!' If anyone, years ago, had said, 'My father was in Mau Mau', they would have been put in prison at once!

Tuesday 4 December
The woman who was imprisoned for fifteen days in the Sudan for allowing a child in her primary school in Khartoum to name one

of the teddy bears Muhammad was released after two Muslim peers from Britain had been to see the President. Of course we've had the whole story all week, an excuse for massive anti-Islam propaganda. She came and said how kind everybody was to her in prison, and how she loved it, she'd love to go back. It was rather like the story of Yvonne Ridley, captured by the Taliban, who became a Muslim as a result.

There's a report from the American intelligence community that they now believe that Iran stopped all work on the atomic weapons in 2003, just like Saddam Hussein, who stopped it in '92, and this has slightly undermined Bush's campaign for an attack on Iran.

The fifty-seventh anniversary of the day I took my seat in Parliament as MP for Bristol South-East.

Wednesday 5 December
I had lunch with Ruth, and then Ruth said, 'Have you ever thought of retiring?' It was a very relevant question because I had agreed to talk to the old-age pensioners ('Older Residents' Forum') in Kensington Town Hall today. Average age seventy, I should imagine, so there was a lot of experience there, and I spoke and did the best I could. But I can't say I was terribly original; I was amusing.

I'd promised to go to David Gentleman's exhibition in Bond Street. So I caught the 94 bus and walked down, and saw this magnificent display of his paintings. If every one of them had been sold, it would have brought in £60,000 or £70,000, I should think, but then that's how he earns his living. I saw Jonathan Miller there (I had to get somebody to tell me his name), whom I hadn't seen for ages, a tall, amusing guy who was one of the original *That Was the Week That Was* team, I think, with David Frost. He said, 'Isn't America awful?'

A distinguished, white-haired man came up to me and said, 'I'm David Dell. I used to be in the Ministry of Technology . . . My job was computers.' He said that he had found my time in the ministry very dynamic, and when he left for another job he followed my model of having meetings of the whole staff.

Thursday 6 December,
By train to Ely and got a cab to the cathedral. They had organised a

buffet lunch before my talk. There were 350 people there, average age sixty-plus, I would think, in the Lady Chapel, with ghastly acoustics! I had to have a hand-mike, which I hate, and there was a massive echo, but I did hear the questions, and Ruth liked it. She is very sparing with her praise.

One of the people who came up at the book-signing was called Audrey Hancock, and she said she had come to work as a temporary secretary in 1949/50 for my dad. She really liked him and said what fun he was. That gave me a huge boost, because that is nearly sixty years ago; she must be eighty now, I should think.

When I got back there were eighty-eight emails, mainly about Viagra; and six telephone messages.

The other thing was that I had a phone call today from *The Observer*, saying would I write an article about my week? Well, it happened to have been a very good week, so I stayed up till one o'clock in the morning typing it, and then found my fax didn't work.

Friday 7 December
I began work today on a debate I've agreed to do with William Shawcross and Liz Cheney, the Vice President's daughter, and others, on the future for Iraq. Google is incredible! I looked up, for example, the phrase 'addicted to oil' because I remember Bush said it in a State of the Union message – and there it was. I googled 'United States and Saddam' and there was a picture of Rumsfeld shaking hands with Saddam, saying, 'We have a common interest.' So I'm going to try and make a measured, quiet demolition of the American case, mainly using American sources.

Channel 4 News are having awards for 'the most inspirational person of the decade'; they trailed it with pictures of Blair and Brown, and of Ken Livingstone and Boris Johnson; of George Galloway, lapping milk in *Celebrity Big Brother*; and just a little glimpse of me on a Stop the War march.

Sunday 9 December
I read all the papers that the Government is releasing on 1 January 2008, under the thirty-year rule, about nuclear power and Iran at the time I was Energy Secretary. I discovered that Jimmy Carter, who

had come over and talked to the Prime Minister, Jim Callaghan, at a meeting I didn't attend, said that twenty-two nuclear-power stations had been cancelled in America because people didn't want them, and therefore Westinghouse had no contracts for their pressurised water reactor. They were pressing Walter Marshall, who was my Chief Scientist at Energy, and the British nuclear industry to adopt the PWR, and I (according to the minutes) was being very indecisive about it. Of course, I wasn't being indecisive at all – I didn't want the pressurised water reactor, and I managed to keep it out until I left office. But Callaghan was angry. One paper to the Prime Minister said that I was too friendly with the National Union of Mineworkers and with Friends of the Earth; and that my wife, an American, was in touch with Brian Flowers, who was opposed to nuclear power. So it was a wonderful insight, and I'll check it all against my *Diaries*.

Monday 10 December
The headline today: Gordon Brown is going to invite Google and 100 major multinational companies to tackle the problem of world poverty, so it is the complete abandonment of any alternative socialist perspective.

I worked further on my speech for the Iraq debate tomorrow, where I've got eight or nine minutes with this huge audience. After I'd completed typing it, it disappeared from my screen! That's where technology really throws you, and I don't know why it happened or what occurred, but the whole thing had disappeared, so I've got to start again tomorrow.

I think I've got to come to terms with the fact that I'm a very old man with serious limitations. I think if I cut back – everyone is advising it – if I cut back, I can cope with what I have to cope with, but I mustn't take on more than I can, because I am exhausted! I pour all this out because you have to say the things you're really feeling.

Tuesday 11 December
Central Hall Westminster for this Iraq debate, organised by Intelligence Squared, which is funded and sponsored by the Rosenkranz Foundation in America. I think it could be a CIA front.

Andrew Neil was in the chair. There were three motions before the meeting, which held about 2,500 to 3,000 people. The first motion before the vote was to go now – leave Iraq now – 533; to go later, 742; and to stay in Iraq, 434.

Anyway, the order of speakers was that I opened; and then a Rory Stewart, who was an ex-army officer, who'd been a Governor or Deputy Governor of a province in Iraq and had come to the conclusion that it was hopeless and that you've got to get out. He wasn't anti-war, but everything just failed. Then Sir Christopher Meyer, the former Ambassador in Washington; Ali Alawi, an Iraqi who had been in exile when Saddam was there and went back as Minister: rather friendly, and he said he'd read my *Diaries* and he was moving to the left as he got older!

The third group were those who thought you should stay: William Shawcross; Lieutenant Peter Hegseth, a twenty-seven-year-old soldier in Iraq, who was now head of Vets (Veterans) for Freedom, very much supported by Bush.

Sir Michael Jackson, the former Chief of the General Staff, bitterly attacked what I had said, that there was no moral difference between a suicide bomber and a stealth bomber. He said, 'Oh, it's quite different – we try to preserve lives!' I said, 'Look, you can't qualify "Thou shalt not kill" by saying one form of killing is different from the other.'

Then I wound up at the end. After the debate: to go now was 668, which was 135 higher than at the beginning; to go later was 866, which was 124 more than last time; and to stay was 630, up 196. So the 'stay in Iraq' group got the biggest vote increase, but still 'go now', at 668, was me, and 630 was 'stay', so we were still above them; but the one that really went up and dominated it was 'go later', the sort of cautious middle view.

I don't think I want to do that again. I'm glad I did it, but I don't want to do any more for Intelligence Squared, of that I'm certain.

Wednesday 12 December
At 2.30 a man called John Manel, who works at the BBC *Today* programme, came along to interview me about these thirty-year government documents involving me.

It is very straightforward: it was at a time when the whole of

Whitehall, and Arnold Weinstock of GEC, and Walter Marshall, my so-called scientific adviser, plus the Prime Minister, were all trying to get me to drop the gas-cooled nuclear reactors (the Magnox and AGR) and adopt the Westinghouse pressurised water reactor. Marshall then said he could negotiate with the Shah, who would build twenty nuclear power stations within Iran – considering the situation now, that's very amusing! – and was prepared to invest in our nuclear industry if we adopted the PWR.

Well, I was absolutely opposed to it, on two grounds: first of all, I didn't want to abandon the gas-cooled reactors in favour of the Westinghouse PWR because the US were cancelling power stations at the time; secondly, because I didn't want to provide American reactors to the Shah, and I had non-proliferation anxieties. But, at that time, the whole of Whitehall didn't care about proliferation; they just wanted contracts and work. My diary entries were full, and so complete, on this.

But what was interesting, in one of the papers that was released, was an attack on me, and on Caroline, by Ken Stowe, the Prime Minister's Private Secretary, in a minute to the PM, saying: Benn is close to the NUM, he works with Friends of the Earth (which, at that time, was treated as a near-terrorist organisation) and he works closely with advisers and won't let papers go round, and so on. Stowe said, 'And his wife, Caroline, is also very anti-nuclear, because she's an American and she's a friend of Professor Brian Flowers.' Now Brian Flowers had published a very important report on nuclear dangers, but to see Caroline attacked by the Prime Minister's Private Secretary, in minutes that must have gone round, was extraordinary.

Thursday 13 December
It's a funny thing to write in the diary, but I actually do think I'm coming to the end of my life. I don't think I'm ill, but I'm just winding down now. I haven't lost my interest in life at all, but I just think my body is wearing itself out. I keep coming back to this thing that, when I was sixteen and did a plan of my life, it said I would die at eighty-two, and that gives me January, February, March . . . three, four more months at most, three and a half months. So I just put it in my diary, out of curiosity.

Today the Treaty of Lisbon was signed, incorporating the new revamped European constitution. Brown is signing it himself. He says Parliament will decide, but he's issuing a three-line whip, so Parliament won't be deciding. It is a king signing a treaty and signing away the rights of the electorate, and it really is an outrage. I don't know what I'm getting excited about: I don't want Cameron to be in power; but I really think it is an outrage and a theft of public rights. So there is a residual political interest in the old man!

Saturday 15 December
Hilary rang from Bali at the World Environmental Conference, and he'll be home tomorrow. It's edged forward but is not a complete success; the Americans were put under very heavy pressure to concede most of what was wanted, although, predictably, everyone else will of course say it's a failure. Hilary played an important part in it.

Sunday 16 December
A cold day, but beautifully sunny. Late lie-in. The Government's in a ghastly mess. I mean, I think there's a 13 per cent Tory lead.

Stephen told me that he'd seen John Major, and Major said that the sale of gold by Gordon Brown has cost the Treasury more than was lost on Black Wednesday. So, I must say, it doesn't look very good for Gordon Brown, but still, if the crisis gets worse, people will rally round the Prime Minister. I think he's more able to cope with it.

Talk about capitalism being wonderful and globalisation being inevitable – the whole thing could end up in the most ghastly smash, and that's when the BNP come up.

Monday 17 December
Well, this morning two days' mail was brought round by the manager from the local sorting office. He said the local postman was ill. There were hundreds of letters!

After I'd had a sandwich I went by bus to the House of Commons. I read Matthew Parris in *The Times*, saying that Hilary should listen to his 'infuriating old father' who did believe the State could do some things well, which was rather amusing.

I had a talk to Michael Spicer, who was, until very recently, the Chairman of the 1922 Committee. He and I agreed entirely about Europe.

Tuesday 18 December

Apparently the Government has now lent Northern Rock, the bank, £56 billion in loans and guarantees. I mean, actually, if you look at the scale of it, it's unbelievable! It just can't be doable, and if another bank goes – apparently that could happen – we're in real deep trouble, and capitalism and market forces and globalisation are being shown up for what they were: a casino! Anyway, I mention that in passing.

Wednesday 19 December

I tackled the packing of 140 presents for twenty-eight family members who are coming on Christmas Day. I could have just put the gifts in plastic bags, but I thought the least I could do was wrap them and, I must say, it's an utterly exhausting job and I had to pause and have a rest on the couch. I tackled it and finished it.

The political situation is very, very strange at the moment. I've got to devote a lot of time to thinking about it. Britain is, in effect, a municipality within a bureaucratic federation. That's what the guys at the top wanted: to isolate democracy from any decision-making. Now, everything is done in Europe, and Europe doing this, Europe doing that really means the Commission has the powers of initiation and the ministers are under pressure to go along with them, and the public are kept completely out! The European Parliament has no particular power – you don't elect Members anyway, you just follow the list system. So you don't have a local representative. The whole thing has been structured to keep the people of Europe from any approval of any stage. There's never been a referendum in Germany; there was in France, which lost, so they're finding another way round it. It is a European federation, of a kind . . . It is an empire being built up, before our very eyes, and what you do about it can't be a nationalist response; it has to be a democratic response. So I've got to think a lot about that in the New Year.

Friday 21 December
Hacking cough all night – felt absolutely terrible! No interest in anything, no desire to do anything . . . I wondered whether this was the beginning of the end.

Saturday 22 December
I imagined last night that I drafted a new constitution for the United Nations. They talk about UN reform, but I thought: What would happen if you really did draft something that was democratic? For example, there are 192 member states in the General Assembly. Well, they certainly should have a vote, according to their population – one vote for every million, or part thereof. So the Chinese would have 3,200 votes and Luxembourg one vote, and that would make it more representative of the world population.

Then there would have to be some representation of the strongest economies in the world, and the others elected by the General Assembly by continent, for Asia, North America, and so on. And then voting by population at the Security Council as well.

And then, there should be powers to elect the Secretary General of the World Trade Organisation, and so on.

It was rather exciting to do it, because it's so bold to think of it. I mean, it's just inconceivable that it would be done, but is it any bolder than it was in 1832 to demand universal adult suffrage? Certainly not. So I think I'll do a little bit more work on that. I'd like to get a few lawyers, but even if I don't get it right, I could work out roughly what it's about, so I'm not really finished.

Tony Blair has become a Catholic, a private matter; but the Archbishop of Westminster – Cardinal Cormac Murphy-O'Connor – welcomed him.

Tuesday 25 December
Ghastly night! Cold, coughed, dreams of all the awful things that I had done in my life . . . moments when I'd neglected Caroline and neglected my mum. I felt absolutely lousy!

Anyway, Christmas Day. The family arrived at midday.

It was a lovely Christmas lunch. The children did everything! They brought the food, they laid the table, they cooked the food, washed up, tidied everything up . . . I did absolutely nothing!

Wednesday 26 December
Another bad night. Got up at 6.30, had breakfast, dressed and went back to bed and stayed in bed till about three or four in the afternoon. Am I having . . . I've written something I can't read . . . having a fit of depression, or am I dying? I just don't know!

I watched David Starkey on the monarchy: the greatest change was under George V when he introduced the new Honours List, with the Order of the British Empire, and how turning the Crown from being the Saxe-Coburg-Gotha to the Windsor family had transformed royalty. It was really poor stuff, and he's supposed to be a professor.

Thursday 27 December
Tidied up. Moved the DAB radio that Ruth gave me down to the office. I unpacked the new telephone that Josh had given me, a lovely phone, and the new heater.

The big news today is that Benazir Bhutto has been assassinated by a suicide bomber.

Friday 28 December
I did, today, manage to change the PIN number on my phone, so I can now dial my home phone when I'm at Stansgate, or anywhere, for messages.

Sunday 30 December, Stansgate
We discussed the problem of the archives, because Stephen brings down boxes and boxes of archives, and I think he's moving them into the containers which were intended for others to use.

After that, I went and sat on the bench by Pixie's grave and thought about her for a long time, and it was a comfort to me, bless her heart.

In the evening, I had an argument with Josh about democracy. Of course it wasn't a serious argument. It was just about whether democracy mattered, whether anybody was interested in it, should there be compulsory voting, and so on.

Monday 31 December

The big event of the year, at home, was that Tony Blair finally went, and Brown won the leadership election. He managed to get so much support he excluded any challenge to his leadership. He did begin by making quite progressive statements about reforming the Government and introducing a bit more democracy and discussion in the Cabinet, and he did withdraw from Basra – actually, we were defeated in Basra, but we call it a withdrawal.

We all expected a November election, and I did indicate to the local party that if there was an attempt to impose a candidate, I'd be available, and Josh warned me about this, but it got into the press that I might want to come back to Parliament, which was a mistake. But the November election was off, so thank God I was spared that!

The world economy is in a very troubled state. There's still the threat to Iran. Bush has got less than twelve months till the election results. We don't know who the candidates are going to be – will it be Hillary Clinton versus Rudy Giuliani, or Barack Obama versus John McCain . . .? We just don't know, but it's a very frightening period, particularly with the possibility of an attack upon Iran, either by Israel or by the United States, or both in combination. So there's that.

Liss is a huge personal supporter and . . . well, she's doing what Caroline would have wanted her to do, and what Caroline would have done, bless her heart.

I find the politics very depressing at the moment. I didn't know how to deal with the next general election. I feel totally out of sympathy with the Labour Party on civil liberties, on the war, on Europe, and perhaps the only answer is to die, which is an extreme thing to say, but I don't quite know how I'm going to cope.

Anyway, these are just the ramblings of an old man, as we approach midnight.

Chapter Three

January–May 2008:
The end of New Labour

Wednesday 2 January 2008
Watched a bit of the film *Gandhi*. I went through all my saved messages and cleared most of them. I haven't got much energy at the moment: what I ought to be doing is tackling my correspondence. I have a mental block about it.

It's now about ten past ten and I think I'll go to bed and read a bit of a book that Lissie gave me for Christmas, *The No. 1 Ladies Detective Agency.*

Friday 4 January
Barack Obama won the Iowa caucus for the Democrats, and Hillary Clinton fell into third place, behind John Edwards. Really good news.

Sunday 6 January
I watched Gordon Brown on *The Andrew Marr Show,* and the plain truth is that Brown is the Managing Director of Great Britain plc. There's no implication or indication in anything he says that he is

listening to us, or being affected by what we think. He's in charge, with a long-term view and a vision, and we've just got to accept it.

Monday 7 January
No cramp and quite pleasant dreams.

Josh arrived, and from 10.00 to 12.30 Pete Williams from UCL and Dr Robert Perks, who is the Curator of Oral History at the British Library, came to discuss the digital indexing of my archives. Robert Perks was particularly interested in *The Diaries* and he did say that the Heritage Lottery team, who had been to see me some years ago, were hostile, but there's a complete change now, implying that money would be available. Josh said afterwards, 'I think this really was an attempt by the British Library to restore their links with your archives.' Anyway, Josh went off, because it was the first day of term and he'd missed a lecture.

I went and did a bit of shopping. I bought for £59 an instant kettle; you just press a button and, three seconds later, a jet of boiling water comes out – an awful waste really, you have to press the button so hard, it's not wonderful. I'll take it to Stansgate.

I've got three things tomorrow: an interview with Gyles Brandreth; an Al Jazeera discussion on the Middle East; and the Speaker's party for a farewell to Chris Pond, one of the senior Commons Librarians. All this activity is beginning to restore my morale a bit.

Tuesday 8 January
At 3.20, three-quarters of an hour late, Gyles Brandreth arrived with a BBC TV crew for a short interview about *The Diaries*. He was very friendly, he always is. As he left, I was picked up by Al Jazeera. It was one of those awful interviews where you sit in one studio and you can hear other people talking, but you can't see them.

Then I went to the Commons, and I saw Ruth briefly, back in the Members' Library.

Then I went to the party for Chris Pond. I saw Betty Boothroyd and had a bit of a word with her, and went into the Speaker's House. Chris made a very good speech, and Ruth and I went and had a bite to eat in the Strangers' Dining Room. Saw David Davis and we had a word.

Home on the 148 bus.

It looks as though Barack Obama has won the New Hampshire primaries overwhelmingly, over Hillary Clinton. She looked absolutely shaken.

Wednesday 9 January

Hillary Clinton actually won in New Hampshire over Barack Obama, which made me very depressed.

There was a little programme on TV on diaries, and an interview with me that lasted about half a minute. I was compared to Pepys and . . . the other guy – the famous one who wrote the English dictionary. My memory!

Thursday 10 January

I had been asked by Rodney Bickerstaffe to the annual Lipman-Miliband Trust dinner. There was a glittering display of old left intellectuals: Tariq Ali, Robin Blackburn, Michael Kustow, Eric Hobsbawm, Gordon McLennan, Susan Watkins, Marj Mayo, and others I didn't know.

In the discussion I said that the left communicate pretty well with themselves and, on the whole, left intellectual life is quite strong at the moment, but how do you get the case across? There are a lot of new media outlets looking for material, for good ideas, and getting them across would be probably the most useful thing we can do.

I added that the most powerful publication this year in the Western world has been Michael Moore's *Sicko*, which was brilliantly researched and has put health at the top of the presidential election campaign.

Then we talked about today's generation of children and I said, 'Well, this is the first generation that knows more than their parents.' I think they're not apathetic; but they don't think anyone listens and they don't believe what they're told.

Rodney walked back with me to the bus in Oxford Street.

Sunday 13 January

I was picked up at eight and driven to Sky News for a discussion on the day's papers, on the Adam Boulton programme. Crispin Blunt, the Tory MP, a former army officer, was also on. It was rather fun.

I had chosen five subjects, not all of which we discussed. We did talk about Peter Hain, because that's the really big news. He's fighting for his political life after failing to disclose £103,000 which he raised for his deputy leadership campaign.

We discussed organ transplants: Brown is promoting the idea that organs should be allowed to be taken, unless you say No.

I brought in the question of Blair, who now wants to be President of the European Union, which of course would mean we had no opportunity to elect him.

Crispin raised Afghanistan. He was in the army. He's now a Whip, and he was very cautious, but afterwards he said he did agree with me.

Boulton began by introducing me as a left-wing member of the Labour Party and former Cabinet Minister. So I said, 'Tell me this: is Crispin Blunt "right-wing?"' 'Oh no, he's mainstream.' 'What about you – are you right-wing?' And I threw Boulton completely.

On the question of organ transplants, I said, 'When I'm dead, I will be happy if any bits of me that are useful should be made available, and of course they will be good left-wing organs.' So, by making a mockery of it, I think I sort of warned him off.

I walked out with Crispin Blunt, who said he had a very high regard for Hilary and he was the leader the Tory Party most feared, if Brown was displaced, which I thought was interesting.

Tuesday 15 January
A very wet day.

Got a bus to Simpson's-in-the-Strand, for *The Oldie* lunch. They had asked Natasha Kaplinsky – I think that was probably to tempt me to go – and she was put next to me at the top table, simply lovely, so I had a long talk to her. She was very sweet and kind and attentive . . . She's got this job at Channel 5, but she is not developing her full talent.

Anyway, I made a speech and it went very well, dare I say it, and then Natasha was going to Chiswick, so she dropped me off at the Commons in a cab.

Had tea with Alan Simpson for an hour and a quarter in the Tea

Room about the major paper he'd written on the Bali conference and the environment. He's absolutely passionate about it.

Thursday 17 January
I felt today I was back in my stride again, and I think all the depression of Christmas, which I stuffed into my diary day after day, is over.

Friday 18 January
I was very, very tired for some reason this morning.

I had the bright idea that I would ring Selina Scott. I had her home number, but it said, 'This number does not receive incoming calls', so I rang her mobile number, which I have had for a while. I left a message saying, 'I'm just phoning to say how much I enjoyed the twenty-fifth anniversary of the birth of *BBC Breakfast*.' Then, later in the day – I'll shorten the story – there was a text message: 'Thank you – you have made my day, bless you.' It didn't say who it was from and I looked up the number and it was Selina Scott's number. So I rang her back and said, 'Oh, I was touched that you should send it through – perhaps I might give you a ring again sometime' and left it at that.

Saturday 19 January
Brown is in Beijing with a lot of businessmen, including Richard Branson.

The Government are so keen for a private solution to Northern Rock that they obviously intend to subsidise a private bid to buy it; so, in effect, in addition to putting £56 billion into Northern Rock to protect it, it will then be protecting the purchaser of Northern Rock in order to avoid nationalisation! What with Chávez, on the one hand, and Bush and the crisis and 'anything but nationalisation' on the other, it looks to me as if the ideological, intellectual tide is turning. I have to keep myself cheerful!

I went to bed watching that lovely Jack Nicolson/Diane Keaton film, *Something's Got to Give*.

Tuesday 22 January
I had a phone call from Selina Scott, who had got my message and

said she'd love to see my latest *Diaries*, so I said I'd send them to her. 'Would you like to have a meal?' I said. 'It'll only be a pizza parlour.' 'Oh, that'll be fine.' I had to go into the Commons, so I dropped the book at the front door of her flat – no response to the bell.

Cab home. As I passed Video City I picked up Saffron's new film, called *Perfect Creature*, about a vampire. I'm dreading it, but I feel I have an obligation to watch it because she's in it.

Wednesday 23 January
I got up at 6.30, had breakfast, and caught a bus to Hyde Park Corner for the protest by the police. What was interesting was that there were 20,000 policemen in plain-clothes, all wearing white baseball caps; they just looked like members of the working class. They might have been dockers, they might have been miners, they might have been railwaymen. I said to them, 'The reason I'm here is that, during the miners' strike, when the police were on duty and I was supporting the miners, I always welcomed the police and said, "And when you're in the front line, I'll be there", so I'm discharging my obligation.' They appreciated that actually. They were terribly friendly! I signed lots of the caps.

There were police from Bristol, from Chesterfield, from the Met. One guy from the Met said, 'When I joined the Met, there were lots of us applying and they asked all of us, "Who's your favourite politician?" and everyone said Mrs Thatcher, the Iron Lady, and I said Tony Benn, and they let me in.'

Anyway, I came home, had lunch, then went to Bladerunners for a haircut, and Assad, who cuts my hair, gave me a long lecture on the difference between the Sunni and the Shia. He said, 'I'm a human being.' Our view on religion absolutely corresponded.

At six Ruth arrived and we set off for the Channel 4 Awards. I'm kind of excited. I think I may be getting an award. At our table was Tom McNally, who used to be Callaghan's PPS and who's now Liberal Democract of course; there was Lindsey German, who had finally got an invitation because the Stop the War movement had been in for the Most Inspiring Organisation; Ruth, sitting next to me. It's a very jolly occasion, and I said to Lindsey, in the course of the evening, 'Now you understand the real corruption of politics.' It's not so much power and cash as it is the feeling that you're part of a little club who govern the country. I quoted what my dad said that what he hated about the House of Lords was all the goodwill.

I saw Jon Cruddas, who won the award for the Best Campaigning Politician. I saw Harriet Harman, with Jack Dromey, a bit quiet. George Osborne, the Shadow Chancellor, I think won an award; and William Hague, the Politicians' Politician.

At the next table were Alastair Campbell and Fiona Millar and Gail Rebuck, who's the Chief Exec. of Random House.

So anyway we sat there, as the awards were announced. Alastair Campbell won the Best Political Book award, and I heard later, from Geoffrey Robinson, who announced the result, that it had been 50:50, three votes for Campbell and three for me, and they couldn't decide, so they agreed to give the award to Campbell and recommend me for a 'Lifetime Award', which Geoffrey Robinson announced, but no further reference was made to it. I thought they might give it to me at the end, but I was relaxed about it.

Thursday 24 January

I had an email today from a man who said I was the biggest hypocrite in politics, so I sent him a message back, saying some nutter had got hold of his email and was sending silly messages.

Anyway, at ten o'clock, Jane Shallice and a guy called Red Saunders, who's sixty-two, an artist and a photographer, came with a plan he had for re-creating the great radical events in British history, using actors and dressing them up and photographing them, so it looked as if they were being photographed at the time. It was a very interesting idea, and I said I would be a patron of it.

The big political news is that Peter Hain has resigned because the Electoral Commission has recommended that the police investigate his expenditure in the deputy leadership campaign.

Just before I went to bed, about eleven o'clock, the BBC rang and said would I do something on the *Today* programme tomorrow morning about Hain? Well, I was very suspicious. I rang them just before midnight to say: Do you want me? And they said No.

Sunday 27 January
World news . . . Well, Barack Obama had a devastating victory in South Carolina, getting more than half the votes cast, more than twice Hillary Clinton's.

Monday 28 January
Drove in to the Commons, and met Colin MacIntyre, who used to be the 'Mull Historical Society' and is now a recording artist in his own right, and he's produced an album called *Water*. I read a poem for his album. He came with a friend and a photographer. I took him to the Broom Cupboard and round Westminster Hall, on the Terrace, over to Portcullis House.

The big news today is that Senator Kennedy and the Kennedy clan have come out for Obama, which will be a huge boost to him. The other news is that Musharraf, the dictator of Pakistan, had tea with Gordon Brown at Number 10 Downing Street, which won't have done Brown any good.

Tuesday 29 January
Big news today is that Derek Conway, the Tory MP, who used his allowance to pay both his sons to work for him as research assistants, for which they didn't do a damn thing, has finally been expelled from the Tory Party. It gives politics such a bad name.

I had lunch, and in the afternoon Patrick McAndrew from Devon came to see me with a book to sign. He's a professional pilot; learned to fly on Tiger Moths and apparently, at an airport in Devon there is a Tiger Moth built in 1943, the very year I flew Tiger Moths. For £200 an hour you can fly it. I'm rather tempted. He was passionately against the European Union, against the smoking ban. Very friendly.

Then I rang Linda McDougall and she said, 'Oh yes, there is going to be a Channel 4 Lifetime Award. There will be a special occasion when it will be given to you.' So that's nice.

Then, in the evening, I rang Ruth, I rang Dave, I rang Hilary.

I had a brilliant idea that houses that are going to be repossessed should be bought by the local council and the owners could become tenants; it would create a whole new class of council-house tenants, and save people being dispossessed.

Wednesday 30 January
To Westminster City Hall in Victoria Street, where I was greeted and taken up to the Annual General Meeting of UNISON. There were about thirty people there, maybe forty, and I gave a little talk and answered a few questions.

The issues raised by trade unions are of fundamental importance and are never discussed in the media at all! One man described how, I think, half the employees working for Westminster Council are now contractors. Some workers had a hell of a job getting trade-union recognition and only get £6 an hour.

The world news today is that Rudy Giuliani, the former Mayor of New York City, has withdrawn from the Republican race, and Edwards has withdrawn from the Democratic race, so it's now McCain versus Romney (I think McCain will win), and Obama versus Hillary Clinton (and I fear Hillary Clinton may win). I can't believe the US will elect another Republican, but the most attractive would be an old man like McCain, straight as a die, fought in Vietnam, right-wing but trustworthy. That's the impression he will create, whereas Obama will be young and inexperienced, so it will be quite an election.

Thursday 31 January
I finalised the referendum letter – that is to say, the letter that Kelvin Hopkins is going to email to all MPs asking them to give me, and everyone else, a vote on the Lisbon Treaty.

In the evening I went by bus to the Curzon cinema for the film *Battle for Haditha*, made by Nick Broomfield. Lindsey German was there, Jane Shallice, David Gentleman, Carol Reagan, Brian Eno, Michael Palin, and I got a kiss from a woman who told me later her name was Sabrina Guinness. I looked her up when I got home and she's the heir to the beer fortune. She's been connected with Prince Charles, Mick Jagger, Bryan Ferry, Rod Stewart and is friends with Paul McCartney. I must say, she was very charming to me, but I can see the danger of getting into the celebrity circuit.

Friday 1 February
Tonight I picked up *The Ghost* by Robert Harris to read a few more

pages, and I stayed up for two and a half hours, till half-past one, finishing the book. It's brilliantly written.

To cut a long story short, it's an account of how the Americans, one way and another, promote their interests through British politics. That's a subject that interests me. Years ago, before I became an MP, I was invited by a Colonel Sheridan – who then worked for the Intelligence Research Department, at the Foreign Office – to work for them for more money than I would ever have got as a Member of Parliament. I was introduced to him by my old headmaster, Carlton, who put me on to Sheridan. And Sheridan said, 'Would you like to work?' and I said, 'Well, I want to be an MP, and I can't have a government job and be an MP.' I realised that there were MPs at that time paid for by the Intelligence Department.

Then, when I got into Parliament and became well known, the American Embassy was always asking me there. I went and talked to the staff there. They may have been thinking, 'Is this somebody we would be happy to promote?' Of course they were wrong and I became the bogeyman in Washington. During the IMF crisis Harold Lever, who was then in the Treasury, was sent to Washington and told them, 'If you don't support Jim Callaghan, Tony Benn will become Labour Prime Minister.' After that, I was the main enemy, and that emerged in lots of ways.

The final bit of the story is that, in 1981, the *New Statesman* reported that Airey Neave, who was himself murdered in 1979, had asked an intelligence officer to kill me, if it ever looked as if I was going to become Labour Prime Minister. That came a week or two before the Guillain–Barré syndrome, which landed me in hospital.

So I just put that into the context of Robert Harris's book. I am going to see him on Sunday.

Sunday 3 February
Emma, from Random House, and I caught the train to Kintbury for lunch with Robert Harris, the author, and his wife, Gill, and their children – Holly, the eldest, seventeen, and then Charlie, fifteen or sixteen, Matilda, seven, and Sam, five. They have got this beautiful old vicarage. Anyway, I was met at Kintbury station by Robert and two of his children.

He can't stand Blair. I suppose he's pro-Europe. He thinks Blair's behaviour in grossing up millions and millions from companies is a disgrace. *The Ghost* is about that, but it's more about the role of American intelligence in controlling British politics.

A lovely lunch, and I had a quiche (Emma had told them I was a vegetarian), and then we sat and talked about all sorts of things. It was a very, very nice day. I really enjoyed it, and I like Robert Harris and his wife. Their boy, Charlie, buys the *Morning Star* and he's active in CND.

Emma and I came back to London and I was collected from home and taken to the Royal Festival Hall to hear the end of the Daniel Barenboim Beethoven recital. He played for two hours on the piano. Absolutely packed!

Afterwards there was a discussion on the stage, with Barenboim, Jude Kelly, Helena Kennedy, Sir Peter Hall and myself, on art in society. I was nervous because I've got not a shred of art in me, or culture of any kind, but anyway I'm glad I went. Barenboim began, and talked mainly about his attempt as a Jew to bring about reconciliation with the Palestinians; he's taken Palestinian citizenship, and he's set up this orchestra where Jews and Arabs play together.

I had a slight clash with Peter Hall because he attacked politicians, and that irritated me a bit. Anyway, it wasn't too bad.

Monday 4 February

I had a phone call from Channel 4 saying they wanted me to go in at ten o'clock to do a thirty-second interview about the bugging of Sadiq Khan, the MP, who was bugged while he was visiting one of his constituents in prison awaiting extradition to America on a terrorism charge. So I said, 'Well, come here.'

So they turned up at 9.30, and I just had time to look at the *Diary*, and I found the occasion I wrote to Merlyn Rees saying, 'Is my phone being intercepted?' and he said, 'It's long been the practice not to confirm or deny whether any MPs have had their phones intercepted', which is completely contrary to the so-called Wilson Doctrine of 1966, where he said there would be no bugging of MPs. Rees also went on to say: 'And that applies even to Cabinet ministers, Privy Councillors or people of distinction like yourself.'

Then I also printed out the interview I had with Jim Callaghan, who said to me that only 139 people were being bugged in Britain, which was ridiculous.

Anyway, when I'd dug all that out, after Channel 4 left – I only got thirty seconds, but it was quite good – I then prepared an article for *The Guardian*, which I faxed off. My fax wouldn't work, so I had to go out and pay for it, which was a bloody nuisance. But I did get it to *The Guardian*, and they won't be able to use it in full, but they might turn it into a letter or something – I don't know.

Then I had a phone call from News 24, saying would I do an interview this afternoon? So that meant I was able to complete my enquiries, and the *Diary* is invaluable for that! Who else could produce, thirty years later, the text of letters or interviews in such detail? I mean, the media do know that about me.

At three o'clock I was taken to BBC News 24. I watched Jack Straw make his statement, in which he said that the bugging had not been authorised by ministers, which is incredible. So here was an MP being bugged on the authority of a policeman! He said he'd do an inquiry. David Davis was very good in coming back.

Anyway, when I got to News 24, I watched all that, and then I did a little interview, and I made the point that this was a police state.

Tuesday 5 February
I spent all morning preparing my evidence to the 'thirty-year rule' review committee at Church House, that Government documents which are deemed confidential cannot be seen until thirty years has elapsed (it used to be fifty).

Paul Dacre, the Editor-in-Chief of the *Daily Mail*, was in the chair. Sir Joe Pilling was one of the members, a former Permanent Secretary; and Professor David Cannadine. I really enjoyed it!

I asked at the beginning, 'May I record this?' and they said, 'Well, we are keeping a transcript.' I said, 'If it's all right, I will,' and they did let me, but they spoke so softly I don't suppose a word they said will be audible.

They just put the usual arguments, which I've heard a million times. Dacre said, 'What about collective Cabinet responsibility?' and then, 'Can there be any confidence, if information comes out?'

Cannadine said, 'If it comes out sooner than thirty years, many more people would have to be employed in the archives.'

I said to him, 'Well, democracy is very expensive, and the cheapest way to run a government is to have a government that gives orders and everybody else obeys them.'

I handed to them my pamphlet based on 'The Right to Know'. I also gave them the Cabinet minutes for the debate on the referendum on the Common Market in 1975, and my diary account for the same day.

I answered the questions very cheerfully. I said, 'You know, the Cabinet, in the old days, properly discussed things, and on one occasion the Prime Minister was outvoted. But the real problem is the trust between the public and the Government: the public feel no one listens, which is true, and they don't believe what they're told.' I said, 'You do need, as a minister, to have access to outside advice', and I gave as an example Windscale and one or two others. What's damaging is malice, rumour, leaks, lies; but truth is never damaging, and you should not underestimate people's intelligence. 'The thirty-year rule means I'll be 113 before I know what the Government's doing now!'

I also said secrecy protects weak ministers and strong civil servants. I think I mentioned *Spycatcher*, and argued that we're voters – we've got to make a decision! There are some real secrets, but most of the decisions of government are ordinary, and if people knew their point of view had been put in the Cabinet, it would strengthen their confidence in government.

Afterwards I had a bit of time to kill, so I went into the Commons and up into the Gallery and heard a bit of the debate on the Lisbon Treaty. It's a complete fraud, because there are days and days of debates, and only two hours allowed for the votes at the end. But I heard Jack Straw – saw Jack Straw sitting there – and a Tory MP raising practical points. It was quite interesting, and I stayed for a bit.

I went and had a smoke, because I was a bit early for the next meeting at 5.30, so I sat where the Post Office vans are, on my little portable seat. Then I went to Labour Action for Peace; truthfully, it is a complete waste of time. They're lovely people. Peace issues are hardly discussed at all.

I feel my contribution as a voter to our government is zero now, and I've got then to think what to do.

Wednesday 6 February
Woke up at six.

Super Tuesday results today. McCain romped home for the Republican nomination – I'm sure he'll win. Both Barack Obama and Hillary Clinton claim victories, but, in effect, they're both in the race.

Jonathan called me from Morocco! I'd tried to ring him thirteen times yesterday for his twenty-first birthday, but each time it either wouldn't connect or a Spanish voice came on, or else somebody would say, 'The person you've called has rung off.' Anyway, bless his heart, he's there with Zohreh, his Iranian girlfriend. He was twenty-one yesterday – I was so thrilled.

Then I had an interview with the *Ham & High* about one of my lectures for Clive Conway.

Then, from 3.45 to 5.00, Peter Kellner from YouGov came to see me. After the big demonstration in March 2003 against the invasion of Iraq, he said that it was just Trots having a day out. Well, if there are two million Trots, the British Establishment should be really frightened.

Anyway, I wanted to be friendly to him, particularly as he said he was writing a book of the best speeches ever made, and he wanted to include my Zircon speech – it was very much a parliamentary event. So I gave him one or two others speeches – or rather a video of my speeches. Also he was very interested in the peerage case, so I gave him the letter from Winston Churchill, which he photocopied, and also the speech that I wanted to make at the bar of the House, which I wasn't allowed to make, in May 1961.

Thursday 7 February
Worked on preparing the press release to go out with my letter to all MPs calling for a European Union referendum on the Lisbon Treaty. Then, just before three, Josh arrived and installed a new printer – took him a few hours and he had to go off and get a cable – he's just a wonderful son and a wonderful man! Time is the most precious thing. I have a huge respect for Josh.

Friday 8 February

Well, the media today have a widespread attack on the Archbishop of Canterbury, Rowan Williams, for saying that the adoption of sharia law in Britain was unavoidable. Ministers have attacked him, Trevor Phillips attacked him, everybody's attacked him! Rowan Williams is an academic who landed up as the head of a failing corporation, the Church of England. I think the statement will have caused enormous anger among the American bishops who are coming to the Lambeth Conference, and probably a lot of African bishops as well. What he was saying was thoughtful – we've got to get together with other religions – but of course the law must be made, in Britain at any rate, by people who've been elected, not by some religious principle. The statement will cause a lot of trouble. On the other hand, maybe he will have a good effect in the Muslim world and maybe, in fifty years' time, it will be seen as a pioneer of global religion or something.

I rang Dave, who sent me a brilliant article he's written for *International Affairs* reviewing a book about Russian history, dealing with Stalin and Khrushchev and Brezhnev and Andropov and Yeltsin and Putin. So I had a bit of a talk to him.

Tomorrow, I've got very little.

So that's the end of Friday 8 February.

Saturday 9 February

At eleven o'clock a young woman called Emily Wilkinson came to do an interview with me about the Boy Scouts. Well, I vaguely remembered going to the Isle of Mull with the Scouts in 1939. But I looked it all up on the Internet and, I must say, the more I looked up on it, the more awful the Boy Scout movement is! It was based on the fact that some young lad was at Mafeking when Baden-Powell was the commanding officer there, and he saved Mafeking from a siege by Africans, but then it went on to say that it was seen as a sort of imperial youth movement. Everyone has to swear to look after and serve the Queen and the country, and the Boy Scouts' oath is like a parliamentary oath. I discovered – which I didn't know – that Baden-Powell was suspected of having been a homosexual, which could well be the case, and also that Hitler had read the Scout manual that he had written, and the Hitler Youth Movement was based on it. Baden-Powell himself had a great admiration for Hitler and Mussolini.

After she left I went out and did something I've been meaning to do for weeks: I bought ten boxes to file my diary archive tapes in. They cost about £31 and I managed to get them all home, though they're very bulky, and then I sat down and I tackled the job, because the tapes were all over the place. It took me about four hours. There was one that I thought was missing, and then I discovered that it was misnumbered, and I put them all in order from mid-2004 to early 2008. Then I labelled the boxes and put them in a filing cabinet, and it does make me realise that, before I die, I have to put my archives in order.

I tried to write one or two postcards in reply to letters, but the plain truth is I cannot write any more. As soon as I'd done about a couple of cards, I got the most hideous cramp. My writing is completely illegible.

Political news, world news today . . .

Some members of the Synod have said the Archbishop of Canterbury should resign. The row has revealed the deep hatred of Muslims (quite apart from the issue of terrorism), which has been built up in the press. All he was trying to do, as he explained on his website, was see how our law could take account of the religious conscience of others. So I think poor old Rowan Williams has probably had his chips. It's rather sad actually. My first reaction was: what a silly thing to say; but the more I thought about it, the more I realised that it was a very important intellectual point to make, made with good intentions – like many of the statements I've made which have led to me being hammered into the ground.

The other news item that interested me, after the alleged bugging of the MP Sadiq Khan when he visited one of his constituents in prison, is that it now turns out (due to a leak from a whistle-blower) that it's a regular practice for the police to bug lawyers when they talk to their clients. Of course this totally undermines the principle of a legal system independent from the Executive. So we're just drifting deeper and deeper into this mire.

Gordon Brown hasn't got a radical instinct in his body. I'm sorry for him because, having been a very 'successful' Chancellor of the

Exchequer, he's now inherited an economy that's going wrong in a huge way and he hasn't got Blair's flair (not that I liked it) to get him through. It's all the most ghastly mess!

Sunday 10 February
Saffron rang and left a message while I was out, and so I tried to ring her back. Eventually got on to her and she has been very unwell. She hasn't been doing any writing. Her TV series – in which she plays a civil-rights lawyer – is getting very good reviews and awards, and she's earning a decent amount of money. So it was nice to talk to her. I'm very fond of Saffron.

I've got three things tomorrow: somebody coming to talk about Paul Robeson; a broadcast on Radio 2 with Steve Wright; and then a public meeting for UNISON in the evening. So things are picking up! I've had four very lazy days.

Monday 11 February
I got a cab to the BBC, and who should I see there but Matt Wrack, General Secretary of the Fire Brigades Union; he was commenting on the fact that firefighters are being attacked by youths while they're doing their job.

Oh, I saw Lisa Minnelli, the daughter of Judy Garland, and so I went up to her and I said, 'Can I shake your hand?' I said, 'I'm your mother's generation – I remember her so well.'

Jonathan Ross walked by. He gets £9 million a year from the BBC.

I did this interview with Steve Wright about the lectures I'm doing for the agent Clive Conway, called *An Audience with Tony Benn*. He was all over me, and he listed all the places I'm appearing at.

Then I got a cab to Tottenham Court Road and bought a DVD camera for £232. It records an hour on a disc.

I took the tube to a UNISON meeting in support of Michael Gavan, a UNISON trade-union rep who'd been sacked by the Labour Council in Newham, whose head is Sir Robin Wales. There were 130–150 people there, and Michael got a standing ovation.

The McCartneys' divorce is all over the place, and the Americans announced they're going to try six people they've held at Guantanamo Bay with responsibility for the 9/11 bombing.

Wednesday 13 February

I spent the whole morning preparing material in relation to the message that Kelvin Hopkins is going to email for me tomorrow. I put a copy in envelopes, with a cover note, to all the Party Leaders and then did another set of envelopes for the political editors of the major newspapers and media outlets. Then I drove to the Commons and I put the letters for the MPs into the internal mail system. I took the press releases up to the Press Gallery. There was a very nice lady who worked for the *Daily Mail*, who took some of them to distribute. The rest were left on the table at the entrance to the room and they may be spotted tomorrow. I don't know if anyone will look at them: the physical transmission of material is so out-of-date now – it's all electronic. Tomorrow I'll have a little blitz on the telephone, with Ruth's help.

Thursday 14 February

St Valentine's Day.

At ten o'clock a very glamorous woman, Celia Walden, from the *Daily Telegraph* came to see me, and all her questions were about Brown, and Mandelson, and Cherie Blair, and nothing political whatsoever! She sat and smiled at me, in a seductive way, and then a photographer came and took pictures.

As she left, I said, 'Have you got a nice boyfriend?' and she said, 'Piers Morgan' (the former Editor of the *Daily Mirror*). So I said, 'You know, he was fitted up by MI5.' She said, 'What do you mean?' 'Well,' I said, 'when a picture appeared in the *Mirror*, allegedly of a torture of an Iraqi, there was a truck in the picture and the Ministry of Defence said that truck had never left Britain . . . they [MI5] obviously set this picture up and then let it be published and then used it to discredit Piers Morgan and get him sacked.' She said she'd never thought of that. It was quite interesting.

I did get four or five replies from Tory MPs in favour of my plan for a referendum on the Lisbon Treaty, and one Labour MP who said, 'I'm not going to support a Tory plan!' So that's what I expected.

Who should I see outside Marks & Spencer but Rory Bremner! While we were talking a beautiful Asian girl came up and asked: was this Notting Hill Gate? So as she left, I said to Rory, 'I assumed she was a fan of yours,' and he said, 'No, I assumed she was a fan of yours.' And I said, 'That put both of us in our place – because she didn't know who either of us was.'

Lord Justice Moses has said that the decision by Blair to cancel the Serious Fraud Office inquiry into bribery in Saudi Arabia by BAE was blackmail by the Saudi Government. Quite extraordinary that all this stuff comes out and it doesn't seem to make any difference to anybody's views. They just take corruption for granted, and in a way they're right, because it does go on, always has gone on. It went on when I was a Minister of Technology.

After eight, I had a call from Natasha Kaplinsky. She said, 'This is a Valentine phone call. Who do you think it is?' So I said, 'Mm . . . not sure . . .' and then she said, 'It's Natasha', and I said, 'I didn't want to suggest that anyone else could have such a beautiful voice as you.'

After a chat, she asked: would I have breakfast with her at a very glamorous restaurant near the Ritz? Well, I said, 'Natasha, if you and I are seen having breakfast at a fancy hotel full of gossip writers, that would do us in.' So she said, 'All right, I'll come to Starbucks!'

Friday 15 February
Up early, for a rather angry BBC Radio Bristol interview about the Iraq war. The interviewer said nobody cares about it, we've got to stay, and I was really quite sharp with him.

I am getting more responses from Tories – all sympathetic – to my proposal, and hostile ones from Nick Palmer, a Labour MP, saying he 'wasn't prepared to play the Tory game', and Gerald Kaufman.

Then I went to Number 10. The Stop the War Coalition had organised to present an anti-war letter. Bianca Jagger was there, Jeremy Corbyn, Louise Christian, Hetty Bower – aged 102 – and a five-year-old boy who had been in his mother's womb when she marched on the demonstration in 2003, so that was very interesting. Also David Gentleman was there and Walter Wolfgang. We walked up to Number 10 and presented the letter, and a lot of photographs were taken. Sky TV covered it later, but not the BBC, predictably. The BBC never mentions the Stop the War movement.

Monday 18 February

Hilary rang to tell me that he attended the National Farmers' Union conference and got booed when he said that he would make a decision about the culling of badgers (to combat TB) in the light of the scientific argument and public opinion. So he had a struggle, but it was all right, I think.

The Northern Rock row is blowing up because Alistair Darling and Brown are being attacked for nationalising Northern Rock. But what else could they do? I mean, if Northern Rock had gone bankrupt, there would have been a complete run on all the banks, so they did the right thing.

Brown is talking about temporary public ownership, but everybody else is talking about nationalisation, which is what it is. So, we shall see – whether it solves the problem is yet to be seen.

Tuesday 19 February

The *Daily Mail* and a couple of other papers absolutely denounced Natasha's Channel 5 News appearance.

Thursday 21 February

David Miliband has had to admit the Government did know that Diego Garcia, which is our base, was used by the Americans to transfer prisoners ('rendition') who've never been tried, to be tortured in other countries. The fact that they lied to us is incredible!

Friday 22 February

I had a message, a phone call, from Mr Thomson, the General Secretary of the Federation of SubPostmasters, about the massive cuts: 169 post offices in London are being lost. I rang him back, and he was cautious, because although they want to save post offices, if there is limited business, he wants it directed to those offices that would survive.

The sub-post offices are now banned from handling TV licences or passport work; Girobank, which I set up, has been transferred; and you can only have a Post Office savings account if you also have a bank account. I spoke to my local sub-postmaster who has been told he cannot petition or speak out publicly and, if he does, he will lose his redundancy payment. He will get quite a good redundancy pay to close his post office business.

So what we're witnessing, and it all emanates from a combination of Blairism and Brussels, is this deliberate destruction of the Post Office network, a public-service network.

Watched *Genevieve*, which must have been made fifty years ago: Kenneth More and Kay Kendall and Dinah Sheridan and John Gregson. Looking at it again, it gave me an insight into the politics of the post-war period. It reminded me of what Britain was like before we had any immigration: all these white people, living it up. It was the beginning of 'Never had it so good'. I understand now why I wanted to marry an American. That wasn't my world; it isn't my world.

Saturday 23 February
I drove to William Rust House, to celebrate twenty-five years of the *Morning Star* and the editorship of John Haylett.

I had looked up Haylett's life story. In my speech to honour him I said he was once a painter and decorator, but he was never a man for papering over the cracks, and he always wanted to get the structure right, and what an amazing twenty-five years it had been . . . beginning with the Cold War, and the early Thatcher years, and Reagan and Thatcher talking about the Evil Empire, the invasion of Grenada, through the Kinnock period, and how things looked better today: Chávez in Venezuela, Northern Rock showing you couldn't rely on market forces; and the Iraq and Afghan wars, which everybody hated. I said the great thing about the *Morning Star* was that it had remained true to its purpose. I said some communists, like John Reid, shifted from Stalin to Blair, and that was the end of him; others went off into the fringe groups. I said my favourite socialist magazine is the *Weekly Worker*, where page one demands political action, and pages two, three, four and five denounce everyone else who attempt it. The thing about the *Morning Star*: they supported working people, and that's what matters. They were true Marxists. I don't know if it went down very well because I'm not really in that left intellectual circle.

The *Morning Star* is the only socialist daily newspaper published in English anywhere in the world. It has a small circulation, but a lot of influence.

The news today is that the Speaker is under attack. His spokesman has had to resign because he misinformed people about his wife Mary's expenses. They really are trying to get rid of him. Michael Martin is hated because he's not the 'right' class to be Speaker.

Monday 25 February
This is dictated on a new cassette recorder – I think it may work better.

I got up at five o'clock and went to do an interview about Michael Martin. I defended him very vigorously. I wrote a letter to him.

But he seems to be surviving. The Prime Minister supported him today.

Tuesday 26 February
I lay in bed this morning and thought: if I die this morning, what a wonderful way to go – I am in bed, I am comfortable and, if I just stop breathing, how heavenly!

Wednesday 27 February
Tube to Paddington and took the train to Shrivenham, where I'd been invited to speak on alternatives to war. They had asked me as President of the Stop the War Coalition. It was very interesting, about thirty, forty people. There were four colonels, four group captains and four naval captains, and there was one rear admiral and an air commodore. I was a bit nervous about it. Their age range was, I should think, between thirty-eight and about forty-five.

They couldn't have been more friendly; they laughed and listened. A couple of them said they thought it was only nuclear weapons that had prevented the Soviet Union coming and invading the West, which I don't believe. I don't think the others really believed it. Anyway, I developed the argument in a way that I think would make a perfectly good chapter for 'Confessions of a Socialist', and I think this is probably the way I'm going to tackle my new book. I'll pick the chapter headings and talk about them.

There was an item in the paper today, about the Numbrella, which is an umbrella you put on your shoulders and it goes all over your head and you don't have to hold it, and I thought to myself: That is a smoker's dream! I'll sit on my stool with that on, and I can smoke my pipe and I'd have a smoking room of my own. I got onto the Internet and there were 747 references to it, but not one of them told you how to buy it! I'll put Josh on to it.

Thursday 28 February
Gave a talk at the Charing Cross Hotel to a group called Government Information, I think – thirty or forty civil servants. One of them was in the Cabinet Office as an adviser, and he said there were ten advisers responsible for delivery – a great phrase that Blair introduced; and there were others who gave orders to civil servants. So they've introduced a completely new layer in government: not elected, not professional, cronies of the leader. The whole thing is a top-down structure, in which the Cabinet is sidelined, Parliament is sidelined, the Party is sidelined. It is really a medieval monarchy operating in an imperial system, where even the monarch doesn't have much control of anything; it's all decided by Europe or by the Americans, or by the multinationals or by the banks, or whatever. When I put to them my points, they looked slightly blank because of course they were young enough, all of them, to have come in long after 1979 when I left office, and it's totally different from what it was then.

My legs are very wobbly now. I've always been slightly unsteady on my pins, but I do find myself swaying about a bit and I hope it isn't anything serious, because if I couldn't walk, I would be in a jam. But there will come a moment when I realise my political life is over.

My hearing is absolutely completely gone! It's lovely, in the sense that I go along the street and I don't hear any traffic noise, but I don't hear anybody saying anything.

Friday 29 February
I was picked up by John Grice, this very nice guy who drives me round to theatres all over the country for the Clive Conway lectures, and he took me to the New Wimbledon Theatre. There were about 600 people there and, before the lecture, I sat in the little bathroom by the dressing room and smoked my pipe – the first time I've deliberately broken the law. I'm going to buy some deodorant so that in the future I'll be able to disguise where I've been smoking. I mean, these laws are intolerable!

I gave the lecture. A lovely girl called Maria, who was sixteen, volunteered to come on the stage with me and help me with the questions, as I am still completely deaf.

The audience were rather quiet – they didn't laugh a lot – but at the end there was a warm response.

Saturday 1 March

I heard the unbelievable news that David Butler's son, Gareth, who's forty-two, had just died.

Sunday 2 March

I rang David Butler about the death of Gareth; I phoned the children to tell them. Hilary is David's godson.

Tuesday 4 March

Lissie was on *Woman's Hour,* talking about *One of Us,* with Lady Rachel Billington, I think, Lord Longford's younger daughter. Lissie was great.

I lost my purse during the day. I looked round the house everywhere and went to the car to see if it had fallen, and then came home and found it in my suit pocket, where I'd put it ready for tomorrow – so that is old age!

Wednesday 5 March

I caught a cab to Euston. Met Ruth and we caught the train to Lancaster.

However, it broke down at Crewe, and we were standing on the platform, not knowing what to do; got on another packed train, to Lancaster, and we were picked up there and driven to Keswick for the 'Ways with Words' Festival. It was a nightmare – exhausting and couldn't sleep on the train, because I worried all the time!

I'm using the lectures now to try out my themes for 'Confessions of a Socialist'. The audience was white, average age sixty-plus, or more, though there were one or two young people. I took the three themes of war, religion and democracy, and then answered questions, and I must say, it did go down well.

Then we were driven to Penrith and I got home by nine! I really was whacked. So that was the end of a ghastly day. I'm beginning to wonder whether I can travel, and indeed, if Ruth hadn't been there, I'd have been in a panic! I wouldn't have known who to ring or what to do, but she organised everything so well. She went for a walk by the lake while I was speaking so that she didn't have to hear me!

Thursday 6 March
Hillary Clinton won Ohio and Texas, but if you count the delegates, Barack Obama is still ahead. Of course the fear many people have is that if Hillary Clinton and Barack Obama do each other such damage right up to the Convention in Denver, this will help McCain, the Republican, to win. I hope to God that doesn't happen. If it does happen, we're in real, real trouble.

Yesterday, I forgot to mention it, the Commons voted *not* to hold a referendum on the Lisbon Treaty. I must say, I felt utterly betrayed by Brown and the Labour leadership. Here is a major decision, which really takes powers from us and gives them to the Commission and people in Brussels, and they wouldn't even allow a popular vote. They argue that it is just a treaty, not a constitution, but it is a treaty making constitutional changes!

Nick Clegg, the Liberal Democrat Leader, lost three of his front-bench people as a result of this, and the Party is divided on it.

You know, I shouldn't get angry at my age because, in different periods of history, people have had different degrees of control over their lives, but this is a significant reduction in the people's control of the laws they're obliged to obey.

I caught the Underground to Baker Street, walked to Daunt's bookshop in Marylebone High Street, and there was a huge party of family and friends for the launch of Lissie's book. Ruth was there, Emma Mitchell came, Tim Owen and Jemma Redgrave, Jim Naughtie and his wife Ellie. Stephen phoned from Washington. Faith Evans, her agent . . . Oh, it was a lovely party! So many faces I knew, but couldn't remember. A speech made by the head of Chatto & Windus, and then by Lissie, a lovely speech.

Bombing in Jerusalem at a rabbinical school, and the whole Middle East thing is going on and on and on, and there's no end to it in sight. The Americans and the British support Israel, and the

Israelis are just dominant, and the Palestinians are really ignored.

I watched *Newsnight* in bed. A survey showed that the white working class don't think anyone listens to them, don't think anyone is interested in their problems, there isn't enough housing, the NHS isn't any good; the white middle class was included, with similar doubts, but slightly less so. Then, Kirsty Wark, who was chairing it, had a panel that included Margaret Hodge, who gushed on about Barking and how she talked to people all the time, had them to tea and gave them chocolate biscuits and how, when you'd had tea and chocolate biscuits, people understood it much better.

Then, blow me down, who did they interview: Nick Griffin, who is the head of the British National Party, the fascist party! He was so quiet and so moderate.

It really, really frightened me. It took me right back to the 1930s, to Oswald Mosley, and I've always feared that if the economy got into difficulties, this would emerge. Of course, if anybody ignores the white working class, it's the BBC, *Newsnight*! They never have any trade unionists on – there's seven million trade unionists. They used to have industrial correspondents, and they don't have them any more. The only time trade unions are mentioned is when there's a strike. I really fear the BBC as an instrument of fascist propaganda.

Friday 7 March
Got up at five o'clock because I was doing the newspapers on News 24. I watched the news bulletins and reports from the stock market in London and Singapore and Washington, and God knows where else.

I was picked up at 6.30. Actually, in the car I had such a cough, I had to ask the guy to take me back in order to get some cough medicine. At the studio I had two hours on my own. I had a cup of tea and I read all the papers and I picked the issues: Israel and Palestine; world starvation (millions are going to die); picked up the white working-class item which had been on *Newsnight*, and the world's billionaires; ID cards; and how Obama might improve relations with Britain.

I went into the studio and had five and a half minutes. On Palestine I said you must talk to Hamas, and they said, 'They're a terrorist organisation.' 'Well,' I said, 'you remember the Omagh bombings in Ireland – how did that come right? It came right because they talked.' Nelson Mandela was a terrorist. So I got the point about Hamas across.

Then, on the world-starvation item, I said, 'Look, we've been told it's all about pollution and CO_2, but it's a critical shortage of food and it raises so many questions.' I made the point about vegetarianism, and the crime of using land for biofuels instead of food, and said we may have to come to rationing.

Then, the white working class. I said that actually, the BBC had a heavy responsibility, because the media simply don't cover working-class interests. I said, 'You have the Dow Jones every morning.' They said, 'Yes, because of globalisation and people moving money.' I said, 'Yes, but people who move their money don't depend upon News 24 – what about all the other news there might be?'

Then the billionaires came up and I said the gap was wider than it had been before. We never got to ID cards.

Sunday 9 March
Travelling through the English countryside, I make it my business to look for churches, and wherever you are in the countryside there's always one spire, sometimes two or three visible, or church towers, and you realise that, in the Middle Ages, the churches were everything: they were the source of information; they were the centre of power because the kings tried to use the churches, and Henry VIII nationalised the Church. Also, it was part of the ritual of marriages and christenings and funerals, and that's the most important thing.

I hardly ever go to church. Seeing those buildings made me think so much about the ongoing role of religion. I don't know how many people actually believe the story of Adam and Eve and the Virgin birth, and the physical ascension and the Holy Ghost and the Trinity, and so on. The teaching of the religious leaders is important and the ritual is important.

Monday 10 March
I forgot to mention that, last Thursday, I had a letter from Gordon Brown, signed by him, in response to the email I sent to all MPs

about the referendum. It was just a standard Government answer, but still, it's interesting to have it.

Tuesday 11 March
John Hutton, Minister of Work and Pensions, made a statement the other day, saying we should celebrate the wealthy because of their entrepreneurial skills. Then, tonight, there was a report that Alistair Darling was unlikely to tax non-domiciled residents with what they earn abroad, because it might drive them to leave the country. Then there were pictures on the television of students taking an oath of allegiance to the Queen and an interview with an Indian who said, 'If we're being taxed, I'm leaving the country.' So if his children had taken an oath of allegiance to the Queen, are they going to leave the country? I don't know. The whole thing is completely rotten and corrupt and medieval!

Friday 14 March
To Smooth Radio. I had been asked to supply six bits of music; it was like *Desert Island Discs*. The last piece was 'Vincent' by Don McLean, and I paid a special tribute to Ruth. They were nice, friendly, soft interviewers.

Saturday 15 March
I caught the 94 to Piccadilly Circus and walked very slowly to the Stop the War rally in Trafalgar Square, which was packed! It is the fifth anniversary of the start of the Iraq war. I sat on the platform – a huge platform that had been erected just in front of Nelson's Column – and I spoke for four minutes and ten seconds. Two minutes was the limit, but I got away with it; they liked the phrase 'Parliament belongs to the past; the streets belong to the future'. They really liked that.

Other speakers: George Galloway; Bruce Kent; Hetty Bower, who's 102, was brought onto the platform; lots of Muslim speakers; Louise Christian; Kate Hudson; Lindsey German.

Then I was taken to the head of the march, down Whitehall. There was another meeting in Parliament Square. There was nothing about the demonstration on either the BBC or ITV that I saw.

One of the worries about demonstrations is the need to have a wee – old age has its problems. I'm feeling a little bit better, a bit more relaxed, less tired, and the job is done, and it was a brilliant achievement.

There were, I think fifty demonstrations going on today, all over the world, and I made a reference to them, from Puerto Rico to Korea, from Iceland to New Zealand, many of them in cities in America, and it was impressive. I'm very proud to be the President of the Stop the War Coalition, and that Coalition has done a fantastic job! The organisation is brilliant.

Monday 17 March
Jonathan Powell, who's Blair's Chief of Staff, has published a book in which he's saying we should talk to Hamas and to al-Qaeda and to the Taliban. So I thought: Well, that must be a breach of the Terrorism Act; so I rang up Liberty. Shami Chakrabarti was out, but I put it to somebody there.

Wednesday 19 March
To Edinburgh Waverley station, and was met by my friend Ann Henderson, who got us a taxi to the Scottish Parliament, where I was greeted by the Labour MSP, Bill Butler.

Then met Alex Fergusson, who is the Conservative Presiding Officer of the Scottish Parliament. I had been invited to give the 'Time for Reflection', which is held in the Parliament every Wednesday. I took as my theme the conflict between the kings and the prophets, which my mum had taught me as we read the Bible, and I delivered it in four minutes. There was applause!

I was taken to see Alex Salmond, the First Minister of the Scottish *Government*, as he calls it. He's a very bright lad, is Alex, and of course he's the Leader of the Scottish National Party. I don't think independence is on the cards. I was asked about it, and I said, 'Well, it's just a matter for Scotland; I mean, the English are not going to try and send an army up – we haven't got one! It's just entirely for you whether you want it or not.'

My impressions of the Scottish Parliament were positive. It is very open, with people in and out all the time, and little security and, I must say, very agreeable, unlike the House of Commons, which is a palace. The only doubt I had about it was the layout of the chamber: like the American House of Representatives and the Senate, in a semicircle, so that when you're speaking you're in a bit of a difficulty because, if you're a minister at the front, you speak and all the audience are behind you. You're just addressing the Presiding Officer. I think the layout does make a difference. The House of Commons has Government and Opposition facing each other, which I think is much more agreeable, but in general I found it very impressive.

My visit was treated as a state visit! Bless her heart, Ann took me to Waverley station and I caught the 5.30 train to London.

Thursday 20 March
Up at seven o'clock.

I wrote and faxed an article, 'Ken for Mayor', for the *Campaign Group News*.

Oh, the other thing is that this credit crunch, or whatever they call it, is a real banking crisis. I mean, in America, I think Bear Stearns, the fifth-largest bank, went bust, and Morgan Stanley bought it up, and the shares have slumped. Today the Bank of England has announced it's going to meet the big banks and provide another £11 billion to keep them going, so there's plenty of money when they want to do it! It's all about confidence, because the whole thing is a complete casino. There was no money for Rolls-Royce when they went bust, but when the banks get into trouble, then there's plenty of money.

Although the commentators are all very reassuring – oh, it's all under control, don't worry, confidence is restored – I'm not sure that's true at all.

This is a turning point in British history, I think, and I've just got to try and think it out. I find it very difficult, but I have got to try starting to think it out again.

Sunday 23 March, Stansgate
A light fall of snow – I mean, really fairyland – and it was lovely. Lissie and I had a three-and-a-half-mile walk, and we talked about the family all the way.

As a result of being away so long, we missed the Easter-egg hunt which Stephen had organised, which is a bit of a ritual. I suppose, in a way, I have drifted into . . . well, complete abandonment of the Church, although the values are important.

Monday 24 March
Up at six. Rang Ruth.

Tuesday 25 March
To St Thomas's. There was a very nice young woman there, a nurse, half-French and half-Croatian. When people do humanise the bureaucracy, it makes such a hell of a difference.

Anyway, I had an electrocardiogram, and saw Dr Cooklin, and he was quite satisfied.

Thursday 27 March
Water poured into the house last night. It's coming from a gutter, I think, through into my bathroom, down into the kitchen, which was soaking wet on the floor. Even in the basement, down the lights – desperately dangerous. I rang Josh and he's called the roofing company who were supposed to have fixed it.

Friday 28 March
Up early because McDonald's, the roofing people, came at 8.30 and cleared the roof gutters, which are blocked.

Tuesday 1 April
In the papers today – it is April Fool's Day – there was an item saying Brown had asked Carla Bruni, the wife of President Sarkozy of France, to come and work in Britain, on British design and dress sense, which must be an April Fool; and, next to it, an article about Piers Morgan interviewing Nick Clegg, for *GQ* magazine, in which Clegg said he'd slept with twenty women, which may be an April Fool – it won't do him any good.

I had an invitation today to meet George Clooney, the American actor. *Harpers & Queen's* invited me. I refused, because I supposed it might be a celebrity event.

Thursday 3 April

If I live to do this diary, it is my eighty-third birthday. When I was sixteen, I wrote in my plan for my life I would die at eighty-two, so I'm dictating this at twenty-two minutes past eleven . . . if I live another thirty-seven minutes, I will have defeated the forecast of my childhood! Ruth arrived with a lovely card, and a very expensive tobacco pouch, which she'd bought in Dunhill's and had had embossed with my initials. It was very sweet of her and we had a lovely day together.

I had home-made cakes from Alison McPherson, who so brilliantly transcribes the diaries.

Natasha phoned. The *Daily Express* today says she's pregnant and, Channel 5 having just taken her on, at a million pounds a year, they must be absolutely livid. But at any rate I said to her on the phone, 'Why don't you become the first newsreader who breastfeeds on the five o'clock news?' and she laughed.

Anyway, then Almaz from Tesco's, whom I helped with her application to stay here, came, and she brought me some lovely presents.

Later Ruth and I watched *The Life and Death of Colonel Blimp*, which is our favourite film.

Saturday 5 April

I caught a Tube and a bus, because the Northern Line was broken, to the Angel, and spent a couple of hours with the London mayoral team. I said a word or two, about how Ken was the most distinguished Londoner of his generation. We walked through Camden Market. It was a beautiful walk – I'd never been before – and met lots of people.

Sunday 6 April

The Olympic torch is in London en route to China. I didn't actually see it. But there were Tibetan protests, a couple of thousand people, they estimate, and the BBC gave it 100 per cent coverage. What utter hypocrisy! When we have 20,000 people in Trafalgar Square, or two million on the streets of London, the BBC plays it down; but the Olympic-torch demo against China, they play it up and play it up.

Monday 7 April

The Diana verdict came on the news, and the coroner – I've forgotten who it was now . . . Butler-Sloss . . . no, I think it's somebody else actually – announced the result, which was a majority verdict that it was an unlawful killing because the driver, Henri Paul, was drunk, and the paparazzi had made it worse.

The Olympic flame was actually extinguished in France – I heard that on the news – but they always keep another flame alive.

Tuesday 8 April

I had a very restless night. I was worried about the Celia Walden article which was to appear in the *Telegraph*, and it was just as bad as I feared it would be. I found it vindictive and sly and cynical. It reminded me of the sort of articles I used to get in the old days, when beautiful women came to interview me for the tabloids and then stabbed me to death.

Someone who works for the National Trust came up to me in Pizza Express and said, 'Have you ever thought of turning your house in Holland Park Avenue into a socialist war room, like Churchill's Cabinet War Room?' He sent me an email and I sent it on to Josh, and it would be fantastic if it could be done.

Wednesday 9 April

Cleared a bit of office backlog this morning. Went to Ryman's to get some office supplies – paper and pencils and things.

To the Transport & General Workers' Union office, at Theobalds Road, for Jack Jones's ninety-fifth birthday. It was a gathering of the old trade unionist elite. Rodney Bickerstaffe; Ken Gill was there – with lung cancer; Neil Kinnock, now sixty-five, laughing-boy Kinnock. Geoffrey Goodman was there, bless his heart – I like him – and his wife, Margit; Bill Wedderburn. I couldn't remember Bill's name. I thought he might be an MP, so when I came home I looked up all the MPs elected in '74, no sign of him; and then it kept coming back to me in little bits that his name began with 'W', and then, gradually, Bill came to my mind. So I looked up the House of Lords and, of course, it was Lord Wedderburn. He's seventy now and looked a bit frail.

People read poetry and sang songs from the International Brigade, and Rodney spoke, and I spoke. I said that I knew Jack didn't want to be reminded of his past because, on his ninetieth birthday, somebody paid a tribute to him and he brushed that aside and talked about the treatment of trade unions and low pay and pensions. 'I put in my diary that he sounded to me like a twenty-year-old shop steward.'

Jack was very sweet. He sat there, smiling. I went on to say that here was Jack: he was born in 1913, before the First World War began, when Keir Hardie was still alive, when the Kaiser, the King and the Tsar were cousins, he lived through the war when people were slaughtered; saw the General Strike, the Hunger March, the International Brigade. 'The thing about Jack is his whole life, in a way, his experience, has been a preparation for the future, because every generation has to fight the same battles again and again and again.'

Saturday 12 April

There was a thunderstorm today and very severe flooding in the house, pouring down the wall of my bathroom, into the kitchen. I should think a couple of gallons came down.

Stephen's back, after being stranded in New Orleans.

Sunday 13 April

I did a twenty-minute programme for BBC Scotland about the court decision to overrule the cancellation of the Serious Fraud Squad inquiry into briberies in connection with British Aerospace . . . BAE's sale of Typhoon fighters to Saudi Arabia.

The polls today show 44 per cent for the Conservatives, 28 per cent for Labour, and one of the things that is causing most trouble is the 10p income-tax change, which means that poor single people pay £254 a year more tax than they did. It was introduced by Gordon Brown as Chancellor a year ago – there's no chance of getting that changed. A lot of Labour MPs who are going to lose their seats are really worried, and *The Sunday Times* had a whole spread about getting rid of Brown and who might succeed him.

Monday 14 April

Train to Wakefield, and was driven to Huddersfield University, for the Harold Wilson Memorial Lecture. I had tea with the Vice Chancellor and the Bishop of Wakefield, and his wife.

Apparently, they had to take another auditorium and pipe through the lecture, it was so booked. Mary Wilson was sitting in the audience, with Robin, Harold's oldest son, who's just about to retire as Professor of Mathematics at the Open University. It was great fun.

At dinner afterwards I sat with Mary. She's ninety-two and a bit frail. At half-past nine, I was picked up and driven home by two drivers, and got back by about 12.45, exhausted.

Friday 18 April
Phil Thompson, from the NUM in Barnsley, came and picked up my miners' banner of Wharncliffe Woodmoor Colliery; they want to borrow it for the surviving miner of the 1936 pit disaster.*

After I was in bed the phone rang – about ten to twelve I think – and I was told that Gwyneth Dunwoody has died. Would I do an interview for BBC *Breakfast* at six in the morning? So I got up and came downstairs and looked up Wikipedia and, blow me down, Wikipedia had already recorded her death, before it was even on the news! I got up at 4.50 and did a little interview. The driver knew Natasha, so I had a talk about that.

I should say that the Pope has been in America, apologising for sexual harassment. Gordon Brown has been in America, much criticised for alleged weakness in support of the American troops in Basra. Brown is in trouble at home because there have been resignations over the 10p tax band, which will mean that low-paid single people will pay more tax. He made a bold speech about reconstructing international institutions and the Atlantic partnership, but the man is in trouble.

Saturday 19 April
Oh, bloody computer problems!

Sunday 20 April
I did a twenty-five-minute interview with Northern Ireland radio on Enoch Powell's 'Rivers of Blood' speech with Jeffrey Donaldson, had an interesting discussion about immigration.

---

* On 6 August 1936, fifty-eight men died in a gas explosion and roof falls at Wharncliffe Woodmoor Colliery, South Yorkshire.

I got myself ready to go to Trafalgar Square about the treatment of ethnic caterers – that is to say, the Indians, Pakistanis, Turkish, Bangladeshi and Chinese – and the difficulties they're having in getting here and being looked after.

Also, I got a note from Stephen saying that Saffron was coming over to do BBC *Question Time*. She hasn't been in touch with me, but it's a great opportunity for her, so I must watch that.

I had a short snooze, and then Lissie arrived, about a quarter past four, and Josh almost immediately afterwards, and we had a marvellous talk!

We made plans for a family court of four to take charge of all the things at Stansgate and here after I die, to arrange for the deposition of the archives, and for the National Trust idea.

Then we planned my funeral. I thought a family funeral, limited to immediate family, Peter Carter and Ruth. A memorial meeting, rather than a service, in the Central Hall Westminster, because Josh thought lots of people would want to come. I want it to be tidy and happy for everybody.

Monday 21 April
I have decided to change the title of my book from 'Confessions of a Socialist' to 'Letters to my Grandchildren', which I think is a much more attractive title. This is a test of my new dictating machine for my diary, so I'll see what it sounds like. Well, that does sound much better, so I'm going to stick to this now.

The huge row over the 10p tax change continues. Of course, if Labour MPs vote against Brown, he might threaten to resign as Prime Minister, but I don't think he could; but he would have to go, and I think it is possible that Brown is now on the slide.

The second thing is that Alistair Darling, the Chancellor, announced today that the Bank of England is providing £50 billion to introduce greater liquidity into the banking system. Well, of course the profits of the banks are absolutely enormous, and it makes me laugh, because if I'd tried to provide a fraction of that sum to keep one of our major industries going in the 1970s – shipbuilding or aircraft, or whatever – it would have been laughed out of court as Old Labour! But things have changed . . .

The third item of news of great importance is that Jimmy Carter has been meeting Hamas, as a result of which the Israeli Government said they wouldn't talk to him. The American Government is very angry. Barack Obama and the others have all distanced themselves from him. Carter was on *Newsnight* with Paxman. He was asked about Obama, and he said, 'Well, when you're fighting an election, it's difficult.' So then Paxman said, 'Who are you endorsing?' and he said, 'All my children and grandchildren are endorsing Barack Obama, but I haven't made a public declaration myself.' Maybe it wouldn't help Obama now if Jimmy Carter endorsed him, so soon after meeting Hamas, but it's a very significant thing to do and I'm so pleased he did it. He's a few months older than me, but it is a perfect example of what an old man can do. I like to compare it in my mind with my visit to Saddam, for which I got criticised of course; at any rate, it was an important mission and will have an effect in shifting world opinion, maybe even American opinion.

But what's interesting is that the Elders, who after all were brought together only last summer to do things like this, can't support Carter because the Americans object to what he is doing; I think the Elders have not turned out to be what they claimed to be, and I think people will do things on their own now. Kofi Annan has been to Kenya on his own, Carter's been to see Hamas, and I've really got to think whether there's anything useful I can do. Writing a diary and books and doing broadcasts and making speeches isn't actually an active political life. It's inadequate.

Tuesday 22 April
I am beginning to think I should come out for a Federal United States of Europe. If we are going to be locked into the European Union, which we are, it must be democratic, and I'd much rather that we had a President and a Senate and a House of Representatives than left it to the Mandelsons and Prodis and all the other Commissioners, who really control everything. I need to develop the argument and hope it will outflank the European Union people on the left.

Then, thinking about the future of the UN itself, you've got to take this bold step for a democratic United Nations, which will probably take 100 years to bring about, but somebody's got to start thinking about it now.

The news continues over the 10p tax rate. There is absolutely no connection between the present government and the inspiration and the purposes of the Labour movement. However, it may be that when the Labour Government is defeated, which I fear it will be, then the movement will come into its own again, and if there's a coalition, which I think must be a possibility, the gap between a government of all the parties and the people will become wider and wider. The danger is that, in the absence of representation, the BNP may grow.

Gordon Brown called the Hunger Summit today at Number 10 Downing Street. Well, it was very much what I said in my chapter for 'Letters to my Grandchildren' about the environment crisis being an argument about shortage.

I looked up the Budget for 1945, and at the end of the war income tax was ten shillings in the pound – that's 50 per cent – but above a certain level of income there was a surtax, which was almost ten shillings in the pound, so in effect the very richest people paid nearly 100 per cent tax on their income. It is a reminder of what people are prepared to do in wartime.

Wednesday 23 April

The Government has done a U-turn on the 10p tax. Despite all the warnings that it couldn't be done, Brown realises he would be defeated in the vote next Monday if he didn't make a change, so of course it's a welcome gain. On the other hand, it's damaged his reputation enormously.

Thursday 24 April

I found an email saying that British Airways wanted to have the audiobook of *Dare to be a Daniel* for their in-flight entertainment for three months starting in September. Well, that's rather nice. It's so long ago since I dictated it, I can't remember what it was like.

Friday 25 April

Having seen a bit of the mayoral debate between Boris Johnson, Brian Paddick and Ken Livingstone, Johnson simply doesn't emerge as having any experience or any capacity to do anything. He's a clever man, but I wouldn't trust him to be able to organise the bicycle shed in my factory. I'm hopeful Ken will win.

Monday 28 April

There's this incredible crime in Austria, where a man of seventy-three fathered seven children by his own daughter and kept them all in a sort of dungeon under the house, with no daylight.

There are reports coming out now about the Israeli bombing of a Syrian plant, which they claimed was nuclear, and there's hardly any comment been made, because America wanted it to happen, probably tipped them off; and it's intended, presumably, to be a warning to Iran that the Israelis would do the same to them. It's a quite incredible world we live in.

I go up and down, but I wonder really whether what anyone does can make all that difference, but maybe writing about it all helps. Because when I look back at people like Tom Paine and the Levellers and the Diggers, who've had struggles like ours and have inspired me, maybe, if we think it out and struggle as well – not as an academic exercise – struggle and think and publish, that will encourage people coming after us who've got problems even more serious than we have.

Tuesday 29 April

Whereas yesterday I almost wasted the day, I had a very useful one today.

At ten o'clock the London-based correspondent of *Europa*, an Italian national daily founded by Romano Prodi, came to see me to talk about the politics of Britain and Europe.

His name is Lazzaro Pietragnoli, forty years old, married, with a child. Very bright. He's a Catholic, and a socialist, a Democratic Socialist. He confirmed that the new Mayor of Rome is a fascist (and it is a bit frightening to consider the shift to the right when you think of the possibility of Boris Johnson winning in London). He described the complete destruction of Bertinotti's Communist Refoundation Party, and said that in the French parliament there is not a single communist.

Kate Hoey, Labour MP, has told Boris Johnson that if he is elected

Mayor, she will work as his Sports Adviser. Unbelievable! When you consider the difficulties that Ken Livingstone is in, for a former Labour Sports Minister to say that is really damaging, and in Lambeth, which she represents, it may have an effect. I never had any time for Kate Hoey. Maybe she's going to defect.

Oh, I spent four hours in the evening – I'm not kidding – filling in the form to apply for a pass to go to the Labour Party Conference, which is a meaningless Conference this year because there'll be no votes, but I felt I should go. I had to fill in my date of birth, my car number (even though I'm not taking the car), my mobile number, my National Insurance number, my passport number, and then, to confirm who I was, my little passport photo has to be signed by Ruth, and then she's got to give her date of birth and phone number. I mean, you'd really think I was going to visit Dartmoor Prison or something! It depressed me no end.

By the end of the day I'd cleared almost all my backlog of emails and letters, so that's a satisfying end to a day.

So that's the end of . . . [yawning]. As you can see, I'm glad to hear it's the end of Tuesday 29 April.

Wednesday 30 April

I caught the train to Greenwich, where I was due to meet Ken Livingstone. I got there about three-quarters of an hour early, and was sitting having a cup of tea when my mobile phone rang and it was Annalisa from Ken Livingstone's office, saying, 'I sent you three messages – it's not in Greenwich, it's in Blackheath.' So I got another train to Lewisham and then back to Blackheath, by which time Ken had arrived, and we walked around Blackheath. Everyone was friendly – a little entourage went with him. We went, in the end, to a little place called Age Exchange, which was a little café full of things from the past – old medicine bottles, old postcards, a picture of Aneurin Bevan. I just felt so old! At the same time I felt quite reassured, in a way. It was very nice.

Then I caught a train back to Charing Cross, walked to catch the bus home and passed one of these tourist shops; I saw a miniature red telephone kiosk and post-box, so I went in and bought them – £5 each, both made in China, of all things!

Thursday 1 May
Polling day for local elections.

Hideous cramp in the night – I was really in considerable pain.

Went and voted at Kensington Temple. I was so early there were a couple of black women giggling away, sticking up with duct tape notices saying 'Polling Station'. I said, 'Do I need to have proof of identity?' and one said, 'Certainly not, Mr Benn!'

Brown yesterday admitted that he'd made a mistake about the 10p tax. It was a bit bloody late, having said that he was not prepared to reverse it.

Friday 2 May
It was quite clear, from the overnight news bulletin, that Labour had been absolutely smashed in the local elections. Indeed, on the popular vote Labour came below the Liberals – 44 per cent for the Tories, 25 per cent for the Liberals, 24 per cent for Labour. We don't yet know . . . we didn't know, early in the morning . . . what would happen in London, but it looks as if Boris Johnson may have beaten Ken Livingstone.

Hilary rang. In Leeds, Labour held all its seats, which is amazing, considering what's happened in the rest of the North, but the BNP came within 150 votes, I think he said, of a victory in one of his wards, and that is the danger – the BNP will pick up dissatisfied Labour, working-class voters.

I went upstairs and turned on the news at 11.30, and they said that the London mayoral election result was about to be announced, so I had a cup of tea and I smoked my pipe, and it was delayed and delayed, and then, at about ten to midnight, the Returning Officer paraded all the candidates and announced the result. On the second ballot, between Ken and Boris Johnson, Johnson had . . . well, 1,400,000, and Ken 1,100,000, so Boris Johnson is the new Mayor of London. Johnson made a very charming speech, paid tribute to Ken, and Ken made a very gracious speech, saying all the responsibilities for the failures were his own, and got warm support, and that was it. I stayed up till about one o'clock listening to it all, getting more and more and more depressed.

It's quite obvious that Ken has been brought down by New Labour, even though he took an independent position. He may have made mistakes – I think he probably did – in quite a number of areas, but he was Mr London, had fought for democracy in London, and is now defeated by somebody who . . . is a very clever man, depicted as a buffoon; he comes across as a posh intellectual having fun, and London will be run by the hard men whom he appoints. He'll just be going round, visiting schools and hospitals and having dinner in the City, and so on.

It was a terrible, terrible day for the Labour Party and, happily, I think, the death-blow of New Labour.

Chapter Four

May–August 2008: Crisis of capitalism

Saturday 3 May 2008

The first email I read today was from a man who said he'd been Labour all his life, but voted Conservative [in the London Mayor's election] because New Labour had destroyed the Labour Party. I've developed my own explanation of it all, but I mustn't pretend that the day when people will listen to my views is close. I think we're going to have a long period of right-wing government. Still, I mustn't talk myself down.

It was Barbara's birthday on Tuesday, so I went and bought her a bottle of wine and a box of chocolates and some flowers.

I did a short interview for Al Jazeera about immigration; about the new controls that are being introduced, a points system. And I did two Sky TV interviews, a short one and then a longer one, down the line, from Osterley. That an old man of eighty-three should be asked to do BBC, Sky and Al Jazeera in twenty-four hours indicates that I have some role still.

I feel 'frozen' today. I've lots to do, but I just can't do it. Boris Johnson has got to prove himself in London, and whether he's capable, I don't know.

Sunday 4 May

The Radio 4 *Today* programme rang and asked if I would appear tomorrow, but all they wanted was somebody to attack Gordon Brown, and when I made it clear I wouldn't do that, they said it wasn't worth having me on. I should just have said, 'Oh, I'd love to do it' and then they would have had me on, live, and I could have said what I liked.

It was lovely to see Melissa and Paul, and the girls. I feel I'm beginning to establish real contact with them. I'm tremendously impressed by them.

Monday 5 May

May Day. Massive floods in Burma – they say 4,000 people died, many more missing and displaced. It depressed me very much, because it reminded me that man's struggle to survive on the planet has always been a struggle against Nature, and if a fraction of the money we spend on Trident and war and ID cards was spent on that, we could make the world a better place. That is the real environmental crisis. It's not using fewer plastic bags. I was very depressed by that.

I managed to check in, after about two hours, online with Aer Lingus, for my boarding pass tomorrow. God, what a struggle! I have two days of meetings in Dublin for the Irish referendum on the Lisbon Treaty.

Tuesday 6 May, Dublin

It was a perfect summer day, absolutely lovely weather – warm and sunny and not a cloud in the sky.

I think, in the course of the day, we must have walked at least three miles. They always said it was quicker to walk – enormously long distances. It was the equivalent of walking to Trafalgar Square and then walking to Oxford Circus and then walking back to Trafalgar Square, and then something. But Dublin was absolutely beautiful – a terribly prosperous city. I've been there many times over the years, but the change is phenomenal. You can see why a lot of Irish people think the Lisbon Treaty and the European Union are good for them.

They were most friendly, I must say. I had to be very careful not to appear to be telling them what to do, so I began by saying it's a great honour to be asked, and the future of my country is in your hands, because we in Britain are not allowed a referendum: it was a flattering approach, and then I concentrated on the democratic case.

Whether it made any impact, I don't know. The poll in Ireland, some time ago, in November, showed a heavy vote in favour of the Treaty, but it had now narrowed to 4 per cent, and, yesterday, one of the electrical unions had come out strongly against. The farmers were coming out against, because they said Mandelson's deal would threaten the farmers with imports from Latin America.

It was quite stressful, but I managed it okay. I can't say I was all that tired.

Thursday 8 May

There was an extraordinary article in *The Oldie* by a man called Edward Enfield, the father of Harry Enfield, the comedian, attacking me violently – the usual mockery about my 'ishoos' and all that, but also saying that I had once said that I darned my stockings years ago, and he wrote, 'I don't believe that, in the home of the Right Honourable Viscount Stansgate, there weren't housemaids to do that.' The usual stuff: Mr Benn is an aristocrat, all that crap.

So I wrote him a little note saying:

> I read and enjoyed your article, especially your reference to the darning of the stockings. It occurred to me you may not remember the last war, where we all had to darn our socks. While I was training to be an RAF pilot, we were all given wooden 'mushrooms' and a sewing kit, and they were very handy. Incidentally, my dad, who had been a pilot in World War One, rejoined the RAF in 1940, while he was still Mr Wedgwood Benn, MP for Manchester Gorton, and got himself trained as an air gunner. This was well before my dad went to the Lords. My mushrooms and sewing kit are still here if you'd like to examine them for yourself.

I put the mushroom and the sewing kit on my photocopier, and out came quite a reasonable photocopy of them, which I enclosed.

Sunday 11 May

Another perfect day – absolutely lovely!

The papers are full of Cherie Blair's book, in which she gives her opinion of Gordon Brown; and John Prescott's book, in which he says that he told Blair to sack Brown, and told Brown to fight Blair from the back benches.

It's all very destructive and doing terrible damage to the Labour Party, and Brown's reputation is now down to 23 per cent, and Cameron has overtaken him in every area.

Monday 12 May

The car came back from the garage, having had its MOT and a new windshield; the cost was £314! Having a car is so expensive. It's not really worth it, but it's just convenient.

A great limousine took Ruth and me to the Grosvenor House Hotel for the Sony Awards – a big event. I'd been asked to present the News Journalist of the Year Award. It's very noisy and there's music and great flashing screens all around, so everybody can see everything.

I was put at a table next to Lady Amos, who was Hilary's predecessor, Secretary of State for International Development. She's had a very distinguished career, degrees and honorary professorships, and so on. She was charming; her niece was there as her guest.

Also at our table was Joan Collins, who was glamorous and cool. I think Lord Reith would have been horrified if he'd seen the way radio had been turned into a sort of celebrity event, but that's true of everything now, including politics.

Anyway, I was called to present the award, and I gave a two-minute speech. It was won by a man called Owen Bennett-Jones, who is a very distinguished World Service guy.

Tuesday 13 May

Blow me down, I had a letter from Richard Ingrams of *The Oldie*, saying he hoped that Edward Enfield, who wrote that article about me in *The Oldie*, would apologise; and a letter from Edward, apologising, so that thing's over. I'm not sorry I wrote.

Thursday 15 May

Lissie rang, bless her heart. Then, just back from Washington, and on his way to the Far East shortly, Stephen rang. He's been in Scotland. Then, in the evening, I rang Josh, who is slogging away at his exams, which will all be over by the end of next week . . . I wonder how many families do keep in touch the way that I do with all of them? I just love it!

I had a phone message today from a man in Dublin, who wanted my advice on the Lisbon Treaty. I rang him back and had a long talk to him – he was very thoughtful, he'd read the whole of the constitutional documents of the European Union and he'd got onto exactly the right point, about democracy.

I was so tired after lunch I had a snooze for about half an hour, and then was picked up and taken to Islam Radio for a half-hour interview with Lauren Booth, Tony Booth's daughter, one of his many children. She lives in the Dordogne in France now and comes over once a fortnight for the radio station, and writes articles.

She had Cherie Blair's book, which has just come out today. There was a reference to me of the time I went to speak for her in Chatham, when she was Labour candidate in 1983; she also said she'd visited Caroline and what a wonderful woman she was.

Friday 16 May, Nuffield College, Oxford

By coach with Ruth to Oxford, and to meet David Butler at the college, and Marilyn, David's wife. I spoke to them of the tragic death of Gareth, their forty-two-year-old son. Marilyn was very sweet, but she was confused then, and at dinner, and David said to me it was the onset of Alzheimer's, which is a frightful additional tragedy for him.

Anyway, we went over to the room where David's annual seminar for the media research fellows is held. I'd been there for the first time in 1957 – fifty-one years ago. David briefly introduced me, What was interesting were the questions: from somebody at the *Washington Post*, somebody from the *New York Times*, an Australian journalist, a Chinese journalist. Ruth thought it went very well. David said, 'Anthony' (he always calls me Anthony) 'has "played the same record" about the media conspiracy', which I thought was a bit insulting, but that is David Butler!

We had dinner in the Hall, with the Latin *Benedictus, Benedicat,* and so on. It wasn't a particularly nice meal. Then to the Senior Common Room and talked for a little bit, and walked back to the hotel.

Saturday 17 May
Ruth went back to London. I was picked up and taken to Burford by a chap called Stephen Cooper, for the annual Levellers celebration.

The other speakers were Giles Fraser, who is vicar of Putney church; Mary Southcott, whom I'd known in Bristol, from the Electoral Reform Society, in favour of PR; and Anthony Barnett, who is one of the founders of Charter 88 and very passionate about Europe (he did support a referendum on Lisbon which was something). Then we had the usual march through Burford. Climbing up the hill I found terribly tiring. At Burford church a choir sang Billy Bragg's version of the 'Internationale'. Now, I really don't see why anyone should rewrite the 'Internationale', and although Billy's an imaginative guy, it slightly upsets me, but at any rate it was sung, and the Woodcraft Folk read a little poem and then laid flowers where the plaque is commemorating the three men who were shot by Cromwell in 1649.

I was driven home with Giles Fraser. I said to him at one stage, 'I think I'm going to have a snooze' and he said, 'So am I', so we snoozed almost all the way home.

Tuesday 20 May
The House of Commons is debating the Embryology Bill: the time limit for abortions, whether lesbians can have IVF, and so on.

But the big news today is that the Tories now have, I think, a 20 per cent lead over Labour in the Nantwich and Crewe by-election, which is on Thursday. It looks as if we're going to be slaughtered, and deservedly so.

It sunk me in a deep depression . . . After we lose the election, which we will in a couple of years, there won't be another Labour Government in my lifetime, and, indeed, probably not for another twenty years. I feel – I'm so tired – I feel bereaved that the Labour Party has gone that way. It has died. It's been assassinated by Blair and Brown. Brown is totally inadequate, but having a new leader wouldn't solve the problem. What are needed are new policies.

Saffron Burrows rang me from California. I send her occasional emails and messages saying: longing to see you. She is living in what she says is a very modest apartment, with no swimming pool or anything; she's really building her career. She's been offered a job in a new American series. I'm very fond of Saffron.

Wednesday 21 May
Caught the train with Ruth to Lewes, where we were met by Mark, who is the Charleston House gardener, and taken to the house, where we had snacks in the kitchen before my show. We were shown round the house. I didn't know anything about it, but it's where the Bloomsbury Group gathered in the '30s, and we were shown the room where John Maynard Keynes wrote *The Economic Consequence of the Peace*. Robert Skidelsky lived near there. There was a portrait of Keynes's Russian ballerina wife. It's a very old house – seventeenth century – beautifully decorated, and I thought to myself: Wait till people walk round Holland Park Avenue and say, 'This is where Miss Ruth Winstone used to work, and that was her room' and 'This is where Mr Benn did his *Diaries*'!

Then into the marquee, where there were 400 people. Ruth, wisely, went round the garden. I was nervous, I don't know why . . . There were some very hard questions from Labour people, who said they're utterly disappointed. I was asked about whether Blair should be tried as a war criminal. They were rather sympathetic, sort of *Guardian/Observer* readers probably.

Then, afterwards, we went back to the kitchen of the hotel for a moment, and Mark drove us back to the station.

Manchester United won the European Cup against Chelsea in Moscow in a fantastic penalty shootout.

If Labour come third in Nantwich and Crewe, I really do think it's possible they'll get rid of Brown. But I can't see anybody else that's any good. I mean, James Purnell is a young Blairite, Jack Straw is a wobbler, Charles Clarke is not serious . . . David Miliband is probably the most likely, and he's a hard Blairite. So I don't see any recovery for Labour, but if the press decide to give Miliband a fair wind, Labour might do better. The whole thing is personality-oriented.

Friday 23 May

Up every two hours to switch on the telly, and at about four o'clock in the morning heard the result that the Labour candidate, Tamsin Dunwoody, Gwyneth's daughter, had been absolutely smashed. There was an 18 per cent swing to the Tories.

In a spare moment Ruth and I sat down and wrote a poem called 'Village Life at Westminster', based on the poem I remember from years back about Abdul Abulbul Amir and Ivan Skavinsky Skavar, who had a terrible fight and both died. We wrote one for the political situation at the moment!

Saturday 24 May

I do have the most awful nights! I have to go to the loo every two hours. I have the most hideous cramp, which forces me out of bed. Then nightmares! I can never remember them, but all I know is that they're always big problems that I have to solve, and I can't solve them. The disadvantages of old age!

Josh worked at my faulty computer for about an hour, and finally sorted it. There were 506 emails, which took me about an hour and a half to read. The email is the communication of the present, and yet, as Josh pointed out, if my dad, who died in 1960, were here and you showed him a computer or email, he wouldn't know what the hell it was about! This is the speed of technical change. I can just about cope, at a very basic level.

Lord Desai has said Brown will have to change his policy or he'll face defeat, but of course what the media are dreaming of is the possibility of a leadership contest, and then they can have months when they don't have to discuss politics at all. It will just be about Alan Milburn or Charles Clarke or David Miliband or James Purnell or Alan Johnson.

I had a lovely letter from Ian Paisley. I'm going to read it into my diary because it was so nice.

Dear Tony,

Thank you for your letter of 29th March and for your gracious words of encouragement and good wishes. I am grateful for the privilege of helping to set Northern Ireland back on the road

of peace and prosperity. I believe that the foundations which
we have laid are strong enough on which to build a secure
future for everyone in the province. It would be a strange world
if we didn't have differences, one with another. The secret is
to overcome them, and agree to differ, and I think that's what
you and I have done. I ought to tell you, my family have always
admired you as a politician, and your son is held in great esteem
in our home. Again, many thanks for your kindness in writing,
which is deeply appreciated.

Now, that really is a very sweet letter. I've known Ian since he was
elected, I suppose, and what interests me about him is that he has
openly and honestly argued in favour of what he believed to be the
interests of those he represented – namely, the Unionist majority in
Northern Ireland; and although I've always been a supporter of Sinn
Fein, and he knows that perfectly well, he's always been . . . we've
always been very respectful to each other.

It's very pleasing because, in politics, I think you have to say what
you mean and mean what you say, and I think Ian did that. I don't
think peace could have been reached in Northern Ireland between
sort of softies like Trimble and Hume. You had to have the hard
men facing each other, and when the hard men agreed, then they'd
nobody behind them to stab them.

Sunday 25 May

In the evening I thought it would be nice to make contact with Ed
Miliband. So I rang his mobile and he said, 'Ed here, leave a message.'
So I said, 'Ed, I know you're going through a difficult time, and I've
been through it all myself, and if it was helpful to have a word, I'd be
happy to do so' and left it at that.

Then I rang Marion, his mother, and had a long talk to her. She's
very unhappy. I was careful about what I said about government
policy, though she shares my view, and she was in Trafalgar Square
when I spoke on Palestine recently; because, although she's Jewish,
she did strongly support the Palestinian case, as I'm sure Ralph would
have done.

It's funny about Ed. I like him very much indeed, but, when I last saw him, there was a sort of glass panel between us – he looked at me in a friendly way, but I didn't think anything I could say would make any impact. Whether he's frightened enough to think a word with me is worth while, I don't know.

Monday 26 May
Bank Holiday Monday – the place is as dead as anything. There's nothing going on. It's pelting with rain. Some of it's come through the roof.

I looked at my emails, but every time I tried a huge red thing appeared on the screen saying, 'You have been attacked by a spy . . . a virus is trying to get your identity.' So I rang Josh. 'Don't do anything!' he said. 'Don't apply for any updates or anything.'

I decided to sew a button on my trousers. I got out my old sewing kit, found a button to replace the one that had broken, pulled out the trousers that Joshua had dyed dark blue, and, in twenty minutes, I did succeed in attaching the button – I was so proud!

I'm thinking of having a little label stuck on things saying, 'Throw this away when I die', because I think that that would help my children.

I realised that your life goes through a period of strangeness, then activity and understanding, and then management, and then old age is to encourage and learn, and then to realise, full stop, you have come to the end of your life! I've no resentment about it. If I died this afternoon, it wouldn't worry me at all.

So, it's half-past six on the afternoon of Monday 26 May.

Tuesday 27 May
I rang Doris Heffer, because Eric died on 27 May (in 1991). She's now in an old people's home.

The lorry drivers, protesting about the increase in the petrol tax when oil prices are rising through the roof, have started blocking the roads in Cardiff and London. As in 2000, I think that's going to be a really, really big issue. The Government has increased taxation retrospectively on bigger cars, which is very unfair – retrospective legislation should not be introduced.

You know, there's a big crisis and I just don't know how Brown and Darling are going to deal with it.

There's a rumour the Americans are going to try and start a
'coalition of the democracies' to replace and bypass the UN, which
would just be the international community, America and its pals.
This is something you've got to watch. On the other hand, it might
open up the possibility of my Convention of the Peoples, in which we
would have the peoples of the world demanding a democratic UN. If
I had the energy, I'd do something about that.

Wednesday 28 May
At eleven o'clock two officers from the National Trust came to
discuss with me and Josh the possibility of the Trust taking over my
house. If they bought it, it would stop it being gutted when I go,
which it would be – developers would take everything out and all
they'd leave is the front. They thought Josh could film the rooms,
make a sort of a tour of the house with my commentary. They liked
the mess in the basement office – they didn't want it to be altered.
Josh says the devil's in the detail, so I wouldn't say more than the
fact that they are interested in it, and compared it to Disraeli's
house, or Churchill's house, Chartwell. I must say, it would be a
wonderful ending.

Thursday 29 May
I ought really to report that the Labour Party is bankrupt. It owes £23
million, and the legal responsibility for that will fall upon members
of the National Executive Committee, including the Prime Minister,
Harriet Harman, Jack Straw, Walter Wolfgang, all the people on the
NEC. The GMB have announced tonight that, because of government
policy, they're withdrawing a million-pound contribution from the
Labour Party. So there is a possibility that the life of the Labour
Party will end this year. I'm putting it rather dramatically, but the
Labour Party, founded in 1906, may end – and God knows how the
Government will handle it, because they can't introduce State funding
legislation to subsidise themselves. On the other hand, the death of
a political party and the bankruptcy of a Labour Prime Minister and
Cabinet would be massive! So, I plant that thought as this diary ends,
on the evening of Thursday 29 May.

Friday 30 May
Well, today, I was still very much shaken by the realisation that the Labour Party might be dying: a bankrupt party, which has lost public support, lost membership, is about to be defeated and will have no money to recover. So that feeling of utter political gloom does overwhelm me a bit.

At 1.30 my driver John Grice collected me and took me to Blackheath, where we picked up Dave, and we went on to Hastings, to meet our cousin, Sylvia Hughes, who is 100 on 8 February next year. We had a lovely talk to her and family members; and then we were driven on to Bexhill, where I was giving a talk in the De La Warr Pavilion. It has just been refurbished. It was a largely older audience of nearly 500, and there were questions and answers and signing of books, and then John drove us back to London. I was absolutely exhausted!

Sunday 1 June
Being a Sunday, I read *The Sunday Times* in bed, took it steadily and then came down to the office. Still depressed.

Just after one, dear old Josh arrived, and for three and a half hours he tackled jobs. He went on the roof and found that the gutters were blocked, which had caused the water to run into the house, so he fixed that. Then he came down and transferred all the email facilities from one computer to the other, so that I don't have to keep running between the two. He's also bought me a new flatscreen TV – he's just wonderful.

I felt like I was watching someone using hieroglyphics, and it so reminded me of my old age and the difficulty old people have in keeping abreast. I really can't cope on my own.

Ruth rang me and said, 'Don't be depressed – take it [the present situation] as an opportunity and a challenge.'

Monday 2 June
A beautiful olive tree, about four foot high, was delivered – from Ursula, for whom I had done something at the Globe Theatre. She worked with Caroline in adult education courses.

Anyway, at 9.30 somebody called Jamie Bennett arrived, thirty-three years old, the governor of a women's prison, to do an interview on prison reform. He'd sent a lot of questions. Interviews force me to think about things I may not have considered before. I had a quick word with Hilary, who was once the Prisons Minister.

Jamie was very nice. I think he was pretty progressive, because his first question was 'How do you define socialism?'

Gordon Brown and Jacqui Smith are having a big campaign on the forty-two days' detention and making little trifling concessions. They may persuade Labour MPs to go along with it. It is an outrage that civil liberties should be denied in this way! I mean, we have far longer periods of detention than anybody else in the world. There's a far greater threat to people that their home will be repossessed or they'll lose their job than that al-Qaeda will blow up a bomb on the train they catch. I mean, the whole sense of proportion is completely wrong, and I must say I'm very depressed.

Tuesday 3 June
For some reason I was absolutely exhausted this morning! I just stayed up in the bedroom. I didn't come down till about eleven o'clock.

Wednesday 4 June
The private management of failed NHS hospitals was announced, and it absolutely horrified me. What do you make of a Labour Government that denies trade unions their rights, that goes to war and then privatises the NHS?

Thursday 5 June
Josh looked in at 12.15, and installed two completely new TV screens and sets, and transferred everything over. Whenever I see him at work, I feel like a Stone Age man looking at a railway engineer. He was so sweet and so helpful and so cheerful.

In the afternoon, I did an interview on the telephone to New York about Barack Obama.

Friday 6 June
Bush has demanded the right to keep fifty military bases in Iraq; to have the right to use them wherever American national interests

are involved, all over the Middle East; to retain, through the oil law, American control of the oil; to exempt all American mercenaries and civil staff from legal action by the Iraqi Government; so Iraq is now a colony again.

And Barack Obama, speaking at the American Israel Public Affairs Committee in New York, said that Israel must have a united Jerusalem as its capital, excluding the Palestinians from their historic place in East Jerusalem; this has driven President Abbas to a desire to talk to Hamas, so it's united the Palestinians, which is not a bad thing.

There was an article today, in *The Guardian*, saying that an opinion poll taken in April revealed that voters would rather have Tony Blair, Margaret Thatcher or me as Prime Minister. The YouGov poll asked voters who they would choose, from a list of politicians at the peak of their power. Only 5 per cent chose Brown. I got 13 per cent, and Blair came second, with 20 per cent, to Thatcher.

Saturday 7 June
Turned on the television for the *Six O'Clock News* and I heard Hillary Clinton's speech, announcing that she was going to support Barack Obama. It was all about her and women . . . the day will come when a woman will . . . and so on, but still, it went down very well. I think it was a bid to be the vice-presidential candidate; whether she will be or not, I don't know, but it will have committed towards Obama a lot of women and white workers who didn't like him.

Sunday 8 June
I caught a cab to Lissie's house, where Hannah and Sarah were sitting on the trampoline in the sunshine, and she drove me to St Paul's, where she was giving a lecture on 'A faith in society – points of common interest in fiction'. I couldn't hear it because of the echo, but as I'd read it beforehand I knew how good it was. She was very confident. The service was full of hymns that had no tunes and old-fashioned words, really revealing the worst of Christian thinking. Anyway, Lissie did very well.

I just had time to thank Canon Warner afterwards, and then got another cab to Marion Miliband's house for dinner; Ed was there, and his girlfriend, Justine, who's an environmental lawyer. She looked about eighteen! He said, 'I owe you tea – we'll have it at the House of Commons one day.' He's the same old Ed, but of course he's locked into this ghastly crisis, and if I do see him, I've got to think what I would say, which is that the Prime Minister ought perhaps to interpret the role of leadership as being to explain the world to people and have a dialogue with the people.

At the dinner was: Tom Snow – a very tall brother of Jon Snow – who works for UNISON, and his wife, who works at the East London University; Rodney Barker from the LSE and his wife; a woman from *Le Monde Diplomatique*, which is now published in English; I haven't been to a dinner party since Caroline died, and it reminded me a little bit of the dinner party sketch with the two Johns, and Frances Barber in the Rory Bremner show. We talked about religion, about the Third Way, about Europe, because I wondered whether the Irish would turn down the Lisbon Treaty. These intellectuals were all passionately pro-Europe. Then we had a bit of a discussion about the Middle East.

Then Marion brought me home, which was very sweet of her, and we had a bit of a talk.

Monday 9 June
I rang Dave, but he was on his way to hospital.

Wednesday 11 June
A little girl of six, Maya Parry, rang me up. She had written to me, and I'd replied with a postcard. She was so sweet! She had all these ideas . . . we want everyone to have enough money, and girls to go to school, and animals to be treated well, and peace.

Anyway, then I drove to the Commons. It cost £35 to part-fill my tank.

I got to the Commons, sat on the Terrace. The result of the vote on the forty-two days (pre-charge detention) was that the Government won by nine votes. The Democratic Unionist Party had been bribed with an offer of money for Northern Ireland.

I did a little interview outside for the BBC saying that it was the repeal of Magna Carta, Osama Bin Laden's greatest victory, and so on. It's no good getting angry about the Government but I was really shattered by it.

I saw Ian Paisley, so I thanked him for his lovely letter and gave him a hug. I said, 'Did you vote for the forty-two days?' and he said, 'Yes.' I said, 'Well, I wouldn't like to say it to a clergyman, but that is selling your birthright for a mess of pottage,' and he gave a nervous laugh.

I won't say this has finally shaken my confidence in the Labour Government, because I don't know that I had any, but it is a democratic crisis. The power of the State is greater than it's ever been. I've got to think the whole thing out. I'm speaking at the Compass conference on Saturday. I'm not going to talk about economics; I'm going to talk about the democratic crisis. I think this government deserves to be defeated and will be defeated.

But I feel alienated from the House of Commons now. When I first went there, I was very impressed by the gravity of it and the seniority and seriousness of the MPs, and now it's a sort of exhibition centre. Tourists pour round. Most power has passed from Parliament to Brussels or Washington, and it's a relic. It's a reminder that all institutions come and go, and this one is going. It has to be resuscitated and it's going to be a very tough struggle, and I'm afraid, as with all democratic struggles, it may have an ingredient of violence in it – not that I favour that, but I don't see how it can be avoided.

Thursday 12 June
Still depressed about the passing of the forty-two-day measure last night. I wondered whether I would respond by getting arrested on Sunday at the Bush demonstration.

On the one o'clock news they announced that David Davis has decided to resign and stand again in his constituency on the question of the forty-two days and civil liberties generally. Should I support him? Stephen advised caution and I think he's probably right.

I wrote a letter to *The Guardian* and they said they'd print it tomorrow, supporting David Davis's stand.

Nick Robinson, the BBC political correspondent, said David's move was a stunt, and that when people said he had principles, they meant he was bonkers. It was so insulting. These media people think they run the world, and they don't like the electorate being involved. It will be interesting to see what happens.

The Liberals are not putting up a candidate. If we don't put up a candidate, then it would be possible for me to go up there and support him, because I couldn't be accused of campaigning against Labour. So that's in the back of my mind.

David and I have a debate fixed for 7 July at the South Bank – I just hope he doesn't cancel it because of the by-election.

Friday 13 June

My letter in support of David Davis did appear in *The Guardian*.

The big news today of course is that the Irish have voted overwhelmingly 'No' to the Lisbon Treaty – fifty-three to forty-six or something – just fantastic! I mean, I never really thought it would happen, but it did, and of course then David Miliband said, 'Oh, we must proceed with our ratification', even though the vote has stopped the Lisbon Treaty from coming into force.

David Davis phoned and said, 'As far as I'm concerned, our meeting in London goes ahead, so long as it doesn't breach election law.' Well, I don't think it could possibly do that, because I wouldn't mention the Haltemprice and Howden by-election and neither would he.

David Davis and the Irish vote on Lisbon really have changed the whole political climate. The press have been revolting! The journalists have been building up the Monster Raving Loony candidate, building up Kelvin MacKenzie, whom Murdoch wants to put up against David Davis. I mean, it's absolutely disgusting. The BBC is as bad as anybody. It's a very big moment, when people are consulted and all the media want is a cosy little discussion on the Westminster village. As far as the people are concerned, they're allowed to say something every five years, and for the rest of the time they should just shut up!

So, that's my mood at 12.45 a.m. in the early morning of 14 June.

Saturday 14 June

To the Compass conference plenary session. Neil Lawson made a soft-left attack on the Government. Then Harriet Harman, followed by Edward Miliband, who walked about the stage all the time and was very matey. He said, 'My first job was with Tony Benn. When I was fifteen and a half I used to work in his basement office, and I'm very glad he's here.' There was tremendous applause.

Sunday 15 June
Caught the Underground to St James's Park, walked to Parliament Square. I did a ton of interviews, with Al Jazeera, Press TV, Dubai, Turkey . . .

I did say to Lindsey German in advance, 'I'll come with you if we're arrested', so there was no question of my opting out of a collective decision to try and get to Downing Street.

I went behind the platform and was put on first. Brian Haw spoke endlessly – there's no emphasis or argument, it's just a rant, but still he's a very courageous man, and he's camped for five years in Parliament Square and he's known all over the world. I saw a very familiar face, Denis Halliday, who of course I'd seen in Iraq five years ago. He used to be Assistant General Secretary for Human Rights, a passionate Irishman, and I had a short talk to him. He said the UN is much, much weaker now, and the Security Council and the General Assembly have got to be restored. I said, 'Well, I agree about that. The vote in the General Assembly should reflect the world's population,' and he said, 'I agree with that; and the Security Council has got to be controlled by the General Assembly.' I agree with that, though whether the Chinese, as an empire, would want that any more than the Americans I do not know.

I asked if he'd been in touch with Kofi Annan. 'Not really, he's such a cautious man.' I said, 'What about Jimmy Carter?' 'Well, he did very well in the Middle East.' Seeing Halliday again takes me right back to the campaigns against sanctions on Iraq and the war – oh goodness me – many years ago now!

Walter Wolfgang spoke, George Galloway, Bianca Jagger.

I'm so glad I took my little backpack stool. I sat, and at the end of the meeting seven people decided to try and deliver the letter to the Prime Minister in Downing Street. Signed by, gosh . . . John Pilger, Harold Pinter, Caryl Churchill, Clare Short, a lot of people.

When we got there the police stopped us, they'd put up barriers. Walter and I and Bianca were at the front, and the crowd piled up behind, and at one stage I thought I was going to be crushed. I had a backpack on, which sort of gave me a little bit of protection, but I thought: If I fall, I'm going to be trampled underfoot. Anyway, I stayed put and I saw young people pushing and pushing and pushing, and pushing the barrier back, and then the police got out their batons and began hitting people, and it looked as if one or two people would get through, but they didn't. The fence that the police had put up was beginning to bend and they looked rather frightened, because there was a great determination and a lot of shouting. All this was going on a few feet away from where I was standing. It was horrible!

Walter Wolfgang was very shaky – I think he was on crutches or he had a stick – so he and I moved out and went our separate ways.

It's difficult to give a proper impression of it, but BBC News predictably was all about Bush's visit, and very little about the demonstration; no mention of who spoke, what it was about, just a mention of protestors 'scuffling' with the police.

I had had an invitation to go and do BBC News 24 and I decided to make that the central theme of my argument. I said, 'Are your instructions not to report public speeches . . . are they in written form? I'd like to see them. The world's media was there covering the speeches, but I didn't see you there.' They were really discomfited. But still, I was polite, and said I passionately believed in the BBC, as an old BBC man. I think it was worthwhile.

Monday 16 June
Today Bush went to Number 10; they had a joint press conference. Brown began – he is, after all, a sitting Prime Minister, and Bush is a retiring President. But Brown, he emerged as a neo-Conservative Republican. He agreed with the United States about everything. He said he was going to send more troops to Afghanistan. He justified the continued presence of British troops in Iraq. He made a threat – but not a military threat – to Iran, about their nuclear programme. He said he was in favour of free trade and against all forms of protectionism. It was just not possible to put a postcard between him and Bush.

I felt distressed because, if I take three items – the Lisbon Treaty, where we were denied a vote and the Irish voted No; the forty-two days, which is a gross breach of civil liberties, where we took the wrong side; and now Bush and Brown on the war – they're just not the views that I hold.

I feel absolutely and completely betrayed by New Labour and by Gordon Brown. I feel so sorry for Hilary, because he's locked into the whole thing. I don't know that I could go and speak at a Labour meeting now, unless they understood what I was going to say.

I had a phone call from Alfredo Toro Hardy, the Venezuelan Ambassador in Madrid. He was in London. He rang up to ask if I would join a seminar in Spain with the Diplomatic Editor of *Le Monde Diplomatique* and a German. I looked through my diary and found I could do 9 July, so I rang back and said, 'I can't easily travel alone now – would it be possible to bring somebody with me?' So I am going to take Ruth and he's going to send the tickets.

Tuesday 17 June
My fifty-ninth wedding anniversary, and how I miss Pixie . . . She was such a source of strength and inspiration. I'm going to do the Caroline Benn Memorial Lecture, the third one to be held. She's had such a huge influence on people, and on me and on the family.

Anyway, I spent the morning on emails, and I collected 200 more cassettes for my diaries and things.

Then I drove to the House of Commons, and my car broke down just as I was approaching Parliament Square. I managed to push it, with the help of a man, just off the road, in front of the Ministry of Justice.

Had lunch with Jean Corston at the Commons. Then I went back with a note to put on the car saying, 'I've called the AA', to find two police horses and two police officers, who had rung to find out who the owner of the car was, discovered it was me and therefore weren't worried. I went over and I saw David Davis about our debate on 7 July. I said I would begin by saying, 'We cannot discuss the election, for legal reasons, or accept any questions about the campaign', and that should settle it. It will all be recorded.

Back to the car and an AA man picked me up, a young guy of thirty-two, bright as a button, and towed me to a garage.

Before I go to bed I must record that, when I was in David Davis's office, I said, 'Look, we share the view that we're being bullied all the time in the nanny state, so do you mind if I light my pipe?' and he said, 'Not at all!' and so I lit it and smoked it for a second. We'd both be fined £1,000! Libertarians can unite in a funny way.

Wednesday 18 June
Ruth looked in and had a look at the finances, and then we had a lot of fun! I dictated an article for *The Oldie* magazine about my seat-case, and what I used to call my chair-case, but Ruth turned that into 'seat-pack'. She edited it beautifully, and then we went out with a camera and she photographed me, pulling both along, sitting at the bus stop, and so on. Everybody laughed as they went by. We had the pictures developed and they are also on a disc. So I posted them off to Richard Ingrams, and he owes me something after the horrible story they printed before, so that was just fun!

Saturday 21 June
The alarm went off just before five so that I could catch the seven o'clock Edinburgh train. Changed at Doncaster for Beverley, on to Beverley for the folk festival. Roy Bailey and I did our two-man *Writings on the Wall* and afterwards I sat and talked to lots of people, and then David Davis turned up and took me to an independent school. There was a little interview with the local paper and with BBC North, and then we went into the meeting. It had been organised at about thirty-six hours' notice by the Conservative Association and it was a mixture of young and old people. David introduced me very generously; I spoke, and then we had questions and answers.

Then I did a BBC interview, and his party chairman, a chartered accountant, drove me home. I got home by ten past eleven, absolutely exhausted! It's been a very good day, and I think David's going to do very well in the by-election. That, plus – possibly – a defeat of the forty-two days in the House of Lords, may kill it off.

Monday 23 June
My dear brother Michael was killed sixty-four years ago. Dave rang me and we had a word about it. He would have been eighty-six, if he'd lived; eighty-seven in September.

On the set of
Will and Testament
in Ealing Studios.

The author returns to
a familiar place in the
House of Commons, 2011.

Tony through the
looking glass – at
Ealing Studios 2012.

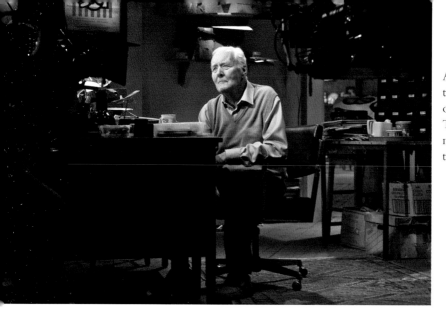

A recreation of the 'basement office' at which TB worked for many years in the family home

Recalling headlines from the days when TB was 'the most dangerous man in Britain'.

On location for *Will and Testament* with Michael Miles (camera) and Mervyn Gerrard (sound) 2011.

Important influences in the life of Tony Benn:
trade union martyrs, the welfare state, tea and miners.

TB's blood, extracted by a doctor when the author inherited his father's title, but refused to leave the Commons for the Lords.

TB with Ruth Winstone and Hutchinson's long-time editor Tony Whittome, who worked on many of the books.

TB confidently handling a racing pigeon: a message had been sent by the Marquess of Bath to the former Postmaster General to celebrate Festival of Stamps in 2010

TB on tour with his editor Ruth Winstone, after the eighth volume of diaries was published.

TB approaching National Treasure status – in Lincoln at least: one of the many honorary degrees bestowed upon him over the years.

Billy Bragg and friends at the Tolpuddle celebration 2013
- TB sporting new beard.

Family and friends say goodbye to the Benn family home
after sixty years.

TB and his brother David camping out in the Benn family home
before its sale in 2012.

Proud father: with, from left, Joshua, Melissa, Hilary and Stephen before leaving the family home for the last time, July 2012

With his only daughter, Melissa (Liss) in the down-sized apartment around the corner from the Benn family home.

I rang Sylvia Jones today: her husband, Fred, was an engine-driver in Bristol. She's eighty in a day or two. The Bristol connection has lasted much longer than the Chesterfield connection – Chesterfield has been lost to the Liberals, the mining community there has died, and that was the radical element in the local party. It's very sad about Chesterfield.

Wednesday 25 June

Well, it's five past twelve and Josh has just rung me: he got a first-class Honours degree at University College! Top of his class – nobody's got a first for two years at University College. He got a first for his exams and a first for his dissertation, and so it's an absolute triumph! I'm overjoyed with happiness. Caroline would have been so thrilled! She always said he'll go back to university; she didn't know of course, because he didn't until five years after she died, but it's a wonderful achievement and it opens up new paths for him.

This morning I had an invitation from a celebrity cruise company to fly to Panama and come back across the Atlantic in a cruise-liner, give four lectures and be paid £1,000.

I went and did BBC *Hardtalk* with Stephen Sackur. It was about civil liberties, and he pressed me quite hard, but what I didn't realise was that *Hardtalk* has an audience of seventy-six million people all over the world.

To Gerry Adams's reception in the Jubilee Room of the House of Commons, and had a word with him, and he thanked me for coming over to Dublin. He made a little statement. His main emphasis now, he said, is to work towards Irish unity. He's interested in getting the Good Friday Agreement fully implemented. He's determined that law and order should be transferred to Stormont, and that the Irish language should be recognised.

Friday 27 June

In the Henley by-election, created by the resignation of Boris Johnson, who has become Mayor of London, the Labour candidate came fifth, below the Greens and the BNP. Tomorrow, I think, is the anniversary of Brown becoming Prime Minister, and his leadership has been an absolute catastrophe, there's no question about it, and at some stage there will be an attempt to get rid of him. It will be painful and a tragedy for him, but he just hasn't done it.

Reflecting on it, New Labour is a continuation of Thatcherism, and so it is the end of New Labour we're witnessing, but everybody knows that; it's also the end of the Thatcherite element in New Labour. So it's the final death of Thatcherism. Of course, David Cameron realises, nowadays, if you want to win an election you've got to sound progressive. He says the gap between rich and poor is too wide, he's talking about things that are completely phoney, one-nation Tory arguments, but he thinks the way to win is to be more progressive than Brown. Brown thinks the way to win is to go on and on repeating the Thatcherite mantra, and no wonder the BNP has replaced Labour because BNP – in its crude and vulgar and dangerous way – represents the working class, and seems to the working class to represent it better than New Labour.

Sunday 29 June
The *Sunday Telegraph* had a whole page of 'national treasures' nominated by their readers. I was chosen as a national treasure for the Magna Carta Award. If I'm a national treasure in the *Telegraph*, something's gone wrong.

Wednesday 2 July
To Leeds today by train where I was met by David Evans, a music teacher who started the Garforth Arts Festival. He drove me there, about eight miles out of Leeds, to a working men's club, just like the one in Chesterfield, and it was a wonderful evening. I don't know how to describe it accurately, except that I felt absolutely at home there. It took me back to the Chesterfield miners' strike and all the friendship. There were one or two young people, quite a few middle-aged people and a lot of old people, but it had all the self-confidence and pride and skill and craft of the real British working class. It reminded me of when I was first elected to Parliament and almost all Labour MPs were like that.

I gave my lecture and they really appreciated it, and then there were lots of questions. I got into difficulty with one man for talking about the Church and the attitude of some Christians to homosexuality. He asked, 'Are you an atheist?' Otherwise, it was a friendly evening. It restored my confidence in the Labour Party.

Saturday 5 July
Lissie spoke at the annual Marxism Conference today, with Lindsey German, about the feminist movement. Also she was invited to lunch by *Private Eye* and talked to Richard Ingrams and to Ian Hislop, whom she liked very much. She's just so busy at the moment! At the age of fifty-one she's now a major national writer and novelist and journalist, and called on to do all sorts of things, and it's just so lovely because she really deserves it. That's what she wanted to do all her life, and she's doing it.

Monday 7 July
I worked on my speech for tonight's debate with David Davis at the Queen Elizabeth Hall.

Then I got a cab to the Venezuelan Embassy. I thought it was a courtesy to go, as the Ambassador has invited me to this international conference in Madrid. The taxi driver was passionate about the problem of population explosion! I said, 'You can't treat people as pollution. How many children do you have?' He said, 'Two.' 'Well, are they pollution?' He got very animated, and I argued with him very hard, and at the end, he said, 'I wish there were more politicians like you!'

I had an hour-and-a-half snooze, and then got another cab to the Queen Elizabeth Hall because it was pelting with rain! I thought I'd get soaked if I took the bus.

It was sold out, 1,500 seats – it was measured and serious, and where we disagreed we said we did. It was quite successful, I think.

It's about quarter to twelve. I haven't eaten, and I'm very hungry and very tired.

Tuesday 8 July
Well, I've got a bit of a cold, and I feel simply awful. I wondered, quite seriously, whether I should cancel my trip to Spain tomorrow. I just didn't think I could do it. Hilary announced that he is not prepared to cull badgers, and is under bitter attack from the farmers,

and warmly supported by the animal-welfare people. In the House of Commons the Tories gave him a really rough time, and Labour supported him.

In the evening I went to the Hinde Street Methodist Church, which is Donald Soper's old church, to give a talk on 'Faith and Politics'. The average age of the audience was about sixty-five, all decent Methodists. Although there were quite a few friendly smiles, I think it was seen probably as an attack upon the Christian faith, in favour of a sort of Pantheism – I don't know. But I'm glad I went because I've got to think about that. I have to be respectful of Christian faith, and not appear to be jumping out of it.

Wednesday 9 July, Madrid
Ruth and I caught a taxi to Heathrow for the plane to Madrid, and were met there by Alfredo Toro Hardy, the Venezuelan Ambassador formerly in London, and driven to the Hesperia Hotel. We decided not to join the official lunch, and Ruth went off to see her cousin, Michael Winstone, who's a sculptor living in Spain with his wife Mercedes and son Miro. I slept – I was just so tired!

The thing I did notice, which amazed me, considering this is a top-grade international hotel, was that there was no kettle in the room! When I asked for tea, they sent up a jug of warm water and a teabag and no milk. So this did make me resolve that I would never go abroad again without my little water heater and teabags and powdered milk and saccharine.

Anyway, we were collected at 6.30 p.m. and taken to the Casa de América to a meeting of about sixty people, and four of us on the platform. One was the Syrian Ambassador; there may have been another ambassador. What Alfredo wanted was to use my presence to overcome the prejudice in the Spanish press towards Venezuela and Chávez.

I was asked to speak first, which I was glad about. I was followed by somebody called Raul Morogo – a man, I should think, perhaps in his late-sixties, who'd been an Ambassador to Venezuela, a very distinguished man. Then Bernard Cassen, one of the early editors of *Le Monde Diplomatique*, who gave a good, radical speech; followed by Carlos Liria, from the University of Madrid, a professor. I hoped it had been worthwhile from Alfredo's point of view; he seemed to think so, and of course the whole obsession was that the press were unfair to Chávez. That was what it was all about, and I tried to address that in my final comment after the questions.

Back to the hotel with Alfredo, who (apart from being the Venezuelan Ambassador to Madrid) is an academic, and he had with him his wife, Gabriella – his second wife – and a friend of hers called Julia, a South Korean widow. She'd married a Frenchman who had a castle in Normandy, and he died at the age of forty-seven in a motor accident. We had a long talk, and they couldn't have been nicer. By then I was relaxed because the job was over.

Thursday 10 July
After breakfast we were collected by Heidi Russell, who is the sort of public-relations director for the embassy, half-Venezuelan and half-English, spoke perfect English. She took us to coffee at the Plaza de Oriente, very near the Royal Palace, and we drove past the cathedral. I must say, Madrid is a beautiful city. It was very hot yesterday and today. I'd taken my light suit, which I haven't worn for years.

Heidi took us to the airport and steered us through all the complexities. I couldn't have done it by myself, without Ruth and Heidi. Ruth was absolutely magnificent. It has been a killing week, but I think Alfredo was pleased, and he will report it back to Venezuela, to Chávez.

I must tidy up before I go to bed. I can't go to bed with such a mess in my office – about a week or more's letters unanswered, many of them unopened, and all these emails.

Friday 11 July
Latish start. Did a bit of shopping for some food. Had a meal.

Caught the Tube to King's Cross, the 2.30 train to Durham, Room 131 at the Royal County Hotel, for the 124th Miners' Gala in Durham.

Saturday 12 July
Up at six. There was a touch of rain – a shower of rain – and I thought: Oh my God, we're going to have the Gala blanked out; but it didn't happen.

I had breakfast in my room, and then I got onto the balcony and stood for three hours on the balcony as all the banners went by. There were forty-one bands, eighty-five banners, and an estimated 50,000 people there, but I have to be honest, nothing like that percentage ever listen to the speeches.

Of course Gordon Brown was asked to attend, didn't reply; Blair, although he was a North-East Member, never came. The last Labour Leader to come was Kinnock, and he – in the 1984 strike – he was so unhelpful to the miners that, when he began speaking, the bands started up and they marched off. But, historically, a Labour Leader had always been there: Keir Hardie was there; Clem Atlee was there; George Lansbury was there; Hugh Gaitskell was there; Wilson was there; Callaghan was there. So it is a break, and I think the simple truth is that New Labour leaders don't want to be seen with trade unionists – as simple as that!

Anyway I stayed, as I say, on the balcony watching the whole of human life go by: babies, tiny little babies; and old miners in wheelchairs, crippled by their life in the pits; and all the banners – 'Fellowship is Life', 'Fellowship is All', 'Suffer little children to come unto me', all about peace; hope, not hate. It's a tremendously moral event really, and I . . . there were moments when I was in tears.

Then I found the Blackhall Colliery banner, which is the one I'm on, and joined them, and they're all so friendly, and I walked with the banner past the Royal County Hotel.

At the racecourse, David Hopper made the last speech. I had written to him last year and said I thought that perhaps we ought to use the Gala to draw up an annual priority list for the movement, a sort of Durham manifesto, and he made a very powerful speech. As he said goodbye, he said, 'There you are, that was the Durham manifesto', so I was very happy, very honoured.

Sunday 13 July
Got back from the Durham Miners' Gala last night. I have been to the Gala since 1961, almost every year. I think I must be the longest-attending person. They're so warm to me. But I do realise my limitations. I had a cough, which didn't help.

Drove to Olympia for the Islam Expo, in the Great Hall at Olympia, full of the most wonderful exhibits of Islamic architecture, art, history, literature, calligraphy, and so on – it was really impressive. There was one little stand there run by the Stop the War movement.

I had been invited to join a panel discussion on democracy and Islam, and I'd prepared my thoughts quite clearly – only about five or six minutes – and there were some questions and answers.

I heard, when I was there, that the British Government had banned any British minister from taking part, which is ludicrous, because it was a great opportunity to show friendship.

There's a bit today in the papers about e-books. For £200 you can buy a piece of flexible plastic which will allow you to read books on it, then fold it up and put it in your pocket. I mean, I find it so hard to keep abreast of changing technology, but Josh is brilliant and is gradually upgrading me.

Nine Americans killed in Afghanistan.

Dr Gene Robinson, the gay bishop from America who has been excluded from the Lambeth Conference, was heckled during his sermon in a church in Putney. I must say, the more you see Christians shouting at each other about women bishops and homosexuality, the more you realise that the Church as an institution is in a state of . . . I won't say terminal decay, but very serious decline. Who could be attracted to go to a church by a man who hated gays or hated women? It's had a very profound effect on my attitude to the Church, which I've always treated with respect, even though my own thoughts have moved on in new directions towards the teachings of Jesus.

Monday 14 July
In the afternoon a schoolgirl called Maria Sheen came to do an interview with me about why the Labour Party gave up socialism – i.e. what New Labour was about. She was a very nice girl, shy, slim, sounded very young, but she was serious, and she had heard me speak and was coming to me, as her sort of guru!

Wednesday 16 July
Ruth tackled a few jobs in the office, but the main thing was she really wanted to talk about her future. She said she might want to work in

a hospice or set up a little business with her sister, and that she was losing interest in politics.

Somehow, this forced me to think about my life. I don't know that I'm going to be able to write the book 'Letters to my Grandchildren'. I've got my diary, but I don't honestly think a year of diary is any interest to anybody. I'm a bit depressed.

I'm feeling extremely tired all the time, and I just wonder how long I'll be able to stay in this huge house. I can't manage the upkeep; the place is becoming a slum. And, to be quite candid, who really wants to read all the junk I'm collecting? And I feel that perhaps my diary and my archives are an attempt to prolong my life in some way.

Thursday 17 July
I had nine hours' sleep, which I think probably did me a lot of good, and today I did not smoke. I won't say I gave up smoking, because I was thinking of nothing else all day, but I didn't actually smoke all day. It was very difficult. I got out an old pipe and sucked it, but I didn't light it or fill it in any way.

I went at 9.30 by car to Kensington Town Hall and talked to the PCS pickets, the second day of the Town Hall strike.

At 10.30 Dr Akbar Etemad came to see me. I last met him in 1976 in Tehran, when I was Energy Secretary. He was then head of the Iranian Atomic Energy Authority, and had been considered as Director General of the International Atomic Energy Agency, which is the key body under the Non-Proliferation Treaty.

First of all we began with the recollections of what was going on at that time, and he filled in a lot of background to me. He said, 'Walter Marshall never saw the Shah – I dealt with him.' He knew exactly my position on nuclear power and also about Jimmy Carter's. It was a rather remarkable opportunity to go back over an interesting period and see it again through his eyes.

Anyway, I asked him about the current situation. I had dug out his statements from the Internet. He's absolutely clear that Iran has the right to have nuclear power. There are no grounds whatsoever why they shouldn't, and I said that to him. I'm against nuclear energy, but that's a different point.

He wanted something done, and so I said, 'Well, I know Hans

Blix, and Kofi Annan and Carter, and maybe we could cook up a statement setting out roughly what it is we believe: that we think Iran has got a right to nuclear power, that the threats to her are a breach of international law and a breach of the Non-Proliferation Treaty, and we call upon nations to support her.' So that was really where we left it. I've now got to do a bit of work. I don't think Carter will sign it, but Kofi Annan might, if Blix is brought in, and so – well, we'll see. Noam Chomsky has agreed to sign it.

Later I caught a bus to a party held by the Editor of *The Guardian* in the National Gallery's Sainsbury Wing. I got there early, at ten to seven, so I sat outside and saw everyone arriving: Emily Maitlis, a very glamorous newsreader; Evan Davis, who's been promoted; Helen Boaden, who's the head of BBC News; Gail Rebuck, the CEO of the Random House Group, my publishers. I saw David Frost; David Miliband, the Foreign Secretary; Matthew Parris; the Chinese Ambassador, a very cultivated lady in her early to mid-fifties, I should think; Simon Hoggart, whom I loathe, so I didn't speak to him.

I saw Seamus Milne, and I had a brief word with him; he said it was pretty difficult at *The Guardian*. Saw, in the distance, the great Polly Toynbee, the voice of the critical but loyal New Labour view.

As I came away, on the bus, I thought: *The Guardian* represents a whole batch of journalists, from moderate right to moderate left – i.e. centre journalists – who, broadly speaking, like the status quo. They like the two-party system, with no real change. They're quite happy to live under the aegis of the Americans and NATO; they are very keen on the European Union because the Commissioners control everything. They are very critical of the left, but would also be critical of a wild right-wing movement. They just are the Establishment. It is a society that suits them well. I should think that probably most of them send their kids to private schools. I should think a lot of them don't use the National Health Service, but they tolerate it as the price you have to pay in order to keep the populace content. They're not interested in me any more because they don't think I have any power, and I can't say I'm very interested in them, except as exhibits in a zoo.

But it did make me realise I'm not important any more. If I was, they'd have been hovering round me. Secondly, I just go on with these lectures and I am earning a bit of money, which is useful, but I'm in a rut.

Also, I'm very frail now. I have to go downstairs with enormous care. I'm finding the house a bit much. I can't maintain it.

Saturday 19 July
Up at 4.30 for the 7.30 to Totnes. As I left the train a man said to me, 'I'd like to congratulate you on your very successful imitation of Tony Benn', so I thanked him and said, 'I have been trying to do it for years.'

There was a rickshaw waiting for me, to take me to Dartington Hall, where the 'Ways with Words' Festival is held. I had arranged to meet Julie Ollis, the widow of John Ollis. John was an architect in Bristol. There was this beautiful girl, now nearly eighty, who came up and introduced herself.

As I was sitting in the garden before the lecture somebody said to me, 'Devon kills ambition', meaning that if you come to Devon you just don't want anything else for the rest of your life. I thought it was rather shrewd.

After my lecture I found myself next to Kate Adie, the BBC correspondent (who lives in Devon).

I must say, going through the West Country – through Taunton, Exeter and Newton Abbot and Totnes – when the sun is shining and you see the cows and the clouds does remind me of my time as a Bristol MP.

Today, Alistair Darling said people couldn't pay any more tax. Well, I don't think that applies to the very wealthy, but at any rate he said that, and there is no more money for schools and education; the recession is more serious than he thought, it'll go on for two years or more. So the great dream – the Brown/Blair dream that you could borrow and spend your way to successful capitalism – has just evaporated; the left have been saying that from the very beginning.

Sunday 20 July
The end of another happy day, in Tolpuddle for the Martyrs' Festival. All these festivals I go to – Burford, Glastonbury, the Durham Miners' Gala, Tolpuddle and then Burston – just keep me going.

That's the real Labour Party, which the Government has absolutely abandoned. It's extraordinary really. I don't quite understand it. But it does mean that, when we are defeated, there is a core support we can go to, and we'll just have to build the Labour Party up all over again, because they've thrown the whole thing away. Alistair Darling's speech yesterday, saying it was worse than he thought, means in effect that he has said capitalism has failed. But he still goes on as if, somehow, if we keep calm, capitalism will recover again. I don't think it will. In that sense there'll be a change.

On the train back there was no food left in the buffet. But I had been given a jar of honey at Tolpuddle so I opened it and drank it straight from the jar, just to keep me going.

Monday 21 July
Some of my trees have grown into the convent next door and are beginning to undermine the ceiling of their chapel. Ruth dealt with that.

Tuesday 22 July
At ten o'clock John Klopacz came to see me. I think I first met him about twelve years ago. He's an American Christian Socialist, and he's gay. He's got a partner of about the same age, and as California law has just been changed, he's going to get married to his partner on 31 July. I said, 'What are you going to call him?' 'Well,' he said, 'I'm going to use the word "spouse", because spouse doesn't have a gender connotation.' He was very well read on theology. He told me Thomas Jefferson had written *The Historical Jesus*, which he's going to send me – it's little more than a pamphlet – which I never knew. We talked about all the current theological arguments, and about socialism, and the war, and so on.

That man – I can't even pronounce his name [Radovan Karadzic] – has been arrested, the Bosnian Serb leader, accused of war crimes. He had concealed himself by growing a beard and appearing as a guru on alternative health. Now he's been captured it will allow Serbia to take steps to join the European Union. The European empire is building itself up by destroying everybody it doesn't like. I remember the former Foreign Minister of Germany saying the break-up of Yugoslavia was his greatest achievement. I never supported the Balkan war, led by NATO, and therefore I'm very suspicious of it now. But war is a horrible thing, and horrible things happen. How he'll defend himself I do not know.

Thursday 24 July

I rang Melissa, and she told me that Hannah and Sarah, with eight friends, were on a train and were attacked by a group of young girls and a ten-year-old boy. Some adults intervened. It was absolutely terrifying for them. They might have had knives!

Friday 25 July

Labour has lost Glasgow East to the Scottish Nationalists – the twenty-fifth safest seat in Britain.

I had been asked to do the papers on the BBC News. It was a sunny morning, so I thought I'd look at all the papers on a table in the garden: the stories that I picked were, first of all, obviously, the by-election; then Obama; and I mentioned the fact that we are about to spend £3 billion on new nuclear warheads. I mentioned the Church at the end, the Max Mosley versus Rupert Murdoch story.

Josh rang to say he'd been appointed as the IT manager of Crisis, the voluntary organisation for homeless people. He said he wanted to stay in public service. He is a wonderful guy!

In the course of yesterday and today I've had an exchange of emails with a man expressing great horror at my attitude to homosexual relations. So I argued with him, and he was quite cordial. He said, 'You're not a Christian.' I said, 'It's not for you to say whether I'm a Christian or not. I interpret it in terms of the teachings of Jesus, and we can take different views, and we may both be wrong.' He was quite courteous about it. But he's a homophobic, Christian evangelical.

I spoke to Dave in the evening and, do you know, my memory really let me down. I was trying to think of the name of the cobbler who lived in a small thatched cottage in Steeple, Essex, and also cut hair. He used to cut my hair for sixpence. I think it was Mr Harrington. But Dave had no recollection of him at all, and I rely on Dave to be my memory.

The news is full of Obama's visit to London, and how Brown wouldn't do a press conference with him, so he came outside Number 10 and did it alone.

Sunday 27 July

The newspapers are full of who will replace Brown. Jack Straw? David Miliband? The Church is going to ban homosexual bishops, so that's a very great advance for humanity. And there was Obama's visit, of course.

The correspondence about Christianity and homosexuality continues. He's obviously a very nice guy, and I ended up by saying we shall know who is right on the Day of Judgement, and Take care, and love and peace. Obviously a very decent guy, utterly persuaded that every word in the Bible is sacred and that anyone who doesn't accept it – or, indeed, accept his interpretation of it, is not a Christian and will go to Hell. The institution of the Church has abandoned the teachings of Jesus about loving one another and concentrated entirely on the irrelevant things, like should you use condoms, and should gays have a permanent relationship, and so on. It's interesting to observe. It deepened my hostility to sectarian Christians and increased my interest in the generalist teachings of Jesus.

Thursday 31 July

Ruth came back from Devon with some flower seeds for the garden, and we went out and bought a sort of pub bench for the back garden.

The article in *The Oldie* about my seat-case invention was published, a whole page, in colour.

Chapter Five

August–December 2008:
Labour in crisis

Saturday 2 August 2008

It was sixty years ago that I met Pixie, at Worcester College. It's incredible! It seems so long ago and yet so recent . . . But it was a day to remember, and I remembered her all day.

Sunday 3 August

The press is full of Brown v. Miliband, and now, today, Jacqui Smith and John Denham and . . . somebody else has come out in support of Brown. There was a whole-page article on the two Miliband brothers. It is what the Westminster villagers are talking about all the time, but most other people are talking about fuel prices, about the cost of the war, about privatisation and pensions, and all that. The media are just on a kick of their own.

Monday 4 August

I'm a bit down. It's partly age, and partly that, when I look back on my life, I've been so obsessed with myself all the time – Benn, Benn, Benn, Tony Benn – and actually I'm just not interesting.

Tuesday 5 August

I got up early, and I went and collected a couple of letters from the post office, which, they said, hadn't been properly prepaid.

The first was an invitation from Windsor Castle, or rather from the Duke of Edinburgh's Award, to go to a dinner in Windsor Castle. Her Majesty the Queen has granted permission to hold two dinners in the sovereign's home and 'We would like to invite you and a guest to join us for either of these galas'. It said the dinners will be attended by the royal family, and 'we know your presence will make it yet more special for all those present'. Other people who had agreed to come were Buzz Aldrin, who landed on the Moon; Sir Bobby Charlton, the football manager; and Sir Roger Bannister, who ran the first four-minute mile. It's a fund-raising dinner. I rang and said I couldn't go.

The second was an invitation from the British Library to a reception for 'national treasures' – the *Sunday Telegraph* has been running a poll as to who are the national treasures, and I've been nominated as one in public life. So I rang and said I wouldn't do that! All is forgiven as you get old.

The Government has given another £3 billion to Northern Rock, which has lost £500 million this year. The absolutely crude propping-up of any company that gets into difficulty, compared to the help for people who are faced with their difficulties, is just a mark of a government utterly committed to save capitalism. But there you are.

Thursday 7 August

Just before ten, Lyn Smith came, on behalf of the Imperial War Museum, to interview me on my experience of war for their archives. I suppose she must have been nearly seventy, worked in the Open University, very progressive, knew Ron Huzzard from the Orpington Labour Party, and she couldn't have been nicer. She'd done a lot of work, and I answered the questions as best I could.

Friday 8 August

The Beijing Olympic Games opened – absolutely sensational performances by performers, and fireworks, which after all the Chinese invented.

At the same time I heard that Russia has invaded Georgia because South Ossetia, which is a province of Georgia, is urging special status for Russian citizens who live there. Of course the real reason, I think, is the Russians are very angry that NATO is trying to get Georgia to join.

Gordon Brown is going to the Beijing Olympics for the closing ceremony to take the Olympic torch from the Chinese, because the next Olympic Games are in London, and we'd have to be very clever to do anything like as spectacular an opening as the Chinese laid on. It was brilliant. In a way it's established China's dominant position in the world. The commentators are all on about human rights in China and Tibet, which is important, but the idea that, after Guantanamo Bay, Bush should warn China to reform human rights is just obscene.

That's the end of Friday 8 August.

Saturday 9 August
I was picked up this morning and taken to BBC Radio 4 to do the *Today* programme on my 'safe seat'. Evan Davis was very charming. I took my backpack and seat-case into the studio, and talked about them a bit.

Afterwards I sat downstairs and smoked my pipe, and lots of people came up and said hello, until it was time to be taken up to the BBC TV News channel. They brought in a travel adviser to sit in, who said what a fabulous idea it was, and I sat on the seat and talked about it. It was just such fun!

As soon as I got home the phone rang, it was the *Mail on Sunday*. So they came and I sat out for about half an hour, three-quarters of an hour, allowing them to take photographs.

Then, just before I went out, the phone rang and *The Sunday Times* wanted to take photographs of the seat-case, so I went out into the street with it again. I was so bloody exhausted by then! So anyway today has been a big breakthrough on the seat-case.

Sunday 10 August
The *Mail on Sunday* and *The Sunday Times* had stories on the seat-case.

Tuesday 12 August

I got a car to the *Richard & Judy* show. It worked like a dream. The show is watched by two and a half million people, which is absolutely phenomenal! They brought in a millionaire from a programme called *Dragons' Den*. Everybody liked it. It was just huge fun.

Wednesday 13 August

George Bush and Condoleezza Rice and David Miliband have denounced Russia for using force in Georgia. I mean, it's just incredible. If it weren't true, you'd think it was a nightmare. It's all because of the attempt by Georgia, which is an American satellite, to get into NATO, and Russia won't let it happen.

Saturday 16 August

I had a letter from Robin Corbett, now Lord Corbett, about my suitcase or seat-case, and he said he had a friend called Grahame Herbert who was an architect and a designer, who'd be happy to help. So I rang Grahame Herbert and he was quite interested, and he's going to come and see me.

Monday 18 August

Went and bought three cartridges for my printer, which last about five minutes. Then I went to Marks & Spencer, and I took with me the details of the suits I wear and bought a replacement.

A car picked me up, by arrangement, at 3.45, and took me to the Almeida Theatre, where I was greeted by Sam West, the son of Timothy West and Prunella Scales, and the cast of *Waste*. It is a play by Harley Granville Barker, about an independent MP, Henry Trebell, who was very keen on the disestablishment of the Church. The whole project came to an end after a scandal in which Trebell made a married woman pregnant, she died after an abortion, and he killed himself.

I was very warmly introduced by Sam West, and then I spoke about disestablishment and the various arguments for it, the political argument and the democratic argument, and so on, and then about morality and the different attitudes towards morality. They asked a mass of questions, and I realised my job was to give them enough detail to enable them to play the parts they have to play convincingly. I enjoyed it greatly.

I watched the last of the three Richard Dawkins programmes about Charles Darwin. I appeared with him last year, in a discussion, and I said, 'Well, I don't care if you don't believe in the Virgin birth, but the fact is: where is your moral teaching in science?' I found him offensive; it was a programme in which he allegedly talked to people who believed in God, but you never heard their argument. I thought it was ghastly.

Sunday 24 August, Stansgate

At three o'clock in the garden we unveiled a bench in memory of Basil Willsmer, who worked at Stansgate for years and who died last year. He was our builder, who built all the sheds and also painted the house. His widow, Heather, arrived, with Basil's sisters, one of whom looked very like Basil, and their daughter and husband, and a little girl who's five, who was absolutely sweet. I made a very brief speech, and then Heather made a speech and unveiled the plaque on the bench.

Tuesday 26 August

David Miliband is going, I think, to the Ukraine tomorrow, calling for a coalition against Russian aggression. I mean, it's just utterly ludicrous! Laughable and pitiful, but very dangerous, and over the last few days the whole atmosphere has built up about a new Cold War and confrontation. Medvedev, the new Russian President, says it doesn't worry him. It does remind me of the summer of 1914, that at some moment we'll suddenly find ourselves pitched into a war nobody wants, with many dying. It is of course an imperial clash: the old declining empire of Russia trying to recover its position, with its new energy strength; Bush – with a desperate defeat in Iraq and Afghanistan, and an economy in a mess, and a presidential election – perhaps trying to create a diversion. It just is very frightening.

Thursday 28 August

At ten o'clock a photographer called Mark arrived to do a photograph, or a series of photographs, for *Engineering & Technology*, which is a serious business magazine that's seen by companies that might be interested in the seat-case.

I caught the 148 to Whitehall. On the bus was a black lawyer who has lived round the corner from me for a long time, half-Nigerian and half-Jamaican, and I found myself sitting next to a Polish primary-school teacher, and in the seat behind a past press officer at the Department of Energy. So we had a lovely talk until I got off to walk to Downing Street. A letter had been drafted by the Stop the War Coalition, to present to the Prime Minister. On the delegation were Brian Eno, David Gentleman, Lindsey German, Chris Nineham and Kate Hudson. Downing Street was completely covered in scaffolding, so we had to push the letter in at Number 11. The press release might be picked up by the media.

Came home on the bus with Brian Eno, and had a very nice talk to him.

Then, at 2.30, Grahame Herbert, an architect and designer, came, having been recommended by Robin Corbett. I looked him up on the Net – he invented a folding bike, which has been a big success. We sat in the garden, and he took photographs of my various attempts at the seat-case and said he'd think about how it could be constructed.

Today Miliband was in the Ukraine talking about another Cold War, and I think it's probably done him damage in the Labour Party because he's the warmonger, and sounded like Blair at the time of the Iraq war. Although Brown is taking a similar line, Miliband is obviously dashing around trying to get a reputation for being tough. The press will love it. I'm not sure the Labour Party will like it very much. I've got to be careful, because of my friendship with Ed and Marion, but I must say, if he was the Leader of the Labour Party, I wouldn't feel any connection with the Labour Party.

Friday 29 August

I had a very nice note from Michael Moore. He asked Penguin, who published his guide to the American elections, to send it to me. He said, 'I've dedicated it to you, and I think you may not realise how much you matter to me.' It was rather nice of him.

The more I think about this Caucasus affair, the more angry I get that NATO should be used to provoke a split in Europe, and then all this talk about isolating Russia. Of course, Russia has one great weapon: if they decide not to supply gas and oil to the West, the West would be in a real mess.

Saturday 30 August
It was a really lovely day today, and I took my lunch out in the garden and had a short rest in the deckchair. The white dog from next door sat on the wall and barked at me, and a black cat from the garden came up on the other side and touched my finger with its nose.

The big news is Alistair Darling's statement that the crisis is the worst for sixty years. What he's done is tell us the truth, and one of the functions of leadership is not to mislead people. Funnily enough, what Alistair said is exactly what I've been saying for months now: that the credit crunch is the 9/11 of the world economy or, put in an ideological way, it's a classic case of the failures of capitalism. So I thought it was interesting.

Apparently Gordon Brown refused to comment. The conflict between a Chancellor and a Prime Minister means that one of them, usually the Chancellor, has to go. Apparently Gordon is pushing the Treasury to do things that would give him a relaunch, and the Treasury don't want to do them. So with Miliband, the Foreign Secretary, out on a limb on the war in Georgia (though Gordon apparently supports him), it looks as if the Government is in meltdown.

Tuesday 2 September
From 4.50 till twenty past six Benjamin Zephaniah came with his Chinese girlfriend, who is twenty-five, and her name is Jin Young Lee and she's an interpreter in Shanghai.

He had a book idea and he wanted to know whether it was sensible. The idea is that there are two children, who hate the world, and they decide to hack into the major economies of the world, the banks and governments, and dislocate them. I encouraged him no end, because of course there's this lad (Gary McKinnon) who is the subject of an extradition order from America for hacking into the Pentagon.

He talked about China. He goes quite regularly to China because he loves martial arts. His girlfriend was shy. I like Benjamin very much.

Saturday 6 September

Ruth and I went to a vegetarian restaurant for a meal and then Barbara joined us and we all went to see *The Edge of Love* about Dylan Thomas, with Keira Knightley and Sienna Miller. I didn't hear a word of the dialogue. Barbara and Ruth talked about it all the way back in the taxi.

Monday 8 September

I had eaten a sandwich yesterday with salmon in it past its sell-by date, and wondered if I was poisoned by it. I had a simply awful night! I was tossing about all night, very cold. I got into a dressing gown, had to go to the loo a million times. I was absolutely exhausted! I thought: I cannot go on like this.

To Brighton for the TUC Conference. I walked from the station to the conference centre, bought a pipe and a couple of cigarette lighters in a pipe shop. I sat outside the centre on my seat-case and smoked my pipe.

I must say, the TUC is a friendly place. What was interesting is how many of them wear ties. As I'm trying to get rid of wearing a tie, I didn't wear one. There were masses of old friends, and I recognised their faces, but I couldn't remember their names. It was ghastly. Anyway, I was very warm to everybody and they couldn't have been nicer to me.

I did four fringe meetings. In the course of the day I saw Bob Crow, Tony Woodley and Derek Simpson, Paul Kenny from the GMB, Bernard Regan, John Hendy, John McDonnell. What's nice about the TUC is there's not all this ghastly security, where they search you and open your bag in case you've got political literature.

My general line at the moment in speeches is to cheer people up. People have been so depressed for so long, I try to give them a bit of a boost – that's what I feel needs to be done. I loved the day, I really enjoyed it, but I did take on too much. Four speeches is quite a lot for a single day.

Tuesday 9 September

To Josh's graduation ceremony as a BSc first-class Honours in information management from University College London.

Hilary, Stephen and Lissie were all there, and William and Nahal. The Vice Chancellor began his speech just boosting UCL competitively against other universities. I found it highly commercial: I felt he was trying to market the UCL product, which I suppose, in effect, he was.

But then all the students went up, and of course every one that went by was clapped and cheered, and when Josh came up we gave a loud hoot, which was noticed. Josh talked to the Pro Vice Chancellor and shook his hand. There were tons of people in gowns, with parents and grandparents and sisters, and so on.

Afterwards to the Bloomsbury Theatre bar for Josh's party – about 125 friends of his, from work, from the university itself, friends from all over the place. I had arranged that I would pay the bill. Josh doesn't know that.

Dave turned up, bless his heart. Emily and Daniel, Sally, Michael, James and Blake and Roger, PC; it couldn't have been nicer.

Dave and I popped out and had a puff.

Then Stephen called for order and made a very good speech about Josh, and I spoke for a few moments, and then Josh made a lovely speech. Altogether, the thing was so moving – but by the end of the day I couldn't stand any more. I've got to recognise I am disabled, I cannot stand.

Hilary couldn't stay; he wanted to see Josh get his degree, but he had to go back to Brighton for the TUC dinner, and I think, later tonight, to Morpeth for the flooding.

Wednesday 10 September
I got up early for a programme called *The One Show,* which is a rather flippant programme, but apparently a researcher has said that it would be possible for people to live to a thousand years. I had done a bit of work because I thought it was an interesting question.

I went out and did shopping for food because I had nothing in the fridge.

The whole evening I spent reading every newspaper in preparation for *Any Questions?* on Friday.

Thursday 11 September
I got up at six o'clock and went out to buy *The Times, The Independent,*

the *Daily Telegraph*, and the *Daily Mail*, which they probably read in Worthing, and I spent all morning going through every one of them and thinking up questions that might be asked.

I sat down and I typed out all the questions, and a few speaking notes, and I'm pretty well prepared. The other members of the panel are David Aaronovitch, Damian Green, the Tory migration spokesman, and Rachel Johnson, who is Boris Johnson's sister.

Friday 12 September
Caught the train to West Worthing. Dinner was at the Ardington Hotel which was full of old ladies with white hair. Aaronovitch, Green and Johnson and I talked at the meal, and every one of us, including Jonathan Dimbleby, had worked for the BBC. Everybody was topping each other with stories. It was all very jolly.

Then we were taken on to Davidson Church of England High School. I'd predicted all the questions: energy policy and fuel costs; should there be a Labour leadership election; the NHS; fourth, should creationism be taught at school; and migration.

The programme wasn't brilliant, but it was okay, and there was quite a lot of support for me.

I came back in the car with Rachel Johnson. She's written a number of novels, one of which is called *Notting Hell*. She's a Conservative, obviously. She said Boris had boundless ambitions, they weren't limited to being Mayor of London, which I thought was quite interesting. I dropped her home in the car the BBC had provided, and she gave me a big kiss on both cheeks. She's a public schoolgirl, nice and a fairly liberal Conservative journalist.

Wednesday 17 September
I got up at 4.45, was picked up by car and taken to GMTV, where I did an interview about Brown's leadership. I said I found the whole thing so boring about who'd be the Leader. The question is: do we stay in Iraq and Afghanistan; what do we do about ID cards, about nuclear weapons? And so on. I argued my case, in a perfectly friendly way, and later on I went to Waterstone's to buy *Notting Hell*.

Thursday 18 September
To the Russian Embassy in Kensington Palace Gardens to see the Ambassador, Yuri Fedotov, a man of sixty. I haven't been in the embassy since the fall of the Soviet Union. I was asked as I arrived not to stay more than twenty minutes, but in fact the Ambassador kept saying, 'No, no, no, please stay!'

I said that I'm an old man, I've seen a lot, I have a great friendship for the Russian people, I knew of all the sacrifices in the war that had made it possible for Hitler to be defeated. I said the Cold War was not real, and I told him the story of going to the Defence Academy, where only two of the officers thought that nuclear weapons had deterred a Soviet attack on Western Europe. He was friendly and respectful, but pompous, I thought.

He told me a very funny story. He said the papers had recently reported a senior Soviet official ringing up David Miliband and telling him, 'You f—ing well did this, you f—ing well invaded Iraq, you f—ing well did that.' It was denied both by the Russians and by the Foreign Office but, the Ambassador said, 'I've no way of knowing what was true, but all I do know is that I had twenty-five letters from people saying, "Thank God someone had the guts to say that to Miliband."'

I gave him the description of my first visit to Russia in 1960, and I said I'd complained about the Soviet invasion of Hungary and about the Soviet control of Afghanistan, but, I said, 'We've now got to have a new security structure in Europe because people are very, very frightened.' He said, 'Well, Medvedev has made a similar suggestion.'

His argument was that you couldn't have a conflict, a new Cold War, now because the interconnection of the world economies is so tight – very much the sort of modern globaliser approach. But still, I think he appreciated my visit.

Monday 22 September, Labour Party Conference, Manchester
Today Alistair Darling made a very strong speech about the crisis, and of course, he got a standing ovation. It was quite a good speech, though he said they'd do all that was necessary to restore the stability of the system. Well, as I'm a socialist, that's not what I want, but he put it very well.

Then David Miliband made a passionate speech, paid a warm tribute to Gordon Brown, got an ovation, and the media are building him up for the leadership.

My reaction and reflections on the Conference? The Party is very worried that they'll be smashed in the general election, which they will. The leadership is very worried, and of course the pressure for a leadership election is coming from people like Hutton – no, not Hutton – Milburn and Charles Clarke and Barry Gardiner.

The Left Convention, which held a meeting here, is very interesting. It's the Labour left, it's John Rees, Lindsey German, people from the Green Party, Respect, and so what we're gradually doing is building up a left centre in the Labour Party. Tonight Billy Hayes said people on the left should now join the Labour Party and take over the local parties and get them going. There'd be a lot of trouble if they did, because the existing members wouldn't like it, but he was very shrewd. John Nicholson's done extremely well with the Left Convention. I think that left unity, which I've always encouraged, is beginning to take place, and I think Galloway would have been welcomed if he'd been there.

I feel that this is a historic Conference in the sense that everything New Labour believed in has been shattered, and what the Left is saying is now relevant again.

Interestingly, the Conference was not allowed a debate on Iraq or Afghanistan or anything – so here are these massive wars in which we're involved, and King Gordon Brown did not want it discussed at Conference, and the Conference accepted it.

So I think we're seeing the death of New Labour, and the birth of ideas that might help us, but we don't want splits, because that will frighten people even more.

Tuesday 23 September
Caught the train to London. I was just so happy to be home!

Watched Gordon make his speech on television . . . Every sentence was punctuated by applause and there were standing ovations all the way through it. Shots of Kinnock smiling. Brown mentioned lots of ministers – Jack Straw, Ed Balls, but he never mentioned Hilary . . . it was all about Brown and his faith, and how 'We're a party of business and enterprise' (he never mentioned the trade unions).

Brown, I think, will survive because there is always loyalty to leaders, and the Party Conference was very pleased he spoke up well.

It took me ages to unpack.

Wednesday 24 September

The news this morning is that Ruth Kelly has resigned as Transport Secretary, and the reason given was that she wanted to devote more time to her family. She has four children under eleven, so it's a perfectly reasonably explanation.

Of course there's a vacancy now Ruth Kelly's gone, and Hilary might be affected, but there's no point in worrying about it. It would be nice for him to carry on until the election, when I feel it's almost certain Labour will be defeated. There might be a coalition, and I think Gordon Brown and Cameron and Nick Clegg would be very happy in a coalition government. That would release the left in an interesting way.

The other big news, and it is enormous news, is that Bush has put before Congress a policy involving a $700 billion bailout of the financial institutions in order to restore confidence in the banking system. Apparently the law would exempt any rules made under this legislation from public review or reference to the courts, so democracy has been suspended for the purpose of this operation, and many Republicans don't like it. I heard it described as 'American socialism', 'financial socialism'.

Obama has been more cautious about it. A lot of the Democrats and others are saying the whole cost of this will be paid for by the American taxpayers. I think they said it would cost the average American taxpayer $5,000 or something. There's absolutely no accountability! If you're going to buy the banks, which is what the American Government is doing, why don't you just own the banks and get the profit as they recover? If this isn't sorted out there will be a total crisis of confidence in the American economy, and that will spread to the world economy.

The news now is entirely dominated by business, particularly by the banking system. Politicians are now treated by the media as people entitled to make a comment, as if they were sort of licensed journalists themselves, but money runs the world and democracy has, to that extent, been suspended.

In 1945, Clem Attlee said the great inter-war crises were not acts of God; they were the sure and certain result of too much power in the hands of too few men who felt no responsibility – I'm just summarising the argument. Of course, in his book *The Labour Party in Perspective* Attlee also said the problem is that the private ownership of the means of production has changed. So the early Attlee was a socialist, and indeed the policies that were followed through, although they weren't presented ideologically, were socialist policies.

If the American banking system collapses, the world banking system will be fatally injured. Then the sort of policies adopted will not be those of socialist governments, but of the likes of Hitler and Mussolini, the national socialists, who nationalised everything and used the power for their own purposes.

Thursday 25 September
Got the Tube to Baker Street and walked to the Royal College of Obstetrics and Gynaecology for the memorial service to Norman Morris. There was a huge crowd there, which included Lucy Morris, his widow, and the children: David, who lives in Canada; Nick, and the two daughters, all four of whom are consultants now. I made my speech.

Saturday 27 September, North Devon
By train to Tiverton Parkway and on to Ruth's house in North Devon.

She had a party for her mum and dad (Joan and Victor); her twin sister Diana, and Di's son Matthew and daughter Nancy; Rose, the librarian, and Tom, the architect who she married a couple of years ago; her neighbours, Ray, who's an engineer, and his wife, Mimi, who's a gardener, and their daughter, Hannah, a very beautiful thirty-year-old who works for an employment agency. Then there was an Air Marshal Peter Walker and his wife, Linda, who taught children with special needs. And then Pauline, who had worked with Marcia Williams when Morgan Phillips was General Secretary of the Labour Party and we had a talk about the old days.

Ruth and I had a lovely late talk. Her friends are very nice, and it's a completely different world; I saw Ruth in a new perspective, I saw her life unfolding in a way that will develop of its own volition.

Monday 29 September
I read the 1945 Election Manifesto, *Let us Face the Future*:

> The great inter-war slumps were not acts of God or of blind forces; they were the sure and certain result of the concentration of too much economic power in the hands of too few men. These men had only learned how to act in the interests of their own bureaucratically run private monopolies, which may be likened to totalitarian oligarchies within our democratic state. They had, and they felt, no responsibility for the nation . . .
>
> The nation wants food, work and homes; it wants more than that, it wants good food in plenty, useful work for all, and comfortable, labour-saving homes that take full advantage of the resources of modern science and productive industry. It wants a high and rising standard of living, security for all against a rainy day, an educational system that will give every boy and girl a chance to develop the best that is in them.
>
> These are our aims. In themselves, they're no more than words. All parties may declare that, in principle, they agree with them, but the test of a political programme is whether it is sufficiently in earnest about the objectives to adopt the means needed to realise them. It's very easy to set out a list of aims; what matters is whether it is backed up by a genuine, workmanlike plan, conceived without regard for section or vested interest, and carried through in a spirit of resolute concentration.

Now that is a brilliant statement, relevant to 1945, but also relevant today! It reminded me that when the nation went to the left in 1945, it wasn't some ideological lunge; it was that the circumstances made it an inevitable and sensible thing to do. People didn't want to go back to the Thirties, they did want all the things listed, and Attlee was the man to do it. So I think I shall be using this more.

The big news today is that the House of Representatives has

defeated the $700 billion bailout that Bush wanted, and the Dow Jones has fallen 700 points, which is the highest ever, and there really is a very serious global economic crisis. A bank in the Netherlands has collapsed, we've nationalised Bradford & Bingley, which was a mutual, and the whole thing is just . . . it's terrifying.

Somebody compared the credit crunch to Pearl Harbor. I'd been comparing it to 9/11, and on the whole, looking back at what I've been saying over the last year, I haven't been too far wrong.

Tuesday 30 September
I got a taxi to do the BBC *Politics Show* programme on the economic crisis. I said, beforehand, 'I hope that, when you introduce me, you'll introduce me factually.' 'What do you mean?' 'Well, I just want to be introduced as the longest-serving Labour MP, eleven years in the Cabinet' (not as a representative of the far left). I made my point. I had worked out carefully the way in which I'd present my case: this is a very serious crisis, people get frightened; in the Thirties it led to mass unemployment and war; and during the war we said we must build up the economy; and I read the extract from the 1945 Manifesto. Norman Fowler, who was also on, was rather superior and when I said we should bring the banks into public ownership, he said, 'Oh no, that would bring a complete collapse in the City of London and Wall Street!' Of course the answer is that if you nationalise the banks there couldn't be a collapse, because the Government would be deciding to whom they lent the money. I was reasonably pleased.

Wednesday 1 October
Very tired all day. Awful dreams. Very depressed.

I did an interview with BBC Radio Oxford on old age, because today is the 'day of the older generation', or something.

I heard David Cameron's speech to the Tory Conference, and I got the full text of it because I did BBC Radio 5 Live this evening on that speech. The other people taking part were Peter Oborne, who's a right-wing columnist on the *Daily Mail*, and Anne Diamond. She said to me afterwards, 'Oh, I'll never forget when I was a local correspondent, at the time that you opened the Hinkley B Power

Station. All the press were there, it was a major event, and you picked me out because I was the local correspondent, and you gave a lot of attention to me. I've never forgotten that. And you sent me a recording of the speech you'd made. I was so touched!' So I'd made a friend for life with her.

Thursday 2 October
Grahame Herbert came, with his tiny model of the seat-case, and photographs, and we had a lovely talk.

I'm so frail now, so tired and depressed, and I think I'm coming to the end of the road. I always said I would die at eighty-two, and I'm now eighty-three, but I must say, if I see out the next twelve months I'd be surprised. I don't know quite how to put it, but I'm very shaky on my pins. I'm too tired to walk, I don't seem to have the energy to get on with what I've got to do, and of course I am extremely busy.

Friday 3 October
The news that's dominated the world today is that Mandelson is being brought back as Secretary of State for Business, Enterprise and Regulatory Reform – in effect the old job I had, at the Department of Trade and Industry. Mandelson, who said he wasn't a quitter, and quit two Government jobs, went up to his Hartlepool constituency and said, 'I'm not a quitter', then quit that, went to Brussels, and he's now quit that and he's coming back into the Government. I don't know who it will encourage, but it will certainly discourage the Party. They have given him a peerage, of course, because he couldn't find a constituency at short notice.

I didn't mention it yesterday, but Sir Ian Blair, the Commissioner of the Metropolitan Police, was forced out by Boris Johnson. Johnson said he had no confidence in him, so the Home Secretary had to accept his resignation, but she has the responsibility of appointing the new Commissioner.

In a crisis governments move to the right, and that's what's happened in Britain; Mandelson represents a substantial vote to the right. They're also setting up an Emergency Financial Committee, a sort of War Cabinet to deal with the economic crisis, with businessmen on it, but not the whole Cabinet. So the Cabinet has been sidelined officially from handling major matters.

I also ought to add that, on the second vote in the House of Representatives, they voted overwhelmingly for the bailout, which they now call a 'rescue plan'. So, in effect, American taxpayers are subsidising the bankers, but of course they won't get any benefit out of it.

So it's a very significant shift to the right in British politics. I'll have to think about all that.

It's now twenty to ten and I'm going to bed, but I hate going to bed too early, for one very simple reason: I have to get up to wee every two hours, so if I go to bed at ten, I think: Oh God, when is the night going to end?!

I'm delighted for Hilary, who's got another eighteen months as a Cabinet minister. I really am delighted, and the family seem quite happy.

Saturday 4 October

I rang Hilary this morning at quarter past seven, and I think he thought it might be the Prime Minister because, yesterday, the Prime Minister did ring him at that time!

Sunday 5 October

I rang Natasha because there was a picture of her baby, whose name is Arla, in the paper, and said what a lovely picture it was, and she said she was having a wonderful time, didn't watch television!

She told me that Selina Scott had actually been offered the job to replace her during her maternity leave, even given a contract, but that the new manager wouldn't have it, so Selina is taking Channel 5 to court for age discrimination. So I rang Selina and left a message – you can never speak to her – and said, 'If you want somebody to come and [give] evidence on your behalf, I'd be delighted to.'

I also rang Blake, James's girlfriend, because it's her birthday tomorrow. I thought she'd probably be working in hospital, but actually she was doing a night-shift tonight, so was at home, and I had a word with her.

I think it's appreciated, as a grandfather, and I just love it of course!

Monday 6 October

In every news bulletin there is a complete meltdown of the world economy! The Icelandic banks are virtually bankrupt. The $700 billion put in in New York has not done the trick. Prices and values are falling everywhere. I think something like £95 billion of shareholders' value disappeared today in London. It is really obvious that the handling of it, the subsidy of the banks, is not going to do the trick. I think the argument for the public ownership of banks is one we've got to consider very seriously.

So I rang Jon Snow, on his office number, just after the bulletin, which was very good, and said, 'Don't you think the moment's come when some alternative ideas should be aired?' Maybe . . . I might make progress.

Tuesday 7 October

The news today is an absolutely major collapse in the shares of British banks, and this so frightened the Government that, all afternoon, they were locked up at Number 10. I think Darling, the Chancellor, was in Europe and flew back, and they are going to announce tomorrow that the Government will put money into the banking system, but will insist on shares. So they will have a voice in the rewards of top banking executives; also, I hope, in guiding where the money goes for investment. It is extraordinary, you know, when you advocated the nationalisation of the banks years ago people said you were absolutely bonkers and dangerous and irresponsible and out of touch with reality, and now, a right-wing government, because that's what it is, has decided that's what they've got to do. Of course, they'll try and privatise it again later, but I'm not sure that will be so easy.

The Icelandic bank which had been attracting investors from Britain for a long time said they won't pay back the money that British investors put in their bank, other than through a compensation scheme, so quite a lot of people will lose a great deal of money.

It's a bit scary really. I feel, in my hearts of hearts, that they couldn't let Lloyds Bank go down the pan; I have my savings in the bank and I always assumed they were safe.

Wednesday 8 October
Up early.

Obama–McCain debate, and Obama seems to have done well.

Fifty billion pounds given to the banks, which is part-nationalisation. I watched Parliament on TV, and John McDonnell raised nationalisation of the banks when the Prime Minister made the statement.

Thursday 9 October
This ghastly crisis has got worse and worse because it turns out £860 million of local government savings had gone to Icesave, this Icelandic company that can't pay up.

Came home and found a message from Rosa Prince of the *Daily Telegraph* saying, 'Would you write an article tomorrow about the credit crisis?' So I painfully typed out 900 words and sent them off to her. She got back to me and said the Editor liked them, but wanted me to add the point that I'd made these arguments before and no one listened. So I did add a little bit. I was really chuffed – actually, I sat and laughed and laughed about it!

Then I heard *The Spectator* wanted to interview me about my time out of Parliament. So it's all sort of coming my way, and I just laughed about all that.

The *Telegraph* said they had less space than they hoped, so they'd have to cut my article by half.

I worked on emails and phone calls.

Friday 10 October
I looked at the *Telegraph* online, and there were over 200 comments about my article, of which all but about two were wildly abusive! 'This socialist millionaire with his stately home and his estate in Wales' and 'Tony Benn, Lord Stansgate'; 'Anthony Wedgwood Benn ruined British industry', 'Communist!' It did remind me that the media hatred, built up over the years, still registers in the minds of lots of people. It completely brushed away the foolish idea I had yesterday that I was now a national treasure, and it did just remind you of the power that newspapers have to poison people against an idea or purpose in such a way that it becomes almost undiscussable. It really

did remind me of the old days – not that it bothers me now, because I don't care what people say, and I'm not trying to be elected again. I printed fourteen pages of abuse, and a couple of friendly comments.

Saturday 11 October
Lissie drove me to the Almeida Theatre to see the play *Waste*, which I had attended the rehearsal of in August, and talked to the cast and tried to explain the political background. It was a very powerful play, though I couldn't hear it all. I knew the rough story, so that helped a bit. I was afraid my breathing would disturb people around me or that I'd go to sleep.

In the interval Sam West brought us a cup of tea and we had a talk to him – very nice lad.

Monday 13 October
If Caroline had lived, she would have been eighty-two today . . . Oh, I think of her all the time. I spoke to all the children.

The Government has nationalised the Royal Bank of Scotland and taken a 40 per cent stake in HBOS – Halifax whatever-it-is – and in Lloyds Bank. Barclays have managed without government money. If I imagined, a year or two ago, that a Labour Government, including Peter Mandelson, would have nationalised the banks, I think I would have merited mental treatment.

The forty-two days vote has been defeated, so David Davis has reason to congratulate himself.

Wednesday 15 October
Kevin Rudd, the Labour Prime Minister of New Zealand . . . or is it Australia, I can't remember . . . has arranged to give huge benefits to people over Christmas, running to over $1,000 each, in order to get the economy going. Quite an interesting idea – much cheaper than giving money to banks! But we shall see.

Thursday 16 October
I got a Tube to Westminster and walked over the bridge to St Thomas's for the conference on multiculturalism organised by Patricia Moberly; a huge crowd of people, probably 50/50 black and

white. There were various talks, including one by a black policeman who's on the Police Complaints Commission, who actually quoted, in his speech just before me, what I'd said about racial intolerance: how if a black has got a job, he's stolen yours, and if he hasn't, he's a scrounger on the Welfare State. Then to 4 Millbank, where I did about seven or eight minutes on the *Jeremy Vine* show, BBC Radio 2, about public ownership of the banks. They put on a ghastly woman who said that politicians were corrupt and a free market was all we needed – didn't sound very credible, but anyway I wasn't particularly angry with her.

The political news today is that the fall in share prices has started all over the world, despite the billions of dollars that's been put in. So that argument is still alive. I do think there's been a big change in people's attitude to public intervention and the public role in banking, and all of a sudden I feel that they're prepared to listen to me. The *Jeremy Vine* show, with a couple of million or more listening, would be a way of getting the case across. I'm not using ideology at all; I'm making a purely practical case for what we're doing, and I think that's what registered with people in 1945 and that's what will register now.

Saturday 18 October
Got up at six, met Ruth at Paddington and we caught the train to Swindon and were driven from there to the Cheltenham Literary Festival. I met Ian Rankin, who was chairing this panel including Tariq Ali and me, but Tariq rang to say he'd forgotten and overslept! Professor Anthony Grayling took part instead. There was a session on the politics of 1968 and of today. It was an absolutely packed meeting.

Monday 20 October
Colin Powell, the former Chairman of the Joint Chiefs of Staff and Secretary of State, has endorsed Obama, and that looks pretty good.

Tuesday 21 October
Hilarious news today that George Osborne, the Shadow Chancellor, was on the yacht of a Russian oligarch, and Mandelson was on the same yacht! The question is: did Osborne ask for money for the

Conservatives through one of the oligarch's British subsidiaries? Well, in September Osborne had leaked the fact that Mandelson had rubbished Gordon Brown just before Brown appointed Mandelson to his Government. So I guess Mandelson decided to get revenge on Osborne. It's just totally corrupt, just stinks – the idea of a Labour minister going on the yacht of a Russian oligarch!

Saturday 25 October
Ruth arrived and I began dictating another preface for the book, but I realised I can't do it – trying to write a book for my grandchildren is nonsense. So I got very, very depressed.

Mandelson is in deep trouble again over this Russian billionaire oligarch, Oleg Deripaska. Mandelson had said he first met him in 2006, but actually it now turns out that he met him in 2004, and he's got to explain why he misled people. The story is building, and I think the *Daily Mail* and the press generally are determined to finish him off. They'll go on and on. Brown can't sack him because, if he did, Mandelson would turn on Brown. On the other hand, Brown must find it acutely embarrassing having this in the news every day.* It was a terrible error to bring him back.

I went round the house and put all the clocks back for tomorrow.

Monday 27 October
Worrying all day about my next book! I think I've found a new way of doing it . . . what Britain was like, or the world was like, when I was born, where we are now, and what we do about it – I don't know if it will work, but I'll try it.

Friday 31 October
I was picked up at 3.45 by John Grice to drive me to Eastbourne. The traffic was absolutely appalling! I got there just as my talk was due to begin. There were about 340 people, in a theatre that would hold 1,750, so it wasn't a wild success. I was driven home by John, got back at midnight and went to bed about one.

---

* Social meetings between Deripaska, an aluminium producer, and Mandelson, the EU Trade Commissioner, prompted suggestions of a conflict regarding European import duties on aluminium.)

I've got a bit of a pain in my chest today. I did wonder whether I'd overdone it.

Saturday 1 November

Up at 4.30, so I had about three and a half hours' sleep. Got a cab to Paddington, Heathrow Express train to the airport, a plane to Manchester, was picked up by a car and driven to Liverpool for a BBC Radio 3 thing called the 'Free Thinking Festival'.

It was quite incredible. I was asked to give a thirty-minute talk to about seventy people in a theatre there, and then the idea was forty minutes of questions and discussion. I picked, as a title, 'Letters to my Grandchildren' to talk about the future. They were pleased. The BBC have never, ever asked me to do a broadcast like that before.

Anyway, after that I had to wait ages for the car to take me back, so I sat in the sunshine, in the street, with my pipe, and masses of people came up. I said, 'What do you do?' 'I'm a teacher.' 'What do you do?' 'I'm a teacher.' Six teachers came up!

A car took me back to Manchester and I was home by 8.45. In the cab home I was driven by a Welsh former miner, who said I could smoke. He said, 'I'm a rebel – I'm not going to be told what I can do!' So I lit my pipe, and when I got home he wouldn't take any money. He said, 'I'm not taking any money from you, Mr Benn.' He looked at my twenty-pound note and said, 'I think it's a dud' – it was rather sweet of him!

Monday 3 November

Ruth and I sat down and I dictated the 'eighty-five-year timescale'. Next year I'm in my eighty-fifth year, and I was born in 1925; eighty-five years before that was 1840, and we'd just had the Opium Wars, to force the Chinese to import opium from us; the Chartists were still struggling in Britain, and only 20 per cent of the population (all men) had the vote.

I was picked up and taken to Al Jazeera for a programme on the Prime Minister's mission to the Gulf States to persuade them to make money available to the IMF for the relief of the world credit crunch. I couldn't see or hear the other two contributors very clearly. I managed to make a few points. First, that if the Prime Minister wants support from the Arab States, the Gulf States, they should say, in return: we expect a different policy on Palestine and a withdrawal of allied forces from Iraq and Afghanistan. I also said the best way of helping people is to take control of your own oil, as Chávez had done, and Norway had done, and we'd done. I also said: do we really want to go back to the casino economy?

Tuesday 4 November
Today was the American election, and mass media coverage! Pages and pages of the newspapers, and hours on the television, and it does show how important it is.

Lissie rang this morning; she said Hannah and Sarah were transfixed by the elections and were absolutely excited by Obama. What Obama has done has been to give hope to whole generations – particularly young people – so he has fanned the flames of hope. I said that the America that had voted for him was the America I knew and loved. I said it was also, of course, the end of Bush and Rumsfeld, of Bolton and Cheney, and also, I think, the end of Blair in a way. Obama had proved that another world is possible, and a black President is a significant thing.

I am in a sort of rut at the moment. I mean, I suppose, as the years go by, my experience is so out-of-date. It's like Mr Gladstone remembering talks he had about the Irish question or the Bulgarian massacre. So I have to be realistic about myself. I'm doing these broadcasts about 'Letters to my Grandchildren', and I must introduce an element of novelty into them.

Thursday 6 November
Well, Obama's victory dominates the press, but there is growing criticism from the left of Obama coming in.

A man called Larry Pinkney wrote a powerful denunciation, saying it's not about colour, it's about class and about the oppression by the rich of the poor, and will anything be done about it? It did plant in the back of my mind the fear, which I think will grow over the months, that perhaps Obama is another Tony Blair raising hopes, but we'll see.

Then, oh, I did an interview for BBC Swindon. The Bank of

England has cut the interest rate by 1.5 per cent. This must be almost over the dead body of Mervyn King, the Governor of the Bank of England, who's been so conservative about everything, and it shows what nonsense it was to make the Bank of England independent.

Monday 10 November
Rodney Bickerstaffe came to breakfast. He's so sweet! He visits every few months and I lay on toast and tea for him, and we have a talk. He's sixty-four now, and he's got ten grandchildren. You know, keeping in touch with people is important, and he makes the effort to keep in touch with me. I'm not so good at it. He's always very supportive, and we talked about what I was doing, and the future, and Obama. He does a lot of work with the international trade-union movement. Then he went off, and I had a short doze.

After lunch I had a doze and at 6.30 Bernard Sanders, the Socialist Senator for Vermont, came with his brother Larry Sanders, who is a Green councillor in Oxford. Bernie is sixty-seven, and Larry seventy-three. We went over everything – Obama's victory, a possible surge in Afghanistan . . . Bernie said, 'You can't negotiate with the Taliban.' I'm not sure I agree with that. They are Polish Jews, by origin, and were cautious on Israel, but felt some progress had to be made.

Bernie Sanders told me he'd been to a conference on the environment today, and Ed Miliband had been there, so he told Ed he was having a meal with me, and Ed said, 'Well, give him my best: I worked in his office years ago.'

I took them over for a meal at Pizza Express, and then I walked back to the Tube station with them and came home.

Today Gordon Brown, all dressed up in a white tie and tails, went to the Lord Mayor's Banquet and warned America against protectionism. I mean, that man's commitment to free trade and market forces is just unbending! But still, he seems to be doing very well, and I want a Labour Government, so there you are.

Tuesday 11 November
Hilary, bless his heart, rang from Beijing.

Rang Josh, and he is transferring me back to my old mobile, because I couldn't use the one he lent me – too complicated, and I didn't get any messages on it and everything went wrong. So that's a bit of a setback.

Thursday 13 November
Hilary rang, or I rang him and he rang me back. He's back from China, so that's all right.

From 9.20 to 12.00, a film-maker, Polly Steele, came – she wants to make a film along the lines of 'Letters to my Grandchildren'. Afterwards I was so exhausted that I just went down to my office and lay on the floor, leaving notices on the front and basement doors saying 'Door open', because I was expecting visitors. I was half-asleep when Colin Leys arrived, and I had a bit of a talk to him, and then Leo Panitch came and we went out and had a meal at Pizza Express.

Leo I have known for years. I have tremendous admiration for him. He's the man who worked very closely with Ralph Miliband on the *Socialist Register*, which is published every year. He's a professor in Canada and very active there, politically. Colin has just published a book on the Health Service which, he says, is being privatised. He is always in a deep political gloom and depression – everything is wrong. Later he said there will not be another surge of progressive activity until the ecological crisis overcomes us and East Anglia is swamped by the rising water levels, and then that will lead to people realising collective action is necessary.

They're two formidable intellectuals, and I like them very much, but talking to them you get the impression that all is hopeless; their analysis is brilliant, but their remedies? Colin thought the answer to the privatisation of the Health Service was to put up Health Service candidates against Labour candidates. Of course, that would just lead to the Tories winning in those constituencies. They are pleased about Obama's victory, he's given hope to people, but they don't have much hope in themselves.

In the evening the front doorbell went and it was a reporter from the *Mail on Sunday*. He said, 'I believe you were Vice Chairman for Labour Action for Peace? There was a woman called Cynthia Roberts who was active in it and who went to Prague and spied for the Czech authorities.' So when he had gone I looked her up in my diaries and there was no reference to her whatsoever. Of course I didn't become

Chairman of LAP till the 1990s and she left for Prague, apparently, in the 1980s. I emailed them to say just that, and that I addressed LAP meetings but I don't think I ever attended any committee meetings. But it was strange that they should try to link me in that way. There is a slight sense of horror when the *Mail* approaches you about anything.

Saturday 15 November
Waiting for a meeting to begin, because I was much too early, I sat next to the Ian Walters statue of Fenner Brockway in the park. It's a brilliant statue and so true of Fenner: the way he's standing, the way he smiles, his spectacles, the way he holds out his arm, and his feet slightly pointing inwards, and the bottom of his trouser legs not even covering his ankles.

After the meeting Lissie and I walked down Southampton Road, found a little hotel and went in and ordered some tea, and we sat out where I could smoke my pipe. She's so sweet, is Lissie, and I'm so close to her. Then she had to go to the National Portrait Gallery, because she wanted to show Paul and the girls her photograph there, so I dropped her off in a taxi.

Came home, and Barbara had left. I'm very, very tired. It's now about twenty past seven, and I realised that I hadn't had a meal.

Just a little addendum before I go to bed – I still haven't had a meal – I rang Josh, I rang Hilary, I rang Stephen, I rang Dave, I rang PC, I rang Ruth, and I left a message for Lissie about today, so that was one, two, three, four, five, six, seven phone calls this evening, and, in the diary, that had better go down as what I call a perfect day!

One final postscript. I had a letter in the post today saying that the network of Socialist Campaign Groups has decided to dissolve and be absorbed by the Labour Representation Committee. I think that is absolutely right. I used to go to the annual meetings and there were half a dozen people, always the same people, nothing really to do, because the Socialist Campaign Group idea is parliamentary in origin, and the Labour Representation Committee is an umbrella organisation. Even that will only really work if it has conferences where it asks pensioners and students and the civil-liberties groups to come. Then it does become a sort of embryonic socialist party.

Sunday 16 November

The *Mail on Sunday* had a major front-page splash, with three pages inside, about this Cynthia Roberts, who'd been involved, apparently, with Labour Action for Peace, and who moved to Prague in the 1980s and, allegedly, was a spy. It was a completely non-story. My little bit appeared in it.

Monday 17 November

Very early start.

At nine o'clock Jarvis Cocker, a pop singer from, originally, the Pulp group, turned up, with a BBC producer, to interview me. They've given Jarvis the editorship of the *Today* programme on New Year's Eve. This guy, who must be about forty-four, asked me, 'I went to the North Pole to see the melting of the ice, and heard the Government should intervene. Could the Government intervene in the economic situation?' It was just such a simple, bare question, so I tried to answer it, but to everything I said he replied, 'Oh, it couldn't be done, it couldn't be done.' I said, 'You're so pessimistic!' and I argued with him a bit.

Anyway, Emily was due at 10.30, but she arrived at 9.30, I think, and was photographed with him.

She and I caught the 'Oxford Tube' – the coach service to Oxford – and I was picked up by Sharon Howe from VERO, the Voice for Ethical Research at Oxford, which campaigns against the study of primates and vivisection of them.

Emily didn't want to be photographed with them because it's rather controversial.

We met my grandson Jonathan and Zohreh for lunch. Then I walked over to New College with Emily, saw her room and toured the college, and she had lots of friends lined up to meet me, and lots of photographs were taken.

I had to leave for Wolfson College at 4.45, for my lecture, and Emily decided to come as well and she brought two friends.

I went and had tea with Professor Hermione Lee, the President of Wolfson College, and then I gave the lecture. It was a very warm reception, rather quiet to begin with. I don't think people believed that someone of eighty-three makes jokes, but at the end they did enjoy it.

Emily had to go off with her friends, and I gave £20 to her.

I had dinner afterwards, and found myself sitting next to Mary Jay, Douglas Jay's widow. Her African friend, Walter, was there, a very distinguished-looking man. Also at dinner was Brian McGee, who used to be a Labour MP, joined the SDP, and he's a philosopher – that's how he likes to be described.

Wednesday 19 November
My pass for use in the Commons is faulty, so I went in to the Pass Office and asked for a new pass; they printed one which didn't say that I had the authority of the Speaker ('Mr Speaker') printed on it. It said 'Ex-Member'. So I tried that and that didn't work, so I went back and in the end they gave me a pass that did work, but it still said 'Ex-Member'. They are going to sort it out. I am the only former Member with a Freedom of the House pass, signed by the Speaker. They were terribly friendly. I said to them, 'You could create an imaginary peer.' You could put all the details in; no one would know who he was because most of the peers don't know each other!

Thursday 20 November
I have nightmares every morning. I am overwhelmed by the feeling that the world – Britain and the world – is going to collapse through shortage of oil. I visualise circumstances where people at the top of tower blocks would find that the lift couldn't be run because there was no energy; doctors couldn't climb twenty-four flights of steps to look after them if they were ill; and the whole of society comes to an end. It's a strange phenomenon, but I have a great imagination, and I can turn it to good things and make good speeches, but when it turns to bad things, nothing could possibly ever go right. But I usually recover by nine.

I spent from nine till one tackling emails, sorting out my trip to Tunbridge Wells on Sunday to speak for the Labour candidate there. He'd said you just get a train from Charing Cross. Well, there is no train from Charing Cross on a Sunday to Tunbridge Wells. I've got to go from Charing Cross to Cannon Street, Cannon Street to Tonbridge, get out, get a bus from Tonbridge down to Tunbridge Wells. And there's no Circle Line in London to get me to Cannon

Street. I've got to leave about ten in the morning and won't be back till about six, so it's a hell of a long time to spend going to a Labour Party lunch.

Friday 21 November
I drove to the doctors and had a flu jab, blood pressure checked (it's a bit high) and a blood test. Came home and had a bite to eat.

Then I was picked up by CNN and taken to their studios in Oxford Circus for a short interview about General Motors, Ford and Chrysler, who've pleaded with Congress to bail them out.

James and Blake came to tea. I don't think I've seen Blake since she qualified as a doctor. She's now in Accident & Emergency. James is well established teaching at his primary school, and he's really enjoying it. His discipline problem is all over, he's doing very well, he likes the pupils, he talks to the parents, and I should think he's going to be a very popular teacher. Blake talked about the problems of Accident & Emergency, and so on. Her folks now live in France, and she would like, in the end, to perhaps become a psychiatrist. I had a lovely talk to them.

I did absolutely no work today! But I made nine phone calls.

Sunday 23 November
Up earlyish. I have now diagnosed my condition. In the morning I'm very, very depressed, always. I don't know why. For about two or three hours I can't focus on anything.

I read the papers today and there were little items, like the number of former ministers who'd got jobs with industry, that made me very cynical. I have to struggle with this. Once the morning is over, I can do a few things, but I'm very tired.

Made the epic journey to Tunbridge Wells. The Circle was closed, so I had to walk from Bank to Cannon Street.

I was collected by Lorna Blackmore, a woman of sixty. Her face interested me, and I realised she did look like Margaret Rutherford, my father's first cousin, the actress. She's in criminal law. Her job is to prosecute people who are engaged in financial crime. A very, very nice lady and I liked her very much indeed – very determined. She took me to the lunch at a luxurious golf club in Tunbridge Wells.

I met Gary Heather, who is the PPC. Heather is fifty-four. He's an engineer, worked with British Telecom. He's on the Executive of the Communication Workers' Union. He did get some academic qualifications. I think he has two children, both of whom went to university.

The average age must have been above sixty-five. There was one little girl of nine, perhaps a couple in their early thirties, maybe a few in their forties, but there were people right up to their eighties, and that is the constituency of the Labour Party in the world in which we live. Lunch was rather fancy, with red napkins in every glass, and there was soup, a main course and a vegetarian option, apple strudel or a chocolate pudding. I sat and talked to them, and then I was asked to speak.

I didn't quite know what to say really. It could have been the type of audience that I meet at my lectures. (I think I did give a lecture in Tunbridge Wells some time ago.) So I tried to relate it as best I could to the circumstances.

I'm glad I don't go round to local Labour parties now, because I just don't think there's much I can do. I cheered them up, made a few jokes, and they were very warm. I don't know how many of them are New Labour, but all you can say is: when you look at them, you realise they are not really a group concerned with political change.

It was icy cold and raining when I left and I'm a bit wet and cold now.

Monday 24 November

After lunch I listened to Alistair Darling make his statement in the House of Commons on the economic crisis and the Government's policy. Much of it had been leaked anyway: reduction of Value Added Tax; help for older people; and so on. He announced that there would be an increase in the level of taxation for those earning £150,000 a year, an increase to 43 per cent, I think, from 40 per cent.

Hilary rang just after that, and I said I thought that Alistair had come across very firmly.

The More 4 channel rang, and sent somebody to do an interview with me on the increased tax rate, and I did the best I could and pointed out that, during the war, the level of taxation on the richest had been 95 per cent.

Tuesday 25 November

I went off to a dinner given by Malloch Brown, in honour of Ian Khama, President of Botswana. I found I had a new suit I'd never worn, and a new shirt, and I dressed myself up very smartly and got a cab to 1 Carlton Gardens, the place where the Foreign Office have their dinners. I think the last time I was there was when Tony Crosland was the Foreign Secretary, and that would be thirty-odd years ago.

I was the first to arrive, and I had a long talk with Alistair Harrison, who is the head of the Zimbabwe Unit in the Foreign Office. Of course Zimbabwe is a very big issue for Botswana and for the British Government, so that's why they wanted the discussion to centre around it. He was very agreeable, like all these Foreign Office people.

Malloch Brown appeared, briefly, and I said I was wearing a United Nations tie as a tribute to him. He said he'd followed my career with a great deal of interest, and of course how wonderful Hilary was when he was at International Development, so that was very agreeable.

Then Ian Khama, the President of Botswana, came in, and he came up and talked to me for about ten minutes. I asked him about the economic situation, and he said, 'Well, it is affecting the diamond trade.'

At the dinner I sat between Lord Triesman, who used to be a communist, then he joined the Labour Party, then he became General Secretary of the Labour Party and then Minister for Africa, and now he's gone and taken some appointment in the football industry. So, when I saw him, I said, 'I see old ex-communists go into football!' 'What do you mean? What do you mean?' I said, 'Well, you and John Reid, who is now the Chairman of Celtic.' I don't think he liked that very much.

I saw Ian Khama last year, when Susan Williams's book about his parents, Ruth and Seretse, was published. He was asked at the dinner to give his view and gave a very thoughtful analysis. He said, 'We're worried about Zimbabwe and we don't quite know how it should be tackled.' He gave a very reasonable assessment of the situation.

The question of whether we should intervene in Zimbabwe came up, and Triesman – Lord Triesman – said he thought the old arguments were over now, that Mugabe in every election was still fighting the British. But the new generation is associated in the minds of Africans with support for the ANC.

It was the cosy, colonial question all over again: should we intervene? I took a contrary view. I don't know whether it went down well or not. I did say also we've got to have an elected United Nations – not China, with two billion, and India, with two billion, having the same vote at the General Assembly as Luxembourg.

So I planted a couple of thoughts. I had decided to go and observe rather than contribute very much. But it reminded me that the old colonial structure is alive and well in Africa. We're the protectorate – we protect them, we help them, we advise them, but of course the real money is in China. China could go in and buy all the diamonds, and Ian Khama would do what he was told.

Anyway I left about twenty past nine, and got home just before ten. I was so tired I jumped straight into bed, in the woollies that I'd been wearing.

That was the end of Tuesday 25 November.

Thursday 27 November
Ruth was in, tackling the VAT and the in-tray.

Three hotels have been bombed in Mumbai, in a sort of 9/11 in India. Nobody knows who did it.

Other news is that Damian Green, the Opposition spokesman on immigration, has been arrested by the police and held for nine hours in connection with information apparently passed to him from civil servants.

Friday 28 November
Worrying like anything about the book! I haven't done anything about it, and 90,000 words are due in in about eight weeks!

I rang Damian Green at the House of Commons, about his arrest, and he told me that the police had taken charge of all his computers and had cut him off from his email, so he couldn't get any letters from his constituency. An outrageous case! I think I rang the BBC,

World at One, next and I did an interview for them. I feel very strongly that it is a case of parliamentary privilege.

Then I rang Jon Snow and said, 'Would you be interested in my doing something this afternoon?' and they did send a car. I went to Channel 4 News and I did this interview with Jon Snow about privilege.

When I got back, Tam Dalyell had left a message saying he was doing *The World Tonight* on it, and could he have a word with me?

Monday 1 December

I rang the Speaker's Office, because I've been asked to do the BBC on Wednesday morning, on the Damian Green business. Michael Martin, the Speaker, is under attack over it, so I thought the best thing to do was to ring up his office and ask if there is anything I could do to help him in the statement he has to make. The more I think about it, it's absolutely outrageous that the Speaker should be told that the police were coming into the House of Commons to search a Member's office! There's a new Director of Security – Ruth spotted this – who is responsible. In a way the House of Commons has become a government department, run by ministers and backed up by the police, instead of being the place which holds the Government to account.

I think this point will be quite clear to make, but the main thing is I'm not going to say anything that could embarrass the Speaker.

Coincidentally I'm going to the Speaker's party at noon – for the opening of Parliament – but maybe that will be delayed, because he may be making the statement.

Lissie rang me while I was trying to watch the news, to say that the *Richard & Judy* show had decided that her book would be the one they recommend for March. Well, it's well known that any book they suggest sends sales through the roof, so her publishers are delighted. She also said that an adviser to . . . a writer who's an adviser to Obama has given him five books to help him come to terms with power, and one of them is Melissa's book, *One of Us*! Well, that's absolutely fabulous news!

As if that wasn't enough for one day, the Speaker rang, and I had half an hour with him. He's terribly worried about this arrest of

Damian Green. Of course it's not a personal issue at all; it's about parliamentary privilege. So I told him he should refer it to the Committee of Privileges. Well, he's seeing the Clerks tomorrow. I think what I'll do is ring the Speaker's Secretary, Angus Sinclair, and send a draft statement in the hope that it's of some use to him.

Tuesday 2 December
Still very, very tired. I must say, I'm beginning to think I'm coming near the end of life.

Mr Khan from the VAT Office came to do an inspection and I was a bit nervous, but of course Ruth had everything totally under control. We had a bit of a talk afterwards. The only thing he discovered was that Ruth calculated VAT as 11 per cent when it was 12 per cent, for a matter of a few weeks, so we may owe about £400, but there's no problem about it.

I read Ruth's novel this morning, and it's so much more colourful than the first draft I read. I had anxieties about it – because of the plot centring on a supposed case of racism by a white civil servant who is caught up in a bureaucratic nightmare – but they have all disappeared. She wants to try and get somebody to take it up and either publish it as a novel, though it's very short, or as a radio or TV play.

I emailed a draft speech to the Speaker, via Angus Sinclair. I told Hilary about it, and he said it was great, and that Charles Clarke had heard me on Channel 4 and agreed with it all.

Anyway the Speaker is making a statement at 2.30. He's not waiting till seven, which is quite right, because it will be raised immediately.

That was a phone call from Grace Crookall-Greening to tell me that Peter Hennessy had done a programme on nuclear weapons and had got access to the archives, and some of the people who would have had the authority to use the nuclear weapons said they would not have agreed to do it – i.e. he identified cases of conscience. I didn't hear the broadcast, but it's a very important one.

Wednesday 3 December
I went into the House of Commons, and the Police Superintendent for the House came up to me and he said he was absolutely shocked

by the fact that the Metropolitan Police had been able to come into the House of Commons; he was answerable to the Speaker, and not to the Commissioner of the Metropolis.

Then I talked to one or two other policemen, who felt exactly the same, so it was very interesting. They felt as defensive of the MPs as MPs themselves.

Then I stood outside the Library because I knew the Speaker's procession would go by, which it did, and I said to Michael, 'Good luck!' because I know how nervous the Speaker is about the statement he's making this afternoon. He clutched my hand in a very warm way.

Went to the Tea Room briefly, and another Tory MP came up and said how much he'd appreciated a broadcast I'd made.

After that I was the first at the Speaker's Party. I thought I might do a little bit of canvassing for the case. Dominic Grieve came up. He's the Shadow Home Secretary, and we had a talk about Damian Green. I think, as a result of my stand on this, I've become very popular with the Tory Party!

While I was standing sort of between the two state rooms, Gordon Brown came by and stopped and had a word with me and I said, 'You're doing very well.' Sarah, his wife, was there, and I talked about her book.

Then I had a long talk to Ed Miliband – this is not necessarily in the right order – who has been appointed Energy Secretary, the first since I was appointed in the 1970s, and so we had a chat about that.

I dashed away, caught the Tube and then walked to Kensington Town Hall, for the Kensington & Chelsea pensioners' forum in the small hall. I always try to go once a year.

Then I went back to the House of Commons because I wanted to see the Speaker's statement, which was available in the Library. I looked at it, and although it wasn't by any means exactly the same as the draft statement I'd given to him, it did include some very important points. He did set up a committee himself, and he did say there was to be no more intervention in the House of Commons without a warrant. I gather the police have now handed back the computer to Damian Green. I felt I was the sort of grandfather of the House on constitutional questions. I was pleased about that.

I also heard that Gordon Brown had made his speech on the

Queen's Speech, in which he said that people who were likely to be repossessed (because they're now repossessing a thousand homes a month, which is an outrage) would have two years' grace to sort out their finances. So that's like the idea of 'the right to stay', which I'd mentioned to Hilary ages ago, in parallel with Mrs Thatcher's idea of 'the right to buy'. So that was worthwhile.

It was a funny experience today, but after having been demoralised the last few days, this cheered me up a bit.

Friday 4 December
I had twenty minutes with Dr Pettifer – blood pressure, cholesterol, all the rest – and she gave me about six prescriptions, which I will go and collect. I like her very much, and I thank God for the NHS. They asked me to fill in an appreciation form. It asked me about thirty questions about my experience at the surgery and I put 'excellent' against all of them.

Saturday 6 December
I went to a Marxism conference on the economic crisis, held in the Friends' Meeting House. They are amazing, the people the SWP get together. There were three speakers at the first session: Professor Jane Hardy, a Professor of Economics, who made a very scholarly and precise and accurate account of the crisis; then Lindsey German spoke; and then I spoke. What got the most applause was when I said, 'This is not just an economic question, it is a moral question – it is wrong for people to be treated in this way. We've underestimated that.' From a left-wing audience, I thought their response was quite interesting.

Lindsey German and John Rees are having a row with the Socialist Workers' Party over their involvement, I think, with the Stop the War movement and with Respect.

Sunday 7 December
I read in the papers that the attack on the Speaker is growing. Bob Marshall-Andrews has apparently come out against, and there is criticism from a former Deputy Speaker.

I designed my Christmas card. It's actually a 'Happy New Year' card and I'm rather pleased. I found a Picasso peace-dove and I added to it what all the great religions of the world say about treating other people as you expect to be treated yourself.

I listened to Peter Hennessy's programme on the mechanics of firing the Trident, and it was a very good programme. He said all sorts of things I didn't know: that every Prime Minister writes four manuscript letters giving instructions in case he himself dies, so the circumstances are such that the Chief of the Air Staff or Chief of Defence Staff might be required to obey orders from a dead Prime Minister, which is quite interesting. He then interviewed a lot of people, including Denis Healey, who was Minister of Defence. He said he didn't think he could ever have used the bomb. Then Peter followed, with meticulous accuracy, the process from the time it appears that we have been attacked, right through where the decision would be taken in a bunker, the Chief of Defence asked to advise the Prime Minister, the Prime Minister would reach a decision, or, if he was dead, his letter would be the basis of a decision which would then be conveyed to the submarine, and then the various people would get it, and then the commanding officer of the submarine would press the button. What you realised from it was that, at every one of those stages – I don't know how many there were, but there could be as many as ten – conscience might intervene, ten 'conscience barriers'.

Anyway, I rang Peter and had a bit of a talk. I told him that, on 3 March 1958, I had resigned from the front bench, when I was the Shadow Defence Spokesman, on this issue.

Monday 8 December
In the course of the afternoon the House of Commons debated a motion, tabled by the Leader of the House, Harriet Harman, recommending that the Speaker set up a committee of seven – four Labour, two Tory and one Liberal – to examine the events of the Damian Green case, but not to start work until the police had completed their enquiries. Well, of course, if Parliament puts itself behind the police, it has conceded the point to start with! There was a debate in the House, of which I heard a part, but the Government issued a three-line whip to Labour MPs to support the motion, and even so, they only won by four votes. Then the Tories and Liberals

said they wouldn't take part in the committee, so actually the whole thing is a complete waste of time.

Michael Martin hasn't handled this well at all. I suggested he refer it to the Privileges Committee, and of course they are free, if they want to, to take it up now. They don't have to wait for the police. The police might take months to complete their investigations, might decide to prosecute Damian Green or not, and I must say, when a really important issue comes up, you can't rely on Parliament to handle it properly.

Tuesday 9 December
Well, I had to go to St Thomas's hospital today, for tests. I had an ECG (electrocardiogram) and saw a doctor who thought my blood pressure might be a bit high. Dr Cooklin, the consultant, looked in very briefly and said I might have to go onto warfarin, because otherwise it might lead to a stroke. So that was a cheerful start to the day!

Then across the bridge to the House of Commons, had a cup of tea on the Terrace and a smoke, and then walked over to 4 Millbank for the BBC *Politics Show* programme. They had asked me to do an interview about protest – does it ever do any good? This is based on the fact that there was a protest at the airport at Stansted on Sunday about climate change, which stopped a lot of planes.

Dawn Primarolo had been on before me, and she's now banning the advertising of cigarettes, so if you go into a shop you won't be able to see any cigarettes on show. I said to her, 'Well, are you banning matches?' She looked a bit discomfited. Anyway, I've know Dawn such a long time – the young radical is now the official minister, and there you are, that's how it happens.

I had a very good discussion about protests. I said of course protest doesn't work. I said, 'As you know, women don't have the vote; apartheid is still in operation, because the protest against all these things was not effective.' And they sort of laughed in an embarrassed way, and then I made the case for demanding: don't protest, demand.

I watched two DVDs of the *Silly Money* programmes made by Vera, Rory Bremner's company, with Rory and the two Johns. I must say, it was absolutely brilliant! It's the best explanation of the financial system I've seen. Funnily enough, Tony Benn was in the last two programmes, commenting every now and again, with my pipe in my mouth.

Wednesday 10 December
James Purnell, the Works and Pensions Secretary, has announced that people on unemployment benefit and people who are disabled will, in effect, be told that if they don't go back to work or do community work, they will lose some of their benefit. It's the most direct attack upon the Welfare State from that end. When you think billions of pounds are wasted or lost every year through tax evasion by rich companies, and they're concentrating on that, it is quite outrageous. It's an absolute Tory policy.

I've now got all my Christmas cards ready to send, but I haven't got a proper Christmas-card list. I'm terrified that I'll send a Christmas card to 'Mr and Mrs . . .' when one or the other of them has died and I haven't noticed it – oh!

Thursday 11 December
Ruth was in, and she found last year's Christmas-card list and printed labels for my Christmas cards. It took her about ten minutes! She printed, I don't know, 350 of them.

We were sitting there all day, waiting for the BT engineer to call to fix my broadband. I found a recorded message saying he wouldn't have to call; then he did call. Then he thought he'd put it right, but he hadn't. He went out, said it was an external fault and came back, and switched it on and it worked! I had about, oh gosh, 300 unread messages.

Saturday 13 December
I caught the train to Chesterfield, arrived in the pelting rain, and was taken to the Winding Wheel. I was a bit overcome, truthfully. I said how moving it was to come back. I felt as if it was only a week or two ago, but it was actually seven and a half years since I left Chesterfield. It was like a bereavement all over again – a political and personal bereavement – because they were so kind to me, and I learned so much in the years I was there. I was there from '83 to 2001, eighteen years, and I worked like a beaver at the

time of the miners' strike. I reconnected today with the old manual working-class movement, but, by God, they've got some powerful intellectuals amongst them.

I came back on the train and got home by about 5.15. I discovered, when I unpacked, that I'd lost my mobile phone, which is an absolute disaster! So I rang Orange and spoke to a very nice girl in Delhi, who told me she would cancel my existing mobile phone. She put me on then to a woman in Durham, who is going to send me a new SIM card that I can put in a new phone.

Sunday 14 December
Brown has been in Afghanistan, Pakistan and India, calling for an end to terrorism. He offered the Pakistan Government £6 million to fight terrorism, which is a laughable sum when you consider that would be a modest bribe by any business company.

Best of all, Bush, in a farewell visit to Iraq, did a press conference in Baghdad, and a journalist took off both his shoes and threw them at him, shouting, 'Dog!' Bush had to duck, and that will be the picture which Bush will be remembered for. It was so funny!

Thursday 18 December
I was in the office this morning, and my mobile phone was returned. A very nice woman called Rachel Smith from Sheffield found it on the train. So I sent her an email, thanking her, and she sent an email back; that just shows how kind people are.

The mail poured in, mainly Christmas cards.

I caught the train to Guy's Hospital to the Urology Department. There were two very nice Zimbabwean nurses there, whom I talked to. After lots of tests I was taken to see Mr Jonathan Glass, the consultant. I'd seen him before, and he recommended an operation.

Friday 19 December
Ruth came in and we had a talk, and I took her off to Paddington because her mother is still very ill in Devon after a car accident. The doctors thought the next forty-eight hours would be critical.

Lissie arrived at two, and we had a couple of hours, and she's such fun! Emotionally, she's the closest to me of all the family. I mean,

Josh is so helpful and we have lovely talks and he's such a friend; Hilary is very affectionate; Steve is supportive; but, with Melissa, it's just lovely. She talked all about Hannah and Sarah, and Paul's new book and everything. She's very over-pressed, with all the family and other things, but, you know, at fifty-two, it's the sort of peak of her life, and she is emerging now as a serious and first-rate novelist.

Saturday 20 December
Still depressed all day – I wish I could control it, but I can't.

The political news today: the Atomic Weapons Research Establishment at Aldermaston has been sold to an American company, so the last pretence of an independent nuclear deterrent has completely gone. The Americans lend the stuff to us, it's produced in Britain by an American company, and Brown's alleged control of the so-called deterrent would be entirely supervised by Washington. So, in a way, we don't have to worry.

I've just heard on the news a moment or two ago: the Americans are sending 30,000 more troops to Afghanistan. Well, as the Russians had 100,000 there and couldn't win, it's just absolutely hopeless, but this is Bush's policy being taken up and launched by Obama.

Wednesday 24 December
Christmas Eve.

Tony Byrne turned up unexpectedly, and while I was away this morning he cut down the big dead tree in the front; I must stop him cutting down the May tree in the back (which is also dead), because Stephen would go berserk.

I dropped a bottle of wine and some chocolates and biscuits in to the Sisters next door, and they sent me in return a beautiful pair of leather gloves. That was very nice.

Thursday 25 December
Harold Pinter died today and, in the middle of lunch, I was asked to make a comment, which I did do, and then the BBC rang me later and asked me to do a short interview about his work, and his passionate opposition to war.

Christmas lunch was absolutely delicious, and sort of the only meal in the year when I have a proper two-course meal – heavy, beautifully cooked Christmas pudding and everything.

I've had this terrible depression. I talked a bit to Sally about it, and she said cognitive thought was the answer: look forward positively; don't go back again and again, all the awful things you've done, or think you've done. Look forward to the things you want to do.

Friday 26 December

I had a lovely long talk to Lissie! She does like ringing me up, and I just adore it. Her Sarah's report on the one-child policy in China is going to be sent to me and I'm looking forward to it. Lissie said, 'You always get depressed in the holidays because you don't get enough attention.' A very shrewd analysis! She said, 'Your nanny, Nurse Parker, spoiled you and you've been looking for attention and admiration ever since, all the time; and you only get it when you make speeches.' Well, out of the mouths of babes and sucklings cometh forth wisdom . . .!

Had a bite to eat. Turned on the telly and *South Pacific* was on, so I watched that. It was with Mitzi Gaynor. It wasn't the original one, which I think was Mary Martin, during the war, but still, I knew every single tune – it was a ludicrous film because war is a brutal thing. It was sanitised to the point that war seemed like a sort of game. Seeing it after all these years, you get a different perspective on it.

I had a talk to Ruth, and her mother is out of danger, which is wonderful news.

Saturday 27 December

Israel has launched a massive military attack, bombing Gaza, and 200 have been killed and 400 injured, justifying it on the grounds that it's self-defence against rocket attacks. But potentially, very, very dangerous . . .

Sunday 28 December

I got a cab to the Israeli Embassy for the Gaza demonstration. It was so bloody cold I dressed up in all the woollies I could find, and an incontinence pad. When I got there, there were over a thousand people. Considering it was only organised twenty-four hours ago, on the Internet, it's amazing. I saw Jeremy Corbyn, Kate Hudson and a lot of Palestinians whom I know, and Moshé Machover, who sends me wonderful material about Palestine. I did four television interviews, with Al Jazeera, Press TV, Kuwait TV and German TV. The crowd moved across the road and blocked Kensington High Street.

Came home and had a bite to eat, and turned on the telly. It was a film called *Diary of a Princess*. It was a film made in 2002, Walt Disney made it, about some girl in a school in America who turned out to be a princess. It was rubbish really, but I enjoyed watching Julie Andrews; apparently her voice is better after she had an operation on her vocal cords, which ended – or interrupted – her singing career. I sat next to her, years ago, at the premiere of *Dr Strangelove* when it was in London.

Monday 29 December
The Israeli onslaught on Gaza continues. Apparently they're shelling from the sea, they're talking about a land invasion, and they've now announced that this is a battle to the death with Hamas, so it's regime change. A hospital bombed, a mosque bombed, children killed – it's ghastly; 300 killed and 700 injured, and no medical supplies. The hospitals are collapsing.

The front doorbell rang and it was somebody who'd worked in the office here sixteen years ago, Claire Bonnin – I remembered her face. She gave me a huge hug. She was with a tall Australian husband and her boy of nine, so we had a cup of tea and a little bit of a talk, and she couldn't have been friendlier. I rang Ruth, who of course remembered all about her.

Chapter Six

January–July 2009:
Brown's nemesis

Friday 2 January 2009, Stansgate
Looking back on the Christmas holiday, it was a lovely three-day family holiday, and they do everything for me! They buy the food, cook the food, serve the food, wash up after the food, and I'm a complete visitor. My only contribution is that I paid about £700 for the food and for the petrol for Josh, so at least they're not out of pocket, but considering how many people were here . . . I think fourteen for three days – it's pretty cheap when you consider the facilities at Stansgate.

Saturday 3 January
March to Trafalgar Square. It was very, very cold.

Bianca Jagger was there, with a young assistant; Annie Lennox, who was a very famous pop star from a group called Eurythmics, and George Galloway; Jeremy Corbyn; John McDonnell; Clare Short; Lindsey German and John Rees; Brian Eno. We marched right down the Embankment, to the House of Commons, turned right and then right again, up Whitehall to Trafalgar Square. I was stuck at the front, so lots of people came up to see me.

All the young Palestinians from behind were pushing and pushing and pushing, and they were kicking my heels and I thought my shoe was going to come off, and then, hanging onto this banner, we surged . . . I don't know what it was like – it was really quite incredible, and I was pushed and shoved, and by the time we got into Whitehall, I had decided to detach myself. Yvonne Ridley, I think, and a man sort of made me their special charge and walked each side of me. I did feel I had reached the absolute limit of my physical strength. I do not think I could do a march like that again. I can walk . . . I could have walked it quietly, but I couldn't cope with the pushing and the shoving, and it really quite frightened me.

What was so wonderful about it was the friendship shown. I did God knows how many interviews: Al Jazeera, BBC Radio 4, BBC TV News, United Press International, Press TV.

I finally walked, with great difficulty, back to the Embankment. On the Tube I ate my cheese bun, and a mince pie and a banana, and tried to sip from my thermos, which was absolutely cold. When I got back I sat with my hands over a fan heater, trying slowly to defreeze.

I just felt it was the world public opinion beginning to shape itself, and of course the Internet keeps us all totally informed about what's happening.

Sunday 4 January
Overnight Israel invaded Gaza, with troops and tanks, and more and more people are dead. It is now, quite obviously, a hideous war crime that people understand.

I had lovely thank-you notes from Hannah and Sarah for the money I gave them at Christmas.

Melissa brought along Sarah's paper on the China one-child policy. I photocopied it and gave it back to her, and I wrote Sarah a little note, saying:

Thank you so much for allowing your mum to bring along your really excellent thesis on China's one-child policy, which

I photocopied and read with great interest. It explains the background, the effect and the consequences in a way that makes it all so clear and readable. Your research is also very impressive. But best of all was your own judgement of the programme, with the conclusions that you reached about it, which gives the thesis a great deal of authority. In all, I think it was a first-class piece of work, and I'm not surprised your teacher liked it so much. I felt very proud to have a granddaughter who could produce such good work. I hope you make a point of keeping the best things you write, because future generations will be interested to read them all.

Lots of love, Dandan.

So maybe, I'll break through to those children. They're very young, but they're very subtle.

Monday 5 January
Bitterly cold.

Tuesday 6 January
Well, the Israeli attack on Gaza has gone out of all proportion. They've bombed a mosque, they've bombed the Islamic University, and today they bombed a school run by the UN or UNRRA. World disgust is really reaching a new peak. Even Blair – and I can hardly bear to mention his name – said that, at some stage, you'd have to talk to Hamas. Here are the Israelis, getting weapons from America, pouring in high-tech weapons, and they're bombing the tunnels which allow the Hamas fighters to get a few rifles and bits of equipment through from Egypt.

Wednesday 7 January
I'll just listen to the news – it's Gaza, Gaza, Gaza all the time! And the crudity of Blair, saying whatever happens, the tunnels to Egypt have got to be closed, Hamas must not be allowed to rearm – Hamas is an elected government, for God's sake!

Thursday 8 January

Some UN negotiations are going on, but I don't know that much will come of it really. But I think they have been forced to recognise that Hamas has got to be brought into the negotiations; you can't say Hamas can't be armed when Israel is being armed all the time. Of course the real problem is that the puppet states of Egypt and Saudi Arabia just do everything Washington tells them to do, just as the maharajas and rajas did when we ran India.

Friday 9 January

The news overnight is that the UN Security Council did pass a resolution calling for a ceasefire, and Britain voted for it, and the United States abstained, so it's the first time that Britain has voted differently to America on Israel, and that's a very important bit of news.

Meanwhile the Israelis have rejected it, and the bombing continues, and Hamas said: we weren't consulted, so it doesn't bind us.

Saturday 10 January

To the Royal Overseas League for Dave's eightieth birthday just before twelve, which was the time it was due to start.

I was freezing cold! Ruth arrived from Bideford safely, and all the family were there, except Daniel, Hannah and Sarah.

There were about 120 people. I had a talk to Peter Hennessy, and to Derek Andrews, who used to be Harold Wilson's Private Secretary. He said his uncle, Sam Andrews, had lived in Bristol. I said, 'You mean Sam Andrews the baker?' 'Yes.' 'Oh,' I said, 'I remember Sam so well – he was a lovely guy!'

Then I talked to Zdenka, the Croatian friend of Dave's from his BBC days.

So it was a memorable day, and Dave enjoyed it so much.

Monday 12 January

A rather disturbed night – cramp and coughs.

I got the bus to St Thomas's and was looked after by a very nice New Zealand doctor, Sarah Hill, who is married to a lieutenant commander in the New Zealand navy. She wanted to do a biopsy on the unhealed wounds in my leg, in case I had skin cancer. Then I went to the Mycology Department, where they checked for eczema.

Turned on the telly and saw a programme on Islamic culture and its contribution to Western European culture, pointing out the fact that the Muslims captured Sicily and got halfway up Spain, and left behind this fantastic architecture. There was a Muslim Empire, just as there was a British Empire, a French Empire and an American Empire, and there will be a Chinese Empire.

Thursday 15 January
The parliamentary news today is that the Transport Secretary Geoff Hoon announced that they are going to go ahead with the third runway at Heathrow. John McDonnell, who has Heathrow in his constituency, got up and said, 'Will there be a vote on it?' and Hoon said, 'No, it's a national issue.' So McDonnell got up, went to the Mace, picked it up and threw it on the Government front bench, and he was suspended. You've got to be careful when you do something like that; on the other hand, he felt so strongly, and Parliament is no longer a place where people have any say – they're just told what to do by ministers. Something's got to happen.

Friday 16 January
Ruth arrived early, and we drafted, together, a press release for my speech in Trafalgar Square tomorrow, listing six things that ought to be done: that we should expel the Israeli Ambassador and withdraw our Ambassador; recognise Palestine as a nation and a member of the United Nations and start talking to Hamas; use the Royal Navy to protect ships carrying food and medicines to Gaza; use RAF aircraft to fly into Gaza those engaged in humanitarian work and include representatives of the world's media, now excluded; ban all Israeli airlines from landing in British airports until Israel withdraws from Gaza; and ask for more balanced reporting from the media.

Saturday 17 January
After going to Trafalgar Square briefly for the rally on Gaza, I was collected by John Grice, in his very comfortable Mercedes-Benz, and driven to the Yvonne Arnaud Theatre in Guildford: my show was

sold out. Excellent questions. I signed books afterwards, and who should come up but a man who couldn't get into the theatre, John Downham, who'd been with me in Rhodesia, in the RAF, flew up with me to Cairo in '45, and came with me to the kibbutz in 1945 on the day that war ended. He and his wife had come, even though they couldn't get in. I had a lovely talk to them!

Sunday 18 January
Up at six. Got a cab to Euston, and a train to Manchester, to visit the Working Class Movement Library. They have a new centre funded by the Heritage Lottery Board. Among the many people I met was Frank Allaun's widow, and also, Ceri Saklatvala, the daughter of the early communist MP for Battersea North, Saklatvala known as 'Sak'. They were so friendly, and the museum shows that there is a history that's been suppressed by the British ruling class.

When I told Josh about Ceri Saklatvala, he said he'd taught her how to use a computer when he set up Communitech, which was a training programme for people using computers. It was such an interesting connection. Sak was the nephew of Tata, the great Indian industrialist; Tata now owns Jaguar and everything else.

So, that's the end of Sunday 18 January.

The Israelis, yesterday, stopped bombing Gaza; so that's called a ceasefire.

Monday 19 January
Very, very cold.

I heard an interview I gave for BBC Radio 4 about Sir Keith Park and the campaign to give him a statue in Parliament Square.

I collected Ruth from Paddington. She's really worried about her mother, who's at the moment in a sort of cottage hospital in Bideford and is moving to a care home in Braunton, which is about twenty-five miles away. She's very distressed.

Anything else? Oh yes, the Government announced a second huge bailout for the banks. I mean, really, it's ridiculous! Brown says you have to do it. Whatever the banks want, we have to do. But if pensioners need money: oh, you can't do that, that'll lead to inflation, you know.

I think the Government is going to be defeated. Now that Kenneth Clarke has been brought into the Shadow Cabinet, he and Mandelson could work perfectly well in a coalition government.

Tuesday 20 January
This is the day that President Barack Obama is inaugurated as President of the United States, and much of the news rotates on that.

Got in the car to go to the House of Commons, because I thought at least I can smoke in the car [laughing]. And in Birdcage Walk I was stopped by the police, beckoned aside. 'We're stopping you and searching your car under Section 44 of the Terrorism Act.' So I didn't argue. I gave my name and address and telephone and date of birth, and so on. The woman who stopped me didn't know who I was, and why should she? She was very young, but I did think to myself: Will that be on police records for ever? Will those police records be accessed through an ID card? I'm going to write to the Home Secretary about it.

I went up to Room 14 for the celebration of the fiftieth anniversary of the Cuban Revolution, organised by Third World Solidarity, and Gore Vidal was there. I introduced myself. 'Oh,' he said, 'of course we've met.' I don't think we ever have actually.

There were a few speeches and afterwards I said to Vidal, 'We must be the same age.' He said, '1925?' So I said, 'Yes.' He said, 'October?' and I said, 'No, April, so I'm six months older than you.' I found him strange. He's a brilliant literary figure. I think he's gay. He's been attacked for all sorts of things. He made a very interesting and amusing speech.

So it was a busy day, and I came home by car. When I got home there were nine phone messages to deal with and, oh God, about fifteen emails.

To live through the day that President Barack Obama was inaugurated was the really big thing, and thank God there was no assassination attempt.

Wednesday 21 January
News today . . . Well, the pound is falling. The banks are bankrupt. Lloyds Bank, the bank where I've banked, has lost a huge value of

its shares. I'm wondering whether I'll take my money out and put it under the bed, but I mean it really is – the whole British economy is in – a desperate situation! Unemployment touching two million . . . I don't think people realise quite the political implications of this, because there are terrible dangers. I'm not saying Brown can do much more, but instead of pouring money into the banks, he should take them all over, give them instructions as to what they should do. Every local authority should be told to prepare a plan of things they want to do locally, and be given the money to do it. That would employ people; and similarly industry should say: if you come up with an idea that meets our needs, we will invest in it. It's a very dangerous situation.

Thursday 22 January
Obama is sending George Mitchell – Senator George Mitchell, who did the negotiations in Northern Ireland and knows the Middle East a bit – to Gaza and the test really is: does he talk to Hamas or not? I watched it on Al Jazeera, which I must say is so much better than the BBC, and of course made up of former BBC Arabic Service people.

Friday 23 January
Wrote to Jacqui Smith, the Home Secretary, asking: will the record of my interrogation under the Terrorism Act be on a database; will it be available if I have an ID card; will it be shared with the Americans and the Europeans; and, if I'm asked have I ever been interviewed under the Terrorism Act, what am I to say? That should put her in a difficulty.

The BBC have banned an appeal by the Disaster Emergency Committee for humanitarian aid for Gaza, on the grounds that it could be controversial and compromise their position of impartiality, which is an incredible decision to take! Douglas Alexander, the International Secretary, said the same.

The BBC rang and asked if I would do the *Today* programme in the morning, about the BBC ban on the appeal. So I've got to be up at the crack of dawn tomorrow! I've also got the conference for the TUC, 'Progressive London', and then I'm going off to the demonstration outside Broadcasting House. God, it's a killing programme at the moment!

Saturday 24 January

I dug out, from the Internet, the postal address of the DEC Gaza Appeal, which the BBC won't broadcast. So when I got to the *Today* programme studio I read out the address, twice. It had an absolutely electric effect, and Edward Stourton and Sarah Montague were perfectly courteous – they tried to interrupt a bit, but not too much. As I left, everybody poured round me and shook my hand.

I got back home and then was asked to do BBC TV News, so I went to the television studios and did exactly the same thing there.

I got a cab to the TUC for the 'Progressive London' conference – lots of people I knew there – and took part in a special session about the Gaza crisis. Back to a demonstration outside the BBC in Portland Place. Then we walked all the way to Trafalgar Square, I should think about a couple of miles. I did speak again there.

I walked to the Embankment, because I couldn't even get a cab. I found the District Line and the Circle Line were closed, so I had to get on the Northern Line to Tottenham Court Road, and by the time I got home I was absolutely exhausted.

It was disgusting to hear the BBC's argument.

So, anyway, a good day's work, and tomorrow I have nothing whatever to do, but I will go and buy all the papers and see what they say.

Came home and went to bed about quarter past eleven. It was a fantastic day: up at five; two major speeches, outside the BBC and at Trafalgar Square; two major broadcasts – that was the *Today* programme and BBC News; and about seven television interviews; and a two-mile march, in the bitter cold!

Sunday 25 January

The *Sunday Telegraph* had a leading article demanding the BBC reverse its decision, because of course ITV and Channel 4 and Channel 5 have agreed to broadcast the Gaza appeal.

The Sunday Times had a picture of the demonstration outside the BBC.

Josh looked at my new TV system, the Freesat, added two new channels – Sky and CNN – and made it possible for me to record on VHS and on DVD from it.

There were about forty-five messages of support for my broadcast appeal to the BBC to allow the humanitarian aid to Gaza to go through, and about four against – one extremely obscene and abusive. So, that's been a success.

Monday 26 January
I was picked up and taken to CNN, when Caroline Thomson, who is the daughter of George Thomson, Lord Thomson of Monifieth, was there. He died last October, aged eighty-seven. She's the Chief Operating Officer of the BBC, and she explained again why the BBC had banned the humanitarian appeal about Gaza. It was disgusting!

I was then interviewed, and the guy played it absolutely fair. I had worked out very carefully what I wanted to say. I said: let's compare this crisis in Gaza with two others. I said: in 1940 there was a Blitz in London, with a population of seven million people, and 30,000 were killed; then in 9/11 in New York, with a population of eight million, 2,900 were killed; and in Gaza, with a population of just over a million, just over a thousand were killed. Putting it in that way did sort of silence him a bit.

Anyway, then I was driven back to the House of Commons, and I saw Lissie. We were going to meet inside, but I sat outside and we went and had a cup of tea. She's been filming all day with Richard and Judy for her novel, *One of Us*; there are 25,000 copies in the bookshops, and I think it's going to do very well, and God, if anyone deserved that success, it's her!

Anyway we went together to Lincoln's Inn, for the 'Forgiveness' Project, sponsored by Anita Roddick of the Body Shop and Emma Thompson. We listened to examples of people who had forgiven those who had committed crimes and had been forgiven; those who had had crimes committed against them and had forgiven; and it's a very moving and Christian idea. I thought it was wonderful.

As I left I met General Ramsbotham, a very progressive independent peer. I've always been a great admirer of his, and he said when we first met and shook hands, he hadn't washed his since. His wife said, 'I shook hands with him after you shook hands with him, and *I* haven't washed since!' All rather silly, but very friendly.

Then I got a lift home with a Professor of Global Hygiene and his wife who was a hospital administrator.

Tuesday 27 January
I must say this: I have been getting emails from all over the world – from Thailand, from America, and so on – from people who've seen the interview I did on BBC TV News about the BBC's refusal to broadcast the Gaza appeal, and so that has sort of gone across the world. People stop me in the street; I went to buy some bananas at Marks & Spencer, and a woman said she was an art collector and she was one of my great fans. I think moral questions and human questions make politics more real.

Wednesday 28 January
I took a couple of Crampex pills last night, and I had no cramp and I slept very, very well.

Thursday 29 January
Didn't come down to the office till a quarter past eleven, and Ruth was there already. I dictated a new section for *Letters to my Grandchildren* on Palestine; and she took out the stitch in my leg where they had taken a biopsy.

Then Stephen collected me, and we drove to Oxford, to New College. While he was unpacking the car I sat there and puffed my pipe, and the porter came out and said, 'You can't smoke in the College anywhere.' So I said, 'Well, I'm a Fellow of the College.' So he said, 'Oh, Tony Benn!' He had a cigarette in his hand, so I said, 'Come and sit down and have a smoke.' He was from Durham, he was the son of a miner, he was possibly sixty-two, he'd been made redundant many times, and he said he loved the job he had. Emily joined us and we had a cup of tea and a talk, and then we walked over to the Union.

I made my maiden speech there sixty-six years ago this month, on the Beveridge Report.

We talked to a few people, and then we went to the dinner. I was sitting opposite Bob Marshall-Andrews, whom I've always greatly admired as a lawyer. Next to Bob was a secretary, a very sort of scatty girl, who was just giggling all the time, and on the left was a beautiful English teacher from St Hilda's. And across the table was Count Nikolai Tolstoy, whom I seem to remember is a historian. He had accused Lord Aldington of war crimes during the enforced return of Soviet prisoners of war to Russia where many were killed.*

After the debate, I drove back with Stephen and Emily, and Peter Tatchell.

I heard the following day that the motion – that this House has no confidence in the monarchy – was defeated, by 155 to 114. I thought we'd lose, and I suppose not bad to get that percentage.

Friday 30 January
At 3.30, Simon Fletcher came to see me. He's forty now. He used to work here when he was a student, under Ruth's wing, and then he worked with Ken Livingstone for the whole of Ken's eight-year term. We had a talk about the future of politics, the way the left would develop, what he might do now – he's a lovely guy, and wants to bring Compass in, which I think is quite sensible.

The news tonight is very important: strikes all over the country because a refinery in Lincoln has brought in Italian contractors, who'll be living in a ship and doing the work more cheaply than British workers. This has exploded exponentially across the country, which gives the BNP the chance they want.

Also, the second thing is that, at the Davos Summit, which Hilary was going to today, Blair was speaking and warning and warning and warning against protectionism – we must make globalisation work – having said, a week or two ago, he wanted British jobs for British workers! So, he's hoist (or foist) on his own petard, as they say.

But what's good about the argument is: it's against Italians and not blacks, so there's no racist element; but also it's an argument about whether the company should have undercut British workers by employing contractors who pay less. So it's a trade-union and a

---

* Lord Aldington, a Brigadier in 1944, won £1.5 million in the ensuing libel case against Tolstoy. The award was overturned by the European Court of Human Rights.

democratic point, and if we're told that, under the European Union, we have to accept it, then that will raise again the whole question of the role of the European Union. It's a dangerous issue, but an important one, and one that's got to be very cleverly and carefully and honestly handled.

Saturday 31 January
Kate Jarvis and a photographer came to do an interview in advance of my visit to Bath on 4 March. She had read all my *Diaries* and *Dare to be a Daniel*, and she had done fantastic research; it was the best interview, in terms of the knowledge of the interviewer, that I've ever had. I liked her very much, and she gave me a book when she left, *A Pacifist's War* by Frances Partridge, who was one of the Bloomsbury Group.

Gordon Brown, at the Davos Summit, has said: whatever we do, we must avoid protectionism. Well, protectionism in the old sense that you don't want to get into trade wars, yes. On the other hand, government is there to protect you, and this concept of globalisation is that the market must preside globally, just after it's failed us nationally, and we've got to think about that very carefully. I think governments should do whatever is necessary to protect their own people, and negotiate with other countries to find a way in which everybody can defend themselves, because the global economy is not going to correct itself. I think I read somewhere that the global economy is $51 trillion in the red, or something – an enormous deficit, and we're heading for incredibly hard times.

Monday 2 February
I woke up this morning to find six inches of snow over the garden – what Caroline would call 'fairyland' – and it was lovely!

I didn't go to the hospital, and when I rang to cancel my appointment there was nobody there. I think the hospital was struck by the snow.

A television crew didn't turn up.

I cleared the snow from the front gate up to the front door, and a very nice young Indian came up to me and said, 'Would you like some help?' He was holding a snowball about the size of a football, and I said, 'I can manage okay.' He said, 'I'm from India. I've never been in England before – I've never seen snow before.' So interesting . . . 'Are you a student?' I asked him. 'No, no, I'm a doctor.'

Later a woman came from right across the road and said, 'Can I help?' It was very sweet of her.

Thursday 5 February

I got on the Tube at Holborn and the driver said, 'I don't know where this train is going' – he said this over the loudspeaker – 'but if you want to go somewhere else, get off at North Acton', and at every station he said, 'I don't know where this train is going.' There'd been complete disruption on the Central Line, and he was just told to drive a train westwards. It was quite funny actually, and everyone on the train was laughing.

Oh, interest rates have been cut to 1 per cent, the greatest cut ever in the history of the Bank of England. I don't think the governments of the world have any idea what to do, but of course Mandelson and Brown are sticking to 'no protectionism'. Although, as the global markets have got us into the mess we're in, why should we worship them now? I mean, it's totally illogical, and I think there will be strikes, and if the Government were to try and use Thatcher's legislation to repress the strikes, I think they'd be in big Trouble, with a big 'T'! So, we'll see.

Friday 6 February

Brian Denny of the RMT union came to the house at half-past eleven about the European elections. To cut a long story short, he told me that Bob Crow had decided that he would put up a list of candidates who would stand in European elections, would not take their seats if they were elected, like Sinn Fein didn't take their seats in Westminster, and it would be against the Lisbon Treaty. They would stand as 'No2EU – Yes to Democracy' candidates.

They have produced a little manifesto, which says: reject the Lisbon Treaty; no privatisation from Europe; defend manufacture; no to social dumping and anti-trade-union rules of the European court; no to racism and fascism, to differentiate it from UKIP and others; no to militarisation; restore democracy; abolish the Common

Agricultural Policy and VAT; scrap the economic policies designed to stop member states from implementing reflationary policies; and keep Britain out of the euro.

Anyway, we had a lovely talk and, in effect, Bob wants me to stand as a candidate. I suggested a slogan: 'No to Lisbon – yes, we can!', the Obama slogan. Of course the whole question is that I'd be expelled from the Labour Party, I presume, but could I get round that because I would be defending Labour policy to have a referendum? I'd have to think of Hilary, of course, and I'd have to think of family and all that, but it is an exciting idea and I was really quite thrilled by it.

Oh, at one o'clock, John Rees and Lindsey German came and we had a talk about what's happening to them, and in effect the Socialist Workers' Party think they have spent too much time on Stop the War and Respect and that has been at the cost of building the SWP. So they're in exactly the same position vis-à-vis the SWP that I am vis-à-vis the Labour Party. We had a lovely talk, lots of jokes, and went over to the pizza parlour for a meal. I told them about the European-election idea, and they were very keen on that as well, particularly about keeping out the racists and UKIP people, and so on.

I looked up on the *Mail* online, and there was this wonderful coverage for Melissa's book, with Richard and Judy's comment, and Sam West and other people. I mean, if that book doesn't hit the headlines, I just don't know what will! It was really, really exciting.

Saturday 7 February
Josh looked in at nine; he cleared the gutters, which had led to more leaking into the house.

We talked about the Euro-elections proposal, and he discouraged me. It brought me down to earth with a bump. His advice is very good – he's a shrewd guy.

I spoke to Hilary on the phone, and I mentioned to him this proposal and he was terribly upset. He said, 'Dad, you'll be expelled from the Labour Party, and anyway, the Lisbon Treaty isn't the same as the constitution' – the official Brown position. So I realised also that if I did go ahead with it, it would be a big break with him and might embarrass him.

Sunday 8 February
Read *The Sunday Times* – just rubbish again.

I rang Brian Denny of RMT to tell him that, although I'd been very excited by his project, I really couldn't get expelled from the Labour Party just for the purpose of helping this campaign, and he understood, to my delight.

Then, in the course of the afternoon, I rang Hilary and told him that the question of my candidature was completely gone.

Monday 9 February
At twelve o'clock John Grice collected me to go to Gateshead. I thought the weather might be bad, particularly coming back, so we agreed to leave an hour earlier than intended. I slept part of the way, and woke up as we got near Gateshead and saw the Angel of the North, which I'd never seen before. It's all rusted over now, and we passed it with the sun just under the wing – it was beautiful.

It was a very strange feeling in the car . . . as I passed Peterlee, named after the miners' lawyer, and Consett and Sunderland and Durham. I had a dream last night that I was dead, and I felt, in the car today, as if I'd come alive and was finding my old life again. I have such warm feelings about the North-East, because of the miners and others.

Got to the Sage Gateshead, which is a beautiful place. Norman Foster, or one of his people, designed it. I was given a liaison officer, called Madeleine, who was about twenty-two, a music graduate I think, and she kept an eye on me all the time. She was very nice. While I was waiting for the lights and sound, I asked one of them backstage where I was sitting, 'What's the origin of the word "Geordie"?' They looked it up on Google, and the answer was they were people in Newcastle and Durham who, in the mid-eighteenth century, supported King George II. It rather confirmed my memory – I don't know if it's true or not, but it confirmed my memory of the idea that the Geordies, although very radical, are also very loyal.

After the show, at about 10.30, John and I left. On the way down to London there was snow, but not heavy, and I got home at three o'clock, and went to bed at 4.30.

Wednesday 11 February
To the Channel 4 Awards. I'd been told in advance that my *Diary* was going to get a Lifetime Achievement Award. Jon Snow was in charge.

When we got there, Hilary was there and, to my amazement, Stephen, Nita and Emily, and the whole table was a Benn table, except for the Labour MP Mick Clapham and his wife.

At the very beginning the first award was to me, and I discovered that Emily had been asked to present it. I didn't even know they were coming. Anyway, she presented it to me, and I made a two-minute speech, paid a tribute to Ruth, and then Jon Snow also made a reference to Ruth, which was very nice.

Among the other people who got awards were: Peter Mandelson; Lord Adonis; John Prescott. Somehow, the whole thing reminded me of the Oxford Union. It was a grown-up version of students laughing about politics. My speech was a serious one. I didn't like it, funnily enough.

Thursday 12 February
I think I forgot to mention yesterday that I had some socks from Saffron, so I rang her up and she answered the phone. She's still with her partner. She's hoping to come back for a few days in late March, so I'll see her then.

Went to Josh's house, and we watched Lissie on Sky Arts, with Mariella Frostrup; and we watched the programme about her on *Richard & Judy*, with Alastair Campbell taking part, and a little vignette about Lissie's life.

One thing Josh drew to my attention is that Vicky Pope, who is the head of climate change at the Met Office, said that a lot of scare stories were being published about Arctic ice melting; I still find the general panic which is going on about climate change a bit of a puzzle.

I gave Ruth my award which I got from Channel 4. I'm going to photograph it, and she'll have the original, which she richly deserves!

Saturday 14 February
Got up early. Caught the bus to Hyde Park Corner for this convoy of 110 vehicles going to Gaza, organised by George Galloway and Yvonne Ridley. Among the vehicles were five or six old ambulances

and an old fire engine. They came from all over the country, and all absolutely packed with Muslims. And of course George Galloway was there, and Andrew Murray and Lindsey German from Stop the War.

There was tremendous affection from all the Muslims who came up and gave me such a hug – they're very affectionate, much more outgoing than the English with their stiff upper lips. I did endless interviews: Al Jazeera, Press TV, Sky TV, BBC TV and various Muslim channels.

Andrew Murray spoke, I spoke and George Galloway spoke, then the convoy went off.

Sunday 15 February
The world news is so grim. The Israelis are now making really serious threats to Iran.

The Afghan war is absolutely unwinnable, and the Russians are offering to help the Americans. They lost 15,000 troops in Afghanistan, and that means America cannot win. The method they're using, of sort of air power to bomb villages, is creating an enormous number of civilian casualties, which is making Karzai's position impossible.

Monday 16 February
A French and British submarine have collided in the mid-Atlantic, because both had switched off their radar so as not to be spotted, and they just hit each other – I mean, a chance in a million, but still, it throws yet another doubt upon the sense of having nuclear deterrents in submarines, and I think it will help the cause of nuclear disarmament.

Tuesday 17 February
In *The Guardian* today David Cameron, the Leader of the Opposition, wrote an article about the need for decentralisation of power from Westminster to local authorities and other bodies, and began by citing me, in my phrase about 'securing a fundamental and irreversible shift in the balance of wealth and power in favour of working people and their families'; and he developed this to mean that local authorities should have more power, which I agree with – indeed, I introduced a bill on it.

It was an interesting idea, and I had an email from somebody saying, 'What do you think of that?' So I sent them an email back saying, 'Give him a peerage.'

Thursday 19 February
I faxed through, to *The Guardian*, my letter to the Home Secretary, Jacqui Smith, on my having been stopped and searched under Section 44 of the Terrorism Act. I think, at this moment, civil liberty is a big issue.

Friday 20 February
Lissie is fifty-two today.

News today . . . 40,000 people have been repossessed in the last year; that is 100 a day. The more I think about it, I mean, it's like war – this crisis is a war crisis, but it's a crisis at home, not a foreign enemy, and 100 people a day thrown out of their homes is unacceptable. I dare say many people would like to buy houses, but can't get a mortgage; just as many people would probably like to get a car and can't get a loan.

Had a bit of a doze, and then I drove up to Lissie's for her birthday. That 'I drove' is very important. For the last few months Josh and Lissie and Stephen and Ruth have all said, 'You've got to give up your car', and it did have a very demoralising effect on me. I wondered whether, when I got in my car, I wouldn't be able to drive, I'd have a nervous breakdown. But I did drive, quite safely, there and I drove, quite safely, back, at night; and I don't think I'm ready to give up the car, because it is that little bit of independence, as today, going up to see Lissie. I couldn't have done it otherwise.

In the news today: Hazel Blears has made a statement saying that she's very worried by the number of members of the Cabinet who are planning leadership bids when Brown goes. Whether it's true or not, and it may be, it's created a great sense of unsettlement, rather like six months ago over David Miliband.

Saturday 21 February
Wrote fifteen letters, because I've been so lazy about tackling my correspondence. Among them, I wrote to Sir Michael Lyons, the

Chairman of the BBC Trust, enclosing a letter I had received from the Chief Executive of the British Red Cross thanking me for speaking up for the Gaza appeal. I gave four reasons why I didn't accept the arguments that Sir Michael had given for upholding the BBC ban, and said now that the armed conflict is over – there are, I think, 100,000 homeless people, including 56,000 children, and they need help now – why won't you give instructions to lift it now?

Clinton is in Beijing, and to see an American Secretary of State almost pleading with a Chinese Head of State on the economy and climate change is quite an interesting reflection on what's happened over the years since Mao's revolution succeeded.

Sunday 22 February
Up at six because, bless his heart, Josh turned up at seven to try and sort out my broadband and my Internet connection. He stayed for nearly three hours and fixed it. So I've now got 170 messages to deal with.

To Marks & Spencer to buy some sandwiches, and who should I see there but Norman Lamont, the former Chancellor of the Exchequer under John Major, responsible for Black Wednesday in 1992. He's probably seventy, with whitish hair. I said to him, 'Norman, what would you do if you were in charge now?' and he said, 'Nobody has the slightest idea what to do.' I said, 'Well, in eighteen months there'll be a coalition.' 'Oh no, there won't – there will be an election and a Tory Government.' I said, 'Yes, yes, of course, but you might want to have Labour there to reassure the nation', so he gave me a funny look. Anyway, it was an interesting exchange.

Thursday 26 February
At three o'clock I was picked up by John Grice and driven to the Severn Theatre in Shrewsbury, a brand-new theatre. The audience was interesting. I've never been very comfortable in the Midlands. Of course, Birmingham was a huge town that grew at a fantastic rate at the beginning of the Industrial Revolution in the nineteenth century, and people came from all over the country and worked in the factories there, so they didn't have any local roots or local pride, as they do in Scotland or in Bristol or in London, for that matter,

though London's changing. Birmingham, in a funny way, has always been Britain's version of America: cynical, brassy . . . I don't know, no collectivity about it.

Some of the questions were very cynical. One man said, 'Why should we vote for anybody? All the MPs are a bunch of crooks just trying to make cash!' I turned on him, and I said, 'Well, that's what Hitler said about democracy.' I kept this theme of cynicism in mind, and trying to give people some hope.

But somebody left some shortbread and tea for me, and a man came up with a big book of Martin Rowson's cartoons.

Got home and to bed about two o'clock.

Friday 27 February

Ruth arrived early this morning and sat on the bed, and she said she wondered whether Mandelson actually wanted the Communication Workers' Union to disaffiliate from the Labour Party. It was a very interesting point. She pointed out that in his book, *The Blair Revolution*, Mandelson had said that he thought it would be better if there was state funding of political parties and the unions were not affiliated to the Labour Party, which of course says it all. It was Mandelson who said he was 'utterly relaxed about people getting stinking rich' in respect of the £633,000-a-year pension that Fred Goodwin, the disgraced Chairman of the Royal Bank of Scotland, was getting.

At lunchtime Marion Miliband arrived, and Melissa, and we went over to the Pizza Express. She's very pessimistic about the political situation, but then she was born in Poland in the 1930s, so I'm not surprised. She's very detached politically from David and Edward, and she has retained her own political position, and I think she quite appreciated the friendship from us. She thought Melissa's book was wonderful, and she likes Ruth, so we had a lovely lunch.

My new photocopier, a Samsung, was delivered, and it looks very good.

I had a snooze. Ruth went off.

Sunday 1 March

I went and bought the *Mail on Sunday* to read the serialisation of Chris

Mullin's book. Also there was a very interesting comment by Clare Short, who said the reason that they didn't didn't release the Cabinet minutes on the Iraq war, under the Freedom of Information Act, was that there *was no* debate about the war in the Cabinet – Blair came, handed out little bits of paper from the Attorney General saying it was a legal war, and therefore there was no discussion about it. That is another reason for keeping things secret: because you don't want to reveal how little discussion there is about a crucial matter.

I drove over to have lunch with Hilary and Sally. Hilary had been in Berlin with Jonathan, and had visited the Nazi headquarters where Goebbels worked, and so on. It would frighten me, even to think about it.

I had a word with Carrie, who's going to be a fashion photographer – she's going to do a course in that.

James was there with Blake. Blake is moving from general practice to psychiatry. Then, afterwards, Hilary showed a video he'd made in Antarctica – fantastic!

I came home and at five o'clock Josh arrived. Then Lissie arrived, with Sarah, who was working on her school paper on Henry VIII. Then Stephen turned up. We had a long political talk, and he's very worried, as I am, about the police state.

Before Stephen went, Josh sorted out Internet domain names and reserved them, for Daniel and Stephen.

He also booked me a first-class ticket to Manchester next Sunday, which I've never done before on the Internet.

Before he went, Josh fixed the security light above the front door.

Rang Dave. He said there was a report on the Internet (in Russian) that a man had set fire to himself in Parliament Square, and there was no reference to it in the British press. He didn't know whether it was inaccurate or whether it had been suppressed. Of course it's exactly the story in Melissa's book, *One of Us*, so I rang her and told her.

So today I saw nine members of my family, out of eighteen. Apart from a very few letters, I did no work and the main priority now is of course the book. I've got to go on giving material to Ruth. She is a brilliant editor!

I had two emails this morning. A very sweet note from a Muslim saying: 'I just want to say how much I love you for the reasons you always stand up for justice', and then: had I thought of becoming a Muslim? I wrote a very friendly note back. Then one from a Buddhist and a great believer in yoga, who told me her father had died. She said how much he had appreciated the message I had sent before he died, which she read to him.

So anyway, that's the mixture of life.

Monday 2 March

I dreamed last night that the house was covered in green slime and fungus, and I went upstairs and in the bedroom was Caroline lying on the bed, and the bed was a complete mess of papers and things. She was absolutely white, her eyes were red, and a fattish woman was cutting huge chunks of bloody meat and giving it to her to eat. I said something and the woman replied, and I said, 'Never speak to me like that again – get out!' and she shouted at me. There was Caroline, with all this meat around her . . . and I woke up and Caroline was gone. Strange!

BBC London Radio rang about my meeting in Catford on Thursday.

I went to the City Temple, where I used to go as a child; it used to be Leslie Weatherhead's church, was bombed in the war and rebuilt. A thousand or more students were in the hall, for one of these sixth-form politics conferences. I had been asked to speak about the crisis. I said that my generation had made a hash of everything and, coming out of the hall, lots of the kids came round. It was lovely.

Got back and Ruth arrived for lunch, but she said she'd had a bit of a heart flutter and was going to see the doctor, quite rightly, I think.

Anyway I had a bit of a snooze, and then I think I may have dictated a couple more bits for the book, and Ruth went off.

At five o'clock, I did a half-hour international discussion on American radio/TV networks with correspondents from America, Ireland, France and Germany, and the theme was: why aren't the American unions doing what the European unions are doing and demonstrating about the crisis? Because I was a bit late I had to get a cab to a meeting in the East End.

Mandelson has made further attacks on Labour people . . . if they want to lose the election, this is the way to do it, but why should he object to the Tories coming in, because they support all his policies? Oh! I think if I did have a video blog, it might be that I could plant a few ideas into people's minds.

Tuesday 3 March

The big story this morning was a little bit of detective work . . . Dave had told me, a day or two ago, that *Izvestia* had reported that a man had set fire to himself in Parliament Square, and Dave was very surprised that it hadn't been reported in the British press. So first I rang the Metropolitan Police Press Bureau and a woman said, 'Yes, I'll send you the statement that we issued after it happened':

At approximately 16:00 on Friday, the 27th of February, a man was seen alight in Parliament Square. Police officers came to his aid, the fire was extinguished, the Ambulance Service attended this 43 year old, taken to a South London Hospital, with superficial burns, not life-threatening. We do not believe anyone else was involved.

Brian Haw has been camping in Parliament Square for years as part of the anti-war demonstration, and so I spoke to him and he told me he was there at the time, and the man was a Tamil; that seven Tamils were going to set fire to themselves all over the world, on the same day, as a protest at the way the Sri Lankan Government had treated them. Brian said, 'We saw him, rolled him over, put the fire out, the Police said it was awesome.' Why did *Izvestia* take an interest? The only guess I can make is that a Sri Lankan may also have set fire to himself in Moscow.

I rang the Press Association and they said they might have reported it, but nobody picked it up.

So that was a bit of very interesting detective work. I told Melissa, who sent a note back saying that he was just about the same age – forty-three – as Jack, the person in her novel who set fire to himself.

Bought Chris Mullin's *Diaries*, which I will read this evening.

Then I had a doze in the office. I've got this very simple white-plastic reclining garden chair, and I've attached to it a fairly thin layer of foam rubber, and I can sleep on it. I must say, I think it is a really useful invention.

Chris is a very skilled writer, wrote the novel, *A Very British Coup*; he used to be very much on the left, but he is a journalist at the heart of government, observing, rather cynically, what goes on. It's not self-justification, just reflections.

Thursday 5 March
Slept reasonably well, and woke up to hear Nicholas Jones, the former Industrial Correspondent of the BBC, talking about the miners' strike, which began twenty-five years ago today. He said he'd gone to the NUM in Barnsley to see Arthur Scargill – nobody answered the door. Then he'd been to Arthur Scargill's house and nobody came out. Then he'd talked to someone from the NUM. He just repeated all the rubbish about Scargill. I thought it was ghastly! I must say, it shook my respect for Nicholas Jones.

Ruth arrived, and I dictated something on the Labour Party for the new book – she thought it was very old and unimaginative; then I tried to dictate something on immigration, and she took the view that immigration really should be limited, because of the cultural effect of it on England. I find myself in disagreement with her about this, so I did another piece on cultural identity to try and show her I understood the point.

After lunch I went and caught the Tube to Cannon Street, and the train to Catford Bridge. Sir Steve Bullock, the elected Mayor of Lewisham, had invited me to meet some of his colleagues, and there were Labour councillors there. He got a knighthood from Blair, and apparently he's the man who rescued Lewisham from a hard-left council, so it is an interesting story.

Anyway, as we walked back to the Catford Broadway Theatre I did feel, as Ruth would have said, very much in the white minority – masses of people milling about, I had the impression that perhaps 80 per cent were immigrant, and I could see how people there might feel. At the meeting itself there were about 450 people, who each paid £17 – the questions were serious. There was one on race and immigration, about Labour and New Labour, and so on. There were quite a number of young people there, that was noticeable. I should think the average age was probably not more than forty. So I got the impression it was a community that had integrated well, and no racial problems of any kind.

Friday 6 March
Grahame Herbert turned up with his prototype seat-case for backpacks and demonstrated it, but it needed modifications. He and Ruth went off to buy a suitcase to try and see if it could be fitted to that.

I had a meal, and had a bit of a snooze, and did emails and letters.

I have put my bus pass inside the right sleeve of my suit, attached with a little clip, and so all I have to do is to press my arm on the Oyster pad – instead of having to find my bus pass whenever I go. It works like an absolute dream!

I caught the train to Bristol, to a packed meeting organised by Stop the War, and caught the 8.30 train home.

Wednesday 11 March
To the Jubilee Room at the Commons for the launch of the People's Charter, a very imaginative idea. It sets out a series of clear aims.

It was quite well attended. Imran Khan, the solicitor, was in the chair. John McDonnell and Alan Simpson and some trade-union leaders were there. I don't know whether there will be any press coverage – it's too interesting for the political correspondents. I linked it with the Chartists' demands in the 1830s: annual parliaments, universal suffrage, and so on. If we got a million signatures, which we could do, I think it could be an influence, and it is absolutely the right way forward: issues instead of personalities; and even issues instead of parties. John McDonnell is a really bright guy.

Sitting on the Terrace with my lunch, a rather nice omelette, I went back into the building for a moment and, when I came back, I found the seagulls had eaten most of it. In the afternoon there was a big Gaza lobby on and I met a couple of MPs from Gaza – Hamas MPs.

Tuesday 17 March

I got the 148 to the House of Commons, and it was diverted just past the Army & Navy because of some road blockage, and the guy would not let me get off the bus until we got almost to the Elephant & Castle – it was bloody awful!

So I had to get a taxi back to the Communication Workers' Union for their meeting calling for a Post Bank: a coalition of local businesses and sub-postmasters and the New Economic Foundation, whoever they are, and the Communication Workers' Union. There was the Labour MP Jon Cruddas; Billy Hayes, head of the CWU; Roger Gale, the Tory MP; Vince Cable, the Liberal Democrat. I tried to give a bit of historical background about the Giro.

And then I went over to the Annual General Meeting of Labour Action for Peace. There were about, I don't know, thirteen people there, average age probably seventy: masses of bureaucracy and no substance! For the first hour: who'd be chairman, who'd be secretary. I was asked to speak, and so I said there are three areas of a peace campaign: one is throwing yourself into the activities on a day-to-day basis, like the Stop the War movement; secondly, working with other Labour organisations, like Labour CND and Labour Against the War, to influence government policy; and the third thing is looking ahead a bit – Russia should be brought into Europe, we should be thinking of some world government that is more democratic than just handing over all the economic powers in the world to the IMF, which is not elected; and they took one or two of those points up.

After an hour and a half, and I slipped out. I came home in a cab.

Wednesday 18 March

Looking at the world today, it's quite clear that the Establishment, the people in power, are desperately trying to safeguard their own position so that the crisis, which is coming, doesn't destabilise them in any way – make a few little concessions here and there, but, otherwise, just carry on as before – and they're terrified of any serious change.

Oh, Natasha Richardson, Vanessa Redgrave's daughter, married to Liam Neeson, the actor, has died, or is dying, following a skiing accident in Canada – very sad for Vanessa . . . Jemma Redgrave, who is married to Lissie's old boyfriend, Tim Owen, is first cousin.

One thing I forgot to mention: Ruth arrived with a birthday card – 'I AM 8', to which she added '4' – and a lovely chocolate cake, which she'd decorated herself . As I'm not going to see her on my birthday in April we sat down and ate the chocolate cake at lunch.

Friday 20 March
Up early, and I went to Guy's Hospital, to the Urology Department, to see Mr Glass, the consultant. Josh came with me, bless his heart. I decided to have a prostate operation in July. It's a bit of a nuisance, I don't want to do it, but the prostate problem means getting up three or four times in the night. The only anxiety Josh had was whether the anaesthetic would be bad for me, but we'll see anyway.

Later I caught the train to Coventry, and was met and driven to the Methodist Central Hall, where I'd been before. Outside were some people representing the Campaign for a New Workers' Party, which the former MP Dave Nellist is associated with – I've always been very friendly towards Dave, who was expelled from the Party in the 1980s.

I went there, and Geoffrey Robinson introduced me, and I paid a tribute to him. I did my *Evening with Tony Benn*. As they were Labour Party people, they were a bit quiet. They weren't anything like as enthusiastic as people at an ordinary public meeting. I can't say it went badly – and I hope I didn't say anything that upset Geoffrey Robinson. But, I thought: If that's the local Labour Party, then I am a bit out of touch with it.

Anyway, afterwards I was picked up and driven, by Colin French, who is Geoffrey Robinson's chauffeur, to the Commodore Hotel in Instow, North Devon. Ruth was there – it was about one o'clock in the morning, I guess – and she took me to my room, Room 15. I don't think I even had a cup of tea, I was so tired.

Saturday 21 March
I got up at six. It was a lovely day! I sat on the little balcony outside the room, overlooking the River Torridge, towards Appledore and the shipyard. Had breakfast with Ruth and her sister Di. James Woolaway, the grandson of Bruce Woolaway (the owners of the hotel), looked after us.

Then we were driven to the Town Hall for the 'Manor Court'; the

Mayor was Caroline Church, a Liberal Democrat who fell out with her colleagues over something or another. I met Geoffrey Cox, the MP. The Manor Court is a medieval institution, and I don't suppose there was much Labour support there, but anyway they laughed at my jokes!

Over to visit Ruth's parents, Joan and Victor Winstone. Joan looked much, much better after her terrible accident in December, which everyone thought would kill her. Then, after that, Ruth and Di drove me to Tiverton Parkway, and I sat on the platform and smoked my pipe and caught the 3.13 back, and was home by about 5.30.

Monday 23 March

I don't put a lot about world news in today, but Obama has decided to buy all the toxic debt of all the banks in America for another trillion dollars. The whole situation is quite incredible! I mean, capitalism is being rejected everywhere. It's a funny way to put it, but I think it is.

Tuesday 24 March

I spoke to Lissie this morning, and told her that the film about the lion called Christian being reunited with his early owners was to be on television tonight, so the girls could watch it. Two Australian lads in London bought a baby lion from Harrods, kept it as long as they could and then released it in Kenya, with the help of Joy Adamson of *Born Free*. They went back, a year later, and the lion came out and slowly recognised them, and just jumped up and hugged them and licked them – oh, it was heavenly! And then Christian introduced them to his 'wife'.

At four o'clock Stephen Kelly, who'd sent me an email about my work as Minister of Technology, wanted to come and talk about a new project for IT software developments in Britain. He brought somebody called Tim Brill, who's a Communications Director of his company, Micro Focus. In effect they wanted me to head up, or join, a campaign to get more government money and support for development of software, involving the universities and adult education. I said I was out of touch with day-to-day developments, but I gave them a steer: I said don't ask for money at the beginning, put it at the end; link it with Europe and America; point out that it's got great export potential and introduce a green element, because, after all, software is very green. They were much struck, and sort of half-hinted they'd like me and Michael Heseltine to launch this campaign. Well, I'm not prepared to do that, but I said I'd give it any support I could.

Mervyn King, the Governor of the Bank of England, has made it clear that he doesn't think any further financial stimulus by the Government is appropriate. Inflation has dropped to zero. So Gordon is under some difficulty, because if the Governor of the Bank of England says you shouldn't do something that he obviously intends to do, it weakens Gordon Brown. On the other hand, it may be the right thing to do. But the more I think about this whole economic thing, the more I think the approach should be to develop projects that will benefit society, that won't necessarily be profitable – build council houses, and so on. But just funding the banks I think is a dead loss. The pound is slipping, and that will have an effect on our economy.

Obama has talked, for the first time, about an exit strategy from Afghanistan, which is good news.

Otherwise, the stories from Gaza are horrific now: Israeli soldiers admitting that they shot children and bombed hospitals. I think the war-crimes charge against Israel is now very strong. I think it is a very dangerous state, and I just hope that we can build up support for a better policy and the recognition of Hamas.

I'm thinking a bit about blogging. Josh is going to come at the weekend with a new high-quality camera, and then maybe I shall be in a position to get on with this project.

I've been thinking a lot about dying. One day I will find myself in hospital – what can I do in hospital that would be useful? I thought: Well, why don't I take a tape-recorder and a lot of blank tapes and go round and talk to the patients in their beds, if they're ready to do so, about their lives. I would put a microphone on them and then record their life story, for their children or grandchildren. It would keep me busy before I die and it would be a useful thing to do. It means I've got to be mobile enough to move around the ward, whereas I might be absolutely incarcerated in bed, but it's nice to think of something to do when you're dying.

I think it would make my death more agreeable, and will also be a way of being useful at that stage.

Wednesday 25 March
Just after nine Anita Bromley, a solicitor, picked me up in a taxi and we went to Wormwood Scrubs for the Phillip Trusty parole-board hearing. I've been interested in his case for some time, we have been in contact – he writes me letters – for ten or fifteen years.

We had to queue up with everybody, had to produce a passport or photograph. I had to hand in my tobacco, my cash, my penknife; I don't think I handed in my keys.

We were taken through the prison, with every door being locked behind – six, seven or eight locked doors – into a sort of open space, where I met the barrister, and someone who was his probation officer at one stage.

Then a man was brought up to me, and it was Phillip Trusty. I didn't realise at once it was him – I've never met him before.

We went into the hearing. Judge John Lindsay was in charge, a man in his mid-sixties I think, white hair; I had looked him up on the Net, and I think he was quite a fair-minded judge. The other two members of the panel were an Indian psychiatrist and an English woman with red hair, I suppose in her late fifties.

Phillip Trusty gave evidence first. He said the whole government's corrupt, they're all Freemasons, and then something about the world's energy problems. He was quite serious, perfectly clear, and the psychiatrist pursued him and brought more of it out. But Trusty was doing himself no good at all. And then the psychiatrist said, 'Well, in the light of that, if you ever met any of these people, would you attack them?' – i.e. to imply he was violent.

The woman asked about his wife (he was sentenced to life imprisonment, escaped, went to Cyprus, married, then came back to England and was re-arrested and had to continue his life sentence). It's a very complicated case.

Anyway, I asked to be heard next. I said I had no special qualifications, but I had been moved by two things: I thought there might have been a miscarriage of justice; and also, on the question of humanity, I thought he was being treated very badly. I said he'd written to me, and I'd written to the Home Secretary, and I'd raised it with Chris Mullin at the Home Office. I said I know it's said that he has a conspiracy theory but, in my profession, I said, with a slight smile, conspiracy theories are rampant – communists, Muslims, left-wing, right-wing conspirators . . . And, I said, as to delusions, in my profession there are people with delusions; and there's one man, for example, who thinks he saved the world.

I don't know whether they took it well, but I think it was the right thing to do, and then I went on to say that the real question of probation is: is he safe in public? You've got to check that, with probation after release, but I said actually Trusty spent five years in Cyprus where he was safe.

I was then released and came home on a bus. I rang Anita this evening, and she said that my evidence had been exactly what they wanted. They had not reached a judgement today, though she had told me when I went there was no hope at all of anything other than a rejection. Of course, today the big news was that Trusty said he would accept probation and be released in Britain on condition that he stayed in Britain, which is a complete change, because previously he'd said, 'If I leave, I'll abscond and go back to Cyprus', so he did make that concession. And, originally, he said he wouldn't come to the hearing, but he did, and I'm glad because I met him.

I had a bite to eat, had a snooze, and then went by Tube to St Mary-le-Bow in Cheapside to initiate a series of lectures called 'Just Share'. It's a Christian initiative in the City of London to persuade City people to have some moral responsibility for the poverty of others.

Friday 27 March
The big news today is that Gordon Brown has suggested that the constitutional role of the royal family should be altered, so that it wouldn't be an offence for a member of the royal family to marry a Catholic, and also that the eldest child – even if it was a girl – would succeed to the throne, rather than the first boy. Of course this opens up all sorts of possibilities, which I've thought about.

Polly Steele came to lunch; and she explained her brilliant idea of video portraits. You ask somebody to sit absolutely quietly for two minutes and you film them, and then you could, if necessary, have what they were thinking about underneath. It might be their wedding, it might be the birth or death of a child, it might be anything. She had already filmed me. I was thinking about the Armistice, because I'd just been discussing the death of my brother Michael. It was a brilliant idea, because you do like to stare at people, but you can't. A silent face, just thinking and reflecting . . . I think I had a tear in the corner of one eye, and she wanted to use it to launch the idea, and we had a lovely talk.

Sky TV asked me to do an interview about the monarchy and I had worked out (I thought rather cleverly) what I'd say about it: that I would strongly welcome the Prime Minister's initiative, and that of course the royal family should be able to marry anyone they like – it would liberate them, and it would have an effect on the Church of England, because a Catholic might be appointing a new Archbishop – even a Muslim Prime Minister. I said it would alter the whole question of the prerogatives and the oath, and it would mean the Commonwealth might redefine the title Head of the Commonwealth, so that it rotated round Canada, Australia, India, Pakistan, New Zealand, just as it does in Europe. I think they were a little bit surprised, but anyway I got my case across.

Then I went over to the BBC and I said the same thing again. If the Palace was watching, it would absolutely make them determined not to make any changes, because the last thing they want is to open up the British constitution based on the oath to a monarch.

Saturday 28 March
I had an idea to take the Parliamentary Standards form on the Declaration of Members' Interests and have it sent to every potential election candidate, saying, 'Will you fill it in before you're elected?' There's not much point in knowing what the interests of Members are after you've elected them – you want to know before. It might influence you. That's an idea I've had for a long time, but it's something somebody else has got to do – I can't do it.

So, that's how I spend the day, sitting and thinking . . .

Very, very depressed this morning, then very, very cheerful, and then sinking into a bit of gloom this evening. I do go up and down like a yo-yo.

Sunday 29 March

The clocks go forward.

According to the news, Jacqui Smith's husband used her parliamentary allowance to buy pornographic videos; it puts her in a real difficulty. That, plus the fact that she says her home is with her sister in London, while her husband and children live somewhere else . . . I think it could be the end of her.

Josh came with a high-quality camera and set up my blog. It's frightfully easy! Beautiful quality. I did a few blogs: one on the G20; one on torture; one on the need for Russia to be in the European Union – about a minute, ninety seconds maybe.

Monday 30 March

I was picked up at seven and taken to BBC Television News to talk about pensioners' bus passes.

These free passes were extended to allow them to be used on other bus services across the country, but the Treasury has insisted they now be cut back, saving a billion pounds. I said, 'Isn't it wrong that the Government should be taking a billion pounds from eleven million pensioners, which is £90 per pensioner per year? Isn't it wrong that this money should be given to the banks to allow their bonuses to be paid? Isn't it better for tourist areas to have pensioners visiting, because it creates jobs in hotels and shops? Isn't it better to build more buses to accommodate the pensioners because that would create jobs? Isn't it a good idea to keep cars off the road?' I did it in a jolly way.

Kate Silverton has got an engagement or a wedding ring – I think she married a Marine.

Wednesday 1 April

The G20 summit is meeting in London and I joined the march to Trafalgar Square. My legs just wouldn't do it, so I got a bus. A number of people spoke and at the very end I said, 'When you're my age, eighty-four, as I am the day after tomorrow, you'll look back on this as a very important demonstration.' As a result of that Julie Felix, the singer who'd performed just before me, began singing 'Happy birthday to you', so 8,000 people sang 'Happy birthday' – it was lovely!

It's been a very important day because of course the world's media are here today to cover Obama's visit, so all the demonstrations will be broadcast worldwide. Also, because of the political crisis and the economic crisis coming together, and the continuing war, the Establishment at the top is trying desperately to re-create the old system under regulation, talking about a reformed capitalism. But people want something different, and I think, if we carry on, it will be rather comparable to what happened in the middle of the nineteenth Century and it will lead to change – not quite the ones we want. There may be a bit of bloodshed. But otherwise, it's an important change, and it gives you a feeling of excitement.

Thursday 2 April
I watched the television, and I saw the Summit in which Obama and Brown spoke, and they've come out with a trillion-dollar plan, mainly channelled through the IMF. I mean, it was so obvious really that their plan is to re-create capitalism on a global basis, with no protectionism, and to make it work; and that's what I doubt. Obama had met the Chinese Prime Minister and the Russian Prime Minister and they'd had discussions on the reduction of nuclear arsenals.

Obama is a nice, decent guy, but what you feel when you look at Obama is he's just an ordinary guy, in charge of a rapidly declining empire – because the Americans are overstretched militarily and politically and economically, and now the Chinese and the Russians are talking about a new international currency to replace the dollar. So, I sort of felt for the Americans. I remember the British Empire declining and how awkward it was for the British when they realised they were no longer top dogs.

Friday 3 April
My 84th birthday, with masses of emails, phone calls, cards – and flowers from Saffron.

Lissie had her big day at the British Book Awards. She dressed up, and was brought round to the front of the hotel in Park Lane in a

Rolls-Royce and walked along the red carpet. Stephen was there, with his video camera, and he went into the Green Room to film.

Monday 6 April
To St Thomas's and visited the Dermatology Department. The treatment they gave me for my eczema on my legs seems to have worked, so I thanked them very much, and came home.

Then the BBC's *The One Show* arrived and did an interview in the garden about Paul Stephenson, the Bristol friend of mine. He's getting an OBE at the Palace tomorrow.

I went off, at 3.30, with John Grice, who drove me to Colchester to a Clive Conway lecture at the Mercury Theatre. I'm getting clearer and bolder in my presentation of the argument. John lives in Colchester, so when he dropped me home in London, he had to drive back there.

Tuesday 7 April
Alice Mahon rang today, the former MP for Halifax. She's left the Labour Party, or she's just about to, she's out of sympathy with so much of what it's doing; but also, the Welfare Reform Bill, which is driving unemployed people, women with young children, back to work and so on, is just back to the Poor Law and she can't take it.

Anyway, John Grice picked me up again at three and drove to Newark for a lecture. I saw Glennys Sanders there, who founded the Guillain–Barré Syndrome Support Group. I had met her years ago, at the anniversary meeting at the House of Commons; I suffered from it in 1981.

Wednesday 8 April
I have been asked to do the BBC's *The World Tonight* on the death of Ian Tomlinson, this newsagent who happened to be knocked down by the police last week, over the demonstrations in the City of London. I think he was completely innocent, he wasn't even political. The police hit him, he fell to the ground, they hit him again and he died of a heart attack. When I did it, George Monbiot was in another studio and he hogged the whole programme, but I wasn't looking for saying more.

Saturday 11 April
I had a very funny voice-message from a man who's absolutely bats. He made no attempt to hide his telephone number.

Message: Friday, April 10th, at 7.59 p.m.
Good evening, Tony, AKA Speaker of the House of Gentlemen . . . Tony, there's only one thing left on my checklist today. The RAF confirmed we did have an early warning stage two of the little moustaches . . . If you would be so kind as to call me on that matter, Tony, I would be most grateful. [Then he gave his phone number.]
. . . It would seem a rough calculation that Room 101, Orwell, Big Brother, 84, Animal Farm, was the [unclear] Politburo and Pentagon in order to spread fear at the Fed and the FTSE – in other words, we know what you're doing, and we've also filmed you turning up at your secret meetings . . . Not long now, when you consider an eight-billion-year opportunity condensed to sixty-five million years' worth of dinosaurs, cavemen, killing animals, and finally, Tony Benn. Got that.'

Well, that was the crazy phone call I had on Saturday 11 April. The children listened to it. Some thought it was serious; some thought it was a spoof; some thought it was threatening; some thought he was mad. He has rung before and since. 'God bless you, Tony – you're my main man.'
Selina Scott wrote an article about her legal campaign against Channel 5 for not allowing her to take Natasha Kaplinsky's place when Natasha was on maternity leave, and she mentioned the fact that I had supported her.

Tuesday 14 April
Tony Whittome from Hutchinson arrived, at six. He's sixty-five this year, and he's retiring. It really was quite weird, in a way. When people twenty years younger than I am are reaching retirement age . . . ! I realised something very obvious: that, although Hutchinson and Random House are my publishers, my real dealings of course have been with Tony Whittome, who's been wonderful, and he's now

thinking: What will I do after I retire? So I said to him, 'You should write a book called "More Time for Publishing"!' Of course, he does want to retain the connection with me. But the financial situation in Hutchinson and in publishing is very tight. They can't have all those trips they had before. Emma Mitchell, whom I adore, doesn't get to many of the festivals.

When I talked to him about the new book, I thought: I'm a very privileged person. I've got a parliamentary pension, I can earn money, my children are all privileged, you know – they went to comprehensive schools, but they're privileged. So I wonder whether my book isn't going to be too soft, sort of a good, kind man doing good works and saying good things. Has it got the cutting edge that a socialist should have? So, I've got to think about that a bit.

Anyway, he gave some very good advice and went off on his bike.

Wednesday 15 April

I have this strong feeling that I'm coming to the end of my life. I'm not ill. I've got this operation in July – don't think there'll be anything in that. But gradually, inevitably, you become detached from day-to-day politics . . . Also, things get much more complicated now – simple things bother me. I can use the computer, but if I don't use it for a few days, I forget how it works. I had to fill in a form for the Labour Party Conference on the computer, and I filled it in several times and, each time, I lost it, and so I've got now to get somebody from the Party Headquarters to send me a form that I can post off. Everything just becomes more difficult. I'm not confused, I don't think, but young people take it all for granted, and I can't.

Thursday 16 April

At 10 o'clock Grahame Herbert came with his prototype seat-case and, I must say, it looked very good. So Ruth's taken on the job of starting the marketing process, possibly with an airline that might be interested. But it's fun working with Grahame – I like him very much.

The police have dropped charges against Damian Green, charges which must have been endorsed by Jacqui Smith, the Home Secretary, who's in deep trouble.

Friday 17 April

I read a piece the other day in the paper saying that, in view of the alleged threat of Barack Obama, there were people in Texas saying Texas should be independent, and that gave me the thought that it's not impossible, looking ahead, that the United States could break up, and so could China. On the one hand, you've got the move towards greater units – e.g. Europe; on the other hand, there is the disintegrating tendency, and God knows what the world would be like if China broke up and India broke up and America broke up. Indeed, the United Kingdom might break up – you can't rule it out.

Anyway, these are random thoughts at the moment, and unless anything happens, I'm going to bed shortly.

Wednesday 22 April

Jack Jones died last night, ninety-six. I felt really, really bereaved. He was a lovely man, absolutely true, had an incredible life . . .

The *Today* programme rang me up and asked me for a comment on Jack, and of course all they did was say Jack Jones was 'the most powerful man in Britain', 'he brought Thatcher to power'. I said, 'Mrs Thatcher destroyed trade unionism, and killed off local government, and privatised everything, and now we have the mess we're in.' They described him as a boss. Now, bosses are not elected. In the old days, they used to talk about trade union 'barons'. Well, they're not elected, either. And so I think I turned the argument, and at the same time said how much I loved Jack.

Rodney Bickerstaffe rang to say that he was actually with Jack when he died yesterday.

Later, I phoned Mick Jones, his son.

Ruth arrived, and at nine o'clock Grahame Herbert turned up, with his prototype seat-case, and we went off, taking photographs: started in Notting Hill Gate, in front of a luggage shop, so it looked as if I'd just bought it there; outside a bus-stop; we got a taxi to Paddington and he photographed me next to Isambard Kingdom Brunel; on the Heathrow Express, at Terminal 5. It was just great fun.

Alistair Darling carried the Budget off very well. He also announced that there would be a change in the procedure for paying MPs, so second-home allowances would be replaced by a daily attendance allowance, which is ridiculous. I don't know whether the Budget will work, or whether this will work.

Thursday 23 April
Up early, and went to collect a package from the local post office: and it was ten cartridges for my computer, each of which lasts about two weeks, and the total cost was £279. Boy, that is a racket!

Friday 24 April
I caught the bus to the House of Commons, to meet Saffron, and getting on the bus was an elderly lady with white hair and a stick and a bag, and it was Shirley Williams! She sat right in front of me, didn't see me, got out before me. When I think of the glamorous young Shirley that I spoke for when she was the candidate years and years ago, and then the Shirley with me in the Cabinet, the Shirley who joined the SDP, and the former Leader of the Liberal Democrats in the House of Lords . . . it's strange, just strange!

Anyway, I got to the House of Commons; there was a huge crowd outside the public entrance, and it was the Gurkhas, and in the middle was Joanna Lumley addressing them – she's espoused the cause of the Gurkhas – and lots of television cameras.

Saffron appeared – just the same. She's thirty-six, very tall, no make-up of any sort, her hair down her back, looking very relaxed, and we went through the new security entrance together. I'd never been through before – it's very efficient – then we went to the shop and I bought her various presents. We went on the Terrace: I just had a cup of tea and a banana, and then she got me a second cup of tea, and we talked from about 10.30 till about 12.30, a couple of hours. I asked about Hollywood, about her life, about her plans, about her writing. She's a nice girl – I like Saffron. She persuaded, or I persuaded, a policeman to take pictures of us. She put her head on my shoulder and it was all very sort of friendly and jolly. She is going to Venice tomorrow for a wedding.

I like her in a way, but there's something unreal about Saffron . . . I don't know how to describe it. Politically, she keeps up-to-date, very pro-Obama, is progressive in a generalised way, and it was nice to see her.

Once I was home, Gary from Midpoint Services just up the road turned up with three Freesat boxes, which he installed: one in the basement; one on the ground floor; and one in the bedroom. He freed my video machine in the bedroom, which had jammed, which was a great relief. He's going to bring me a DVD for the bedroom as well. Watching him, I just felt totally out of touch, as I do when Josh works on my computer. I suppose, if I sat down, worked hard, I could learn it all and understand it, but I don't particularly want to – too time-consuming. But I felt as my grandmother must have felt when she saw her first motor car: This is impossible, incredible, how can anyone drive it? Or how can anyone fly a plane? Well, I did fly a plane!

Saturday 25 April
I got up at six, got on the tube to King's Cross and walked to the Annual General Meeting of the Stop the War Coalition. Jeremy Corbyn was there, and he whispered to me, 'I think it's possible that John McDonnell and I are going to be expelled from the Labour Party for voting against the Government so many times.' He said, 'Keep it to yourself', which I will. But if that is true, it's a serious development. It reminds me of the 1930s, when Attlee was trying to build up a credible opposition, and they expelled Stafford Cripps from the Labour Party for working with the communists; and Michael Foot, Aneurin Bevan, and also Jim Mortimer, who later became General Secretary of the Labour Party, for working with Peace for China or something.

Monday 27 April
This flu from Mexico, this bird flu, which has already killed sixty people, might be a global pandemic. It is terrifying to think about . . . nothing you can do, but it may wipe us out.

At ten o'clock a man called Eric Brownsmith arrived. He'd sent me an email saying he'd read all my *Diaries* and wanted to have a talk about them, so I said yes. I didn't know what to expect. I thought he might be a student. He was a sixty-nine-year-old retired prison governor, and he arrived with a box containing the most beautiful scale model of a Spitfire, which he presented to me. We had a talk for about an hour and a half, about the *Diaries* and about politics. He couldn't have been nicer really. He's a Scot. I said, 'Why did you come to London?' 'Mainly to see you.'

Thursday 30 April

At eleven o'clock Professor Matthew Jones, from Nottingham University, came on behalf of the Cabinet Office to do an interview with me about the history of the Chevaline project – that was the Polaris upgraded to Trident. I gave him some uncut diary extracts, and he left a list of other things he'd like. I was a bit suspicious of him before he arrived – I thought he must be an intelligence man – but actually he's a clever academic who's concentrated on American and Canadian studies and written a lot about nuclear weapons, so they asked him to undertake this job.

Then the man with the aerial arrived. This is part of the new equipment – he extended the aerial up a few feet, because I am getting a poor signal, and reconnected the new recording device. To be candid, I can't make it work. I wanted to watch a DVD, but I couldn't make it work, and so Josh will have a look at it on Sunday, bless his old heart.

This evening, I've got the job of preparing for Jack Jones's funeral, and also my speech for May Day. When I'm at full bat I'm happier than when I'm gazing at a huge pile of unanswered letters and dozing off because I'm so tired.

Friday 1 May

May Day.

I got a cab to the Honor Oak Crematorium in South London for Jack Jones's funeral. It was a beautiful, beautiful day. Neil Kinnock and John Prescott were there.

Harriet Harman came up to me and said, 'I just want to let you know that I'm trying to model myself on you.' I said, 'That's a bit of a mistake, because I was a great failure.' But anyway she was trying to be friendly, and obviously her Leadership campaign is well advanced.

Rodney Bickerstaffe presided over the whole thing. Derek Simpson was there; I remember he said to me at Durham, years ago, 'I'm just a simple Sheffield communist.' There's something funny about him.

We went into this chapel – small, but packed. Mick Jones, Jack's son, had got a lot of recordings organised and pressed buttons, and so on. Another son, Jack, looked just like his dad! It was quite extraordinary. To look at him, you wouldn't believe Jack was dead! Tony Woodley spoke; Geoffrey Goodman; Marlene Sidaway, Secretary of the International Brigade; Manus O'Riordan, from Ireland; and then I spoke.

I was very emotional. I began by saying, 'I'm utterly bereaved' and I ended by sort of half-singing, 'I dreamed I saw Jack Jones last night, alive as you or me, says I; but Jack, you're two weeks' dead; I never died, said he.' Anyway, there you are, that's what I did, and I was a bit tearful.

I got a lift back with Tony Woodley, and got a bus up to Trafalgar Square, sat on Nelson's plinth for the May Day rally.

Jonathan has been offered a place at the London School of Economics to do an MA in the philosophy of science, if he gets a 2:1, which I'm sure he will.

Really sensational news: Phillip Trusty has been released on parole. I went and gave evidence for him a few weeks ago. He's written to me for fifteen years. I'm so thrilled. He is to be released to live with his sister.

Then Ruth and I went off to Marion Miliband's for dinner, and Ed Broadbent, the former leader of the New Democratic Party in Canada, was there, with his friend Ellen Wood, a writer. We had a lovely talk, including talking about the future of the Labour Party, and left about a quarter to eleven.

Sunday 3 May
Hazel Blears, in *The Observer*, said something about the Gurkha decision and the MPs' expenses, which was being interpreted as an attack on Brown.

We've had Charles Clarke saying that the expenses scandal had made him ashamed to be a member of the Labour Party; and David Blunkett, who also said something very critical.

So it looks to me as if there is a build-up to try and get rid of Brown. I don't think it can possibly succeed, because getting rid of Brown would be very messy and would damage everybody. Secondly, the leadership election would lead to bitterness and would damage everybody. Thirdly, whoever did win the leadership election would have to call an immediate general election, and that would be messy. So I think Brown will just stumble on till polling day. The Blairites – because Blears and Blunkett and Clarke are all Blairites – are trying to destroy Brown, and then, if Labour loses the election, they'll say, 'We told you so – only Blair could win an election,' and the Blairites will try to resume control of the Party. That's the situation we're in at the moment.

I have come to the conclusion that the trade-union leadership in Britain is part of the Establishment, and they don't want strikes. Strikes are illegal, would get the leaders into trouble if they supported them. It embarrasses the trade-union leaders, just as when Keir Hardie proposed that there be a Labour Party he was described as 'an irresponsible man, bringing division to our ranks'. So, one mustn't think that Tony Woodley and Derek Simpson and all that are going to help the left, because they aren't. They don't even like John McDonnell and the Labour Representation Committee. I've got to put it in a delicate way, or it is going to get me into a lot of trouble.

But you see, Tony Woodley is absolutely locked in with Derek Simpson. Derek Simpson, this old Sheffield communist (as he always tells me), doesn't want to take any action. Unite, the union, has actually employed Charlie Whelan as their Chief Press Officer – Charlie Whelan, of all people, who worked with Gordon Brown!

So one has to see the trade-union leadership quite clearly in that light and try and explain that everything comes from underneath, not just politically, but also in the trade-union movement, and I hope that makes sense.

Monday 4 May

I think I'd better go to the dentist because my teeth are worrying me a bit, and I think I'd better have my ears dealt with because my deafness is getting worse – all the problems of old age!

I turned on the television and found on the *Parliament* programme that they were re-broadcasting, in full, the BBC coverage of the general election of 1979, when Jim Callaghan was defeated and Mrs Thatcher became Prime Minister. It was absolutely riveting! First of all, seeing all sorts of faces: Robin Day, who's now dead; Bob McKenzie, who's now dead; David Butler, who now isn't used any more; a young and rather pompous David Dimbleby; John Sergeant as a young reporter, standing behind Mrs Thatcher on the day she was elected, just as he was there eleven years later, on the day that she was removed.

There's no doubt whatever that a contemporary programme shown again is so much more effective than these retrospectives. What you want to see is the raw material again.

It also reminded me that, thirty years ago this very day, my job as Secretary of State for Energy ended. I don't think I went back to my Department – I might have done. But that's my last glimpse of office, and Hilary is now near, possibly, the last year of his ministerial experience.

The other thing that I was impressed by – and it's so obvious it's hardly worth mentioning – is that the whole British Establishment is about public schoolboys and successful upper-middle-class people. And although Tom Jackson, the General Secretary of the Post Office Workers' Union, was shown talking to some industrialist, the working class, the trade-union movement, is hardly ever mentioned on the media. It's almost revolutionary or way-out even to suggest talking about it. Jackson, who was very right-wing, was sitting there, with his big moustache; the trade unions were discussed a bit more then, because they were seen to be powerful, but now you hardly ever hear them mentioned.

It made me wonder whether the whole democratic process isn't some sort of a fraudulent device for pretending to people that they can change things, whereas, actually, all they can do is to replace one government with another government, with the same policy under another name, which gets there by abusing the previous government and attacking it for the very things they would have done if they'd been there at the time. These are very pessimistic conclusions, but I'm thinking about how you do change things, and that's going to be my task over the next few years. I have just got to think it out afresh, and that's one of the themes coming out of my book, *Letters to my Grandchildren.*

Tuesday 5 May
Political news . . . Lady Uddin has been accused of claiming that her home is a flat in Maidstone, which apparently she never visits. So that's going to damage the Labour Party because she's a Labour peer, but also the House of Lords. Corruption in the Commons is bad enough, but when it's in the Lords, and none of them have been elected and they're getting tons of money . . . I think this is going to lead to some sort of constitutional change.

Friday 8 May
The *Daily Telegraph* has bought, I presume quite illegally, a list of Cabinet Ministers' expenses, and it does look terribly bad – people have claimed for all sorts of things. Hilary comes out absolutely bottom with a small claim for food. He phoned, and we talked a little bit about it. But the expenses affair has done deadly damage to Parliament and the reputation of Members of Parliament, just before the European elections, the local-government elections and, of course, the coming general election. It's just possible that this is a major crisis for democracy.

Tuesday 12 May
Saffron arrived, and she drove me to the Cuban Ambassador's residence, where I was presented with the Medal of Friendship, which had been signed by Raúl Castro. It was a great honour.

The left and trade-union movement were there in force including Benjamin Zephaniah, Helena Kennedy, Michael Mansfield, Ken Loach, Yvette Vanson. Saffron met a lot of old friends, and of course she speaks Spanish.

The Ambassador made a very elaborate speech, a wonderful sort of obituary.

I was picked up by *Newsnight* later to do an interview on MPs' expenses. Cameron has said to Tories, 'If you don't repay your expenses, you'll be sacked.' Brown has said people should repay their expenses.

Hazel Blears, who did not pay capital gains tax on the sale of a home, produced, on television, a large mock up of a cheque which she said she'd sent to Inland Revenue.

I made a few points, and I did say to Paxman, at one stage, casually, 'Well, you're a public servant too – I don't know what you earn, but you're paid for by the licence-payer, just as I have been by the taxpayer.' He looked very uncomfortable. I said, 'You should simply publish your income-tax returns, and your pay and allowances should be settled independently and all expenses claims should be published, so everybody knows what they are.'

Thursday 14 May
Ruth is working on the new book, *Letters to my Grandchildren*. Tony Whittome had made a few suggestions, and she checked one or two of them with me, but I was so tired! I don't think I've ever felt so tired before.

Elliot Morley has been suspended from the Parliamentary Labour Party. Andrew MacKay, who was Cameron's close friend and his adviser, has resigned because he was caught doing something or another.

I feel utterly dejected and disgusted by it. I can't tell you! And the fact that I was an MP is now a source of embarrassment really!

Hilary is absolutely in the clear, as you'd expect. I am arguing that all expenses claims should be published as soon as they are made, and then they can be scrutinised, and the Register of Members' Interests should become a Register of Candidates' Interests, so you know all about your parliamentary candidates before you vote for them. And that democracy is the transfer of the people's power, on trust, to an MP for five years, for a parliament, and when that MP is elected, he owes an obligation to his constituents, to his colleagues in the Party and to his conscience, and those three loyalties have to be made clear and public.

It's no good paying back the money you've improperly taken. I mean, it's like robbing a bank and then, when you're charged by the police, you give them a cheque for the money you stole and hope it's all over! I don't want to sound censorious, I don't want to get into muck-raking and I don't want to discuss individuals, but I think certain principles can be established.

Saturday 16 May
The MPs' expenses story goes on and on. Gerald Kaufman asked for
£8,000 for a TV.

Sunday 17 May
John Grice picked me up at 11.30, got me to the Warwick Arts
Theatre at the university campus in Warwick at about quarter past
one, and I did the sound-check and the lights and all that. Then I
went and sat in the open and smoked my pipe and met people as
they came in. It's a lovely way of doing it! A guy called Steve, who's an
Associate Professor of Politics at Warwick, sat on stage and repeated
the questions to me. I began with my opinion of the expenses' crisis
– I feel so angry and disgusted and disappointed, and also I see this
now is being developed into a major attack on democracy – oh,
everyone's corrupt and all that. I rang Ruth when I got back because,
when I was there, one of the people who asked me to sign their book
was the actress (Patricia Gallimore) who plays the part of Pat in *The
Archers*, so I thought Ruth would be pleased about that, which she
was, being an *Archers* addict.

I began reading the proofs of the new book and, I must say, it's not
bad . . . it isn't bad . . . I think it's going to be all right.

Monday 18 May
The car was returned after its MOT: £701! I think this is my last year
of the car, because I've had a lot of taxis, and I still have to pay the
tax, the insurance, the parking permit, the petrol.

I had lunch, and was so tired after lunch I had a bit of a snooze.

The Speaker was confronted today. He made a statement and was
confronted with eighteen Members of Parliament who've put down
a Motion calling for him to resign. He said as it was an Early Day
Motion there is no requirement to debate it. Well, my understanding
was: if you put down a Motion of censure on the Speaker or the
Deputy Chairman of Ways and Means, it automatically is debated.
So I think he's been advised wrongly about that. But the question
is: what will the political parties do? If Gordon Brown threw his
weight behind it, the Speaker would have to go, but I think a lot of
people may feel, as I do, that he's being made the scapegoat to take

attention off MPs and their fiddles. Anyway, we shall see.

The NEC is meeting in the morning to discuss reselecting candidates. The Party is thinking of expelling candidates, and that's right. We're in a state of complete confusion, and it's frightening. It's a turning point in British parliamentary history – of that I have absolutely no doubt.

I heard today that Esther Rantzen might be standing against Margaret Moran, and if that sort of thing were to happen – if the end product is that serious political parties are replaced by stars and entertainers, like Arnold Schwarzenegger in California – then it would be the end of the whole democratic system as we know it. I think the whole parliamentary structure is now simply collapsing.

Tuesday 19 May
At 2.30 the Speaker announced his resignation. It was a brutal treatment of him by the House of Commons, but he hasn't been handling the difficulties as well as he might. But it's partly class prejudice and partly that they've got to find a scapegoat.

We've entered a new era. Politics are never going to go back to where they are now. What the outcome will be, I don't know, but the total discrediting of Parliament is a major feature of it all. I'm going to try and come out with positive ideas, and go further and say get rid of the Lords and have an English Parliament and a Federal Senate.

Monday 25 May
Well, it's about quarter past ten, and I'm just going to post my letters, and I hope to get to bed by 10.30 or 11.00, but if I get time I might read a bit more of Chris Mullin's *Diaries*, which are a perfectly amusing account really of the corruption of a New Labour Government. But he writes very well and, to do him credit, his expenses were absolutely zero.

At 6.55, on Channel 5, I watched the 'No 2 EU' broadcast by Bob Crow's group, who are putting up candidates in the European elections. They had a lot of comments from a lot of people against the EU, including mine.

Alan Johnson, in what is widely interpreted by the press as a leadership bid, called for proportional representation in elections

– the list system. Ed Miliband has been joining in discussions with Helena Kennedy. It takes people's minds off the economic crisis a bit, but of course the hatred of MPs that is being stimulated is really quite frightening, and in a way it's a hatred of the democratic process, which the powerful have always hated because it challenges their power. So we'll have to watch this one very, very carefully.

Thursday 28 May
I haven't been reporting the Expenses scandal news but, today, Julie Kirkbride, Andrew MacKay's wife, decided not to stand again. Margaret Moran also decided not to stand again – she was a former Whip. It's simply ghastly! But I don't think anything very serious, by way of reform, is being contemplated by the people at the top.

Friday 29 May
The Guardian this morning reports that fifty-two Labour MPs have asked for peerages. These are the ones who think they'll be defeated. I don't know whether or not any of them are involved in the scandals about expenses, but fifty-two Labour MPs! They just regard a peerage as something they're entitled to, and it's all part of the whole racket. I don't think Brown could do it. I suppose the Speaker will be made a peer, because that's part of the tradition, but I think all that will end, which means there'll be a lot of bitterness among Labour MPs who thought they were entitled to peerages.

Sunday 31 May
Well, it was another perfect summer day, absolutely beautiful! It was yesterday, and is forecast for tomorrow.

If Brown goes, I think Alan Johnson would succeed, with Ed Miliband as Number 2. Things might improve, but I doubt it.

Tony Byrne turned up this morning, bless his heart, and he put up a rail along the path so that I won't slip on the ice and break my hip.

Monday 1 June
The first day of summer today. I set the alarm for four, woke up at three and had breakfast and a bath and shaved and slowly dressed,

and came downstairs and packed for Hull and Middlesbrough. It's now half-past seven in the morning.

John Grice picked me up at eight and took me to the Ramada Jarvis hotel to address the Humberside Institute of Directors – there must have been 300 there, sitting around tables. I spoke. I was a bit nervous, made a few jokes – it went down very well. There was a very nice guy called Philip who looked after me.

Then John drove me up to Middlesbrough, to the Crypt of the Town Hall – about the same number of people. It looked rather like a miners' welfare, with people sitting around tables. I spoke there, and that went well.

We got home in four hours, so that was a 23.5-hour day, and I was absolutely exhausted!

Tuesday 2 June
Stephen told me that David Miliband has refused to move from the Foreign Office to make room for Peter Mandelson, and if that's true, it's another example of the failure of Gordon Brown. I think it must be quite likely now that Brown will have to introduce his reshuffle just after the European and local-election results are announced, and if he can't force it through because people won't go, then I think he's going to go, and then we're going to have Alan Johnson and a September election. So I think that's the way that New Labour will finally die.

Alan Simpson rang. He was so infuriated by the way that Ian Gibson had been treated! Ian was called to a 'Star Chamber' of three members of the Executive and two officials, told he couldn't bring anyone with him except a silent witness, so he brought the chairman of his local party; his local party supported him 100 per cent, but the witness wasn't allowed to say anything. Ian said that what he'd done had been specifically and explicitly approved by the Fees Office; but the 'tribunal' ruled that he couldn't stand again as a Labour candidate. Alan was absolutely incensed by this, and said that he felt inclined to support Ian, if he forces a by-election and fights the seat as an independent, which he might just do.

Wednesday 3 June
Hazel Blears has resigned from her Cabinet post. I must say, I

personally was very delighted because I greatly dislike her, but of course it has started a new explosion of rumour and gossip and stories in the media on eve-of-poll for local elections and Europe.

I was picked up about ten o'clock and taken to the Skinners' Hall by a cab driver. The Worshipful Company of Skinners in medieval times used to trade in fur – only the aristocracy could trade in fur, common people traded in rabbit or wool. Of course that all disappeared, but they're very, very wealthy, and I was told when I was there they are actually funding two academies: so medieval money is still distorting the cause of democracy – so interesting.

Anyway, it was a beautiful place, like a palace! Glorious, and apparently it's used now for events. I was there to be filmed by RTE, about the Irish crisis in '69. I did about a half-hour interview with them. What was interesting, and I never knew it before: documents have come to light that Jack Lynch, the Taoiseach, the Prime Minister of the Republic of Ireland, had said that he might possibly intervene militarily in Northern Ireland. I didn't think for a moment that the British would have wanted to go to war; the Americans would have intervened, and so on. I gave the best answers I could.

To College Green opposite the Commons, where I found Jack Straw and Michael Heseltine giving interviews. I developed the argument that I thought the power of anger to get rid of MPs was a very positive thing. People were angry, not just about this, but about the Lisbon Treaty, about the war, about bailing out the bankers and not helping industry.

I said I didn't think Gordon Brown would go (I've changed my mind since yesterday!), because the Tory Party give all their Leaders a ten-minute standing ovation and then put a knife in the back when they fail, but in the Labour Party we elect Leaders, argue with them till the day they go, and they go the day they want to go.

At the end of it Jon Snow said to me, 'I agree with every word you said.'

Oh, I had an email from Gordon Brown – just a standard email, sent to everybody. It said 'Dear Tony', and how all the money I'd given to Party funds had humbled him and so on.

Tomorrow is polling day and, at the moment, I think I'm going to vote for Bob Crow's 'No 2 EU, Yes to Democracy' candidate. I think this really is a vote I should have been allowed to give in the Lisbon referendum, which they wouldn't allow me to do. So, I put it in my diary, honestly and truthfully. I feel guilty about doing it because I'm a Labour man through and through, but that betrayal on the Lisbon Treaty is an outrage and I don't have any option.

Thursday 4 June
Today was the day of the European poll and some local elections, though not in London.

Walking in the bright sunshine to the polling station and back, my thoughts were on democracy and how important it is and how it's being eroded.

I had two letters today. One was a long manuscript letter from a woman who said that, in the Sixties, she worked for the Post Office as a telephonist, got married and then gave up the job. She was then divorced and applied for it again, and they said they couldn't give it to anyone who'd been employed before. So she raised it with Derek Page, her local MP, and he raised it with me, and apparently it was all sorted. She said she'd never written to thank me. It was a lovely letter!

The second letter was from a man somewhere in England, signed John Bull, bitterly attacking me and Parliament, and saying Enoch Powell was driven out, and ending up with 'You are a traitor'.

The BBC ignored the election almost completely. Tomorrow, when we know the results, the whole thing will be covered: 'another crushing blow for Brown'. It is not a good public-service organisation.

Friday 5 June
The press are going berserk about Gordon Brown: could he survive, will he go, who'll take over.

The reshuffle is going on today, with more resignations – I forget who they all are. Caroline Flint has gone. Geoff Hoon has gone.

All the speculation today is: can Gordon survive? When I was asked, I simply said, 'Well, if you've just lost your job, your home might be repossessed, you've got a son in Afghanistan – do you really worry who's in or out of the Cabinet? What's wrong is the policies are wrong. We don't want to change the leadership, but change the policies!' Of course all the journalists knew it was true, but they didn't like my saying it.

Saturday 6 June

Up about six. Went to get myself breakfast and forgot to light the gas. It was quite funny.

I then got a cab to the Central Hall Westminster – I shouldn't have done, but I was so bloody tired – for the Liberty seventy-fifth anniversary (that's the old National Council for Civil Liberties). I was invited by Shami Chakrabarti, who is the Chief Executive, an old friend of mine.

Lord Bingham was there; he is a former Lord Chief Justice and a very strong supporter of Liberty. He made a very powerful speech in support of the Human Rights Act – pointed out how the police had treated the unemployed in the 1930s, and the miners and so on. I suppose he's a bit younger than me because, when I spoke to him afterwards, he said that, as a student, he'd come to hear me present my case on the House of Lords, in court in 1961. So he probably is seventy now, I should think, just retired.

In the order of speaking: Jack Straw; Dominic Grieve, who is the Tory Shadow; Ken Macdonald, QC, who is a former Director of Public Prosecutions; Kevin Maguire; and, finally, Yasmin Alibhai-Brown. Each spoke for only about five minutes. Jack Straw said to me, 'You and Caroline founded New Labour', which I thought was a load of rubbish, but still!

Sunday 7 June

European election results are not in yet, but it's obvious that Labour is going to do badly – low turnout. It will give another great surge to the anti-Brown campaign. And Monday, tomorrow, the Parliamentary Party is meeting, and there will be criticism. Brown is entirely dependent on Mandelson now. He brought Mandelson in to save him from Miliband. He's now promoted Mandelson, as a compensation for not making him Foreign Secretary, which David Miliband would not agree to, so Mandelson is now Lord President of the Council, First Secretary of State, and he's taking over another department. If Mandelson, at this stage, were to say publicly that Brown should go, he would go. Brown has to do everything Mandelson wants, so the Post Office part-privatisation will go ahead, and Mandelson is on all the bulletins, looking very confident, whereas Brown looks worried. Some people booed him when he arrived in France for the D-Day celebrations.

The way I look at it is: the Tory press wants, obviously, to have a Tory Government following right-wing policies, and if they can't have that, and couldn't at the end of the Major Government, they'd rather have a Labour Government introducing Tory policies. But now, when the Labour Government is unpopular, they don't want to support that, so they'll go back to the Tory Party and hope that, if Tories get there, they'll get Tory policies again.

I'll never see a Labour Government again in my lifetime, but it's an interesting period, and my *Diaries* will cover quite an interesting period: the beginning of Brown, after Blair goes in 2007, right up to the development of British politics after a couple of years of the Tory Government, and that will be a very interesting period to record.

Monday 8 June
There were programmes all night about the European elections. Labour was behind UKIP and the Tories, and, in the West Country, was virtually assassinated. Two BNP candidates were elected. We got 15 per cent of the vote cast, but only 35 per cent of the electorate voted, so the Labour vote, as compared to the whole voting population, was 5.3 per cent! Quite incredible!

I had a phone call, just after eight, from Jean Corston, saying that Peter Townsend, her husband, died at midnight, and she just wanted to let me know. She said, 'I can't speak now.' But she married him in 1985 and . . . he was a great and a most distinguished socialist, thinker and progressive – a remarkable man.

Then Ruth went off, and my grandson Jonathan came to lunch. He'll know his final results on Monday.

At the Parliamentary Labour Party meeting tonight, where Brown was supposed to have been removed, only two people spoke against him: Charles Clarke and Fiona Mactaggart. He got thunderous applause from the PLP because they realise that, if they ditch him now, they are absolutely finished. So, undoubtedly, we will go on to an election next May, when I imagine we will be very severely defeated, and then that's a whole new era in British politics.

Tuesday 9 June

I had a phone call that my car was impounded this morning. I had to go to the Chelsea Car Pound to collect it. It cost £260. The guy who took all the particulars was reading the Bible, so I commented upon that, and he was a Nigerian Pentecostal. He said the Bible is absolutely true, and gay activities are condemned in the Bible, and the Bible is the spirit. I said, 'Who created God?' and he said God was a spirit that had always been there, and God didn't create the world in seven days, he created it in six days, and on the seventh day he rested. Quite an interesting theological discussion.

Then, a Ghanaian, who took me to my car; he was a Catholic and told me that, in Accra, there was an exhibition commemorating Kwame Nkrumah. So a little theology in the middle of a horrible experience of having your car impounded made it more tolerable.

Thursday 11 June

I rang Miriam Karlin, the actor, who had written to me. She was terribly low. She said she wanted to die. I think she's had mouth cancer, and she broke her hip; a couple of days ago she said she had a duodenal ulcer that burst, and she was absolutely desperate to die. She said one of the doctors whose signature is required to go to Dignitas or whatever has refused to sign, so I cheered her up as best I could.

Friday 12 June

Tony Whittome arrived, just after 9.30, on his bike, on his way to work, and we gave him the typescript of *Letters to my Grandchildren*. I was so relieved! Ruth has done a phenomenal job. It's not ghost-written, because I threw the ideas at her, but she's shaped them up in a fantastic way, and I said in the acknowledgements that Ruth is my very best friend, which is true.

The next – possibly last – volume of *The Diaries* is going to be called 'The Dawn of a New Era', a suggestion Ruth made! It was lovely, and we had lunch.

Then, in the afternoon, at two o'clock, Grahame Herbert came to discuss the Benn safe-seat. He's so charming and friendly, and we did agree, in effect, that the prototype he had made need not include a little pull-up handle because most modern suitcases have them, so it would then be a more simple attachment to a suitcase. I said we should have five prototypes made: one to attach to a very decorative suitcase; one for a backpack; and so on. It is a very slow business.

Then Hilary rang this morning on his way back from the Cabinet and said they'd had a good two hours.

Oh, wait a minute – one thing! Hazel Blears appeared on television tonight apologising for resigning just before the elections, which might have damaged the Party. She apologised for so many things, and I think the reason that she's done so is that there's a lot of criticism of her in her own constituency, among Party members, because they feel that she let the Party down, which of course she did. Although she may have some support among the officers locally, it could damage her in the next election if she stands, so I thought that was amusing. It confirmed what I've always thought about Hazel Blears, who's a complete empty-head.

Saturday 13 June
Miliband gave an interview, in *The Guardian*, in which he said he very nearly left the Cabinet but decided to stay. Peter Mandelson, in the *Telegraph*, said there would be a new threat to Brown in the autumn. What Mandelson was really saying was, 'You still need me.' And what Miliband is saying is, 'I really agreed with Purnell, but didn't leave the Cabinet.' I think, probably, the Blairite plotters said to Miliband, 'Don't you resign – stay in the Government, because we will need you for our Leader later.' I imagine that's what it's really about.

Hazel Blears, meanwhile, is in terrible trouble because, as a result of resigning when she did, and wearing that brooch that said 'Rocking the boat', she's really annoyed her local party. Next week she faces a vote of no-confidence, so she's now all over the media, regretting and apologising.

Anyway, I went and caught the 148 to the House of Commons, met Ruth, and Alison McPherson, who's typed all my *Diaries*, joined us with her husband, Ross, and their ten-year-old daughter, Jade. We had arranged to take them round the House of Commons, but found it was shut and locked, so I had a word with the police and they said, 'You're always welcome', so we got through! When we went through the security, there were about eight or ten plain-clothed men in a group and I asked, 'Who are they?' and they said, 'They're armed policemen who are going to do service in the House and they're being trained in security.' It was rather weird. Anyway, we couldn't get into the Lords' Chamber or the Commons' Chamber, but we wandered round and saw quite a lot. Then we went and had lunch in a restaurant in Whitehall where, when I went to pay, they said, 'We don't take plastic', so, fortunately, I had enough cash. Caught a taxi and dropped them off at Regent's Park because they were going to a play, and came home and sat in the garden.

Sunday 14 June
I didn't come down till nearly eleven this morning.

Read the papers. *The Observer* is rubbish! It's just gossip, gossip, talk, talk – it's an awful paper! I think I'd rather have the *Sunday Telegraph*.

The Iranian elections got good coverage this morning, and of course all the media coverage was that the elections were fixed; people shouting in the streets of Tehran. If it had been people shouting at the G20 of course, in London, it would be 'violent behaviour'. But I then watched Al Jazeera, which was much more balanced. It did say there were critics, there had been incidents, but it said that 24 per cent of the GDP (the Gross Domestic Product) in Iran goes to food subsidies for the poor, so I expect Ahmadinejad does have substantial support and the people you saw demonstrating are all middle-class people.

I rang Mrs Mac because she's eighty-one today.

I watched *Notting Hill*, which I've watched a million times!

Monday 15 June
Ruth led a clean-up of the kitchen and the hallway. We went through it meticulously together and threw out tons of stuff, and it was really successful.

At 3.30 I heard the Prime Minister announce there would be

an Iraq Inquiry, which is really a secret Iraq Inquiry, with four civil servants and academics; they're going to deal with the whole history of our relations with Iraq, over about ten years. It's just a commissioned official government history, and doesn't deal, critically, with why we went to war with Iraq. It's in secret – a complete fraud.

I heard that Jonathan has won a first at Oxford Brookes – it's absolutely fabulous! I rang Hilary.

Tuesday 16 June
The Iranian crisis is developing in a very interesting way, because there now seems to be some indication of a recount in some areas, although nobody is disputing that Ahmadinejad has won. Well, people are disputing it, but, worldwide, it's accepted that he is the President. I'm . . . looking at it quite independently, I think a lot of this may be a resistance of the people to the Islamic revolution, which leaves the clerics in charge of everything, although the elections allow presidents to emerge who have political power, but the overall control is in the hands of the clerics, and I think that may be being challenged. It's very interesting.

Wednesday 17 June
Turned on the telly, and I saw Michael Martin making his farewell speech as Speaker, and presiding over Prime Minister's Questions, the last for him. He paid tribute to all the people who'd helped him in his office, and so on – he's like a shop steward – and then he did make one or two critical comments of the way the House had handled the expenses business. Later in the day, I rang to see if I could pop in and see him, but he'd already gone home to Glasgow.

I was collected by car and taken to the Islam Channel to have a discussion on the Iraq Inquiry, announced by the Government. Anas Altikriti, a Muslim whom I know very well, was in the chair. Jonathan Freedland from the *Guardian* was in the studio with me, and Frank Judd was at a remote interview, and somebody called Professor Miller, who'd written a book about distortion by the media – a very interesting discussion, and we reached complete agreement.

Taken to the Commons. Went to Portcullis House and had tea with Ruth and Paul Flynn and his assistant, Jayne. We were sitting right next to my portrait, which has been put in the atrium of Portcullis House.

Thursday 18 June
I wrote a letter to the Speaker, Michael Martin, and thanked him very much for his friendship.

I also did a draft letter to the Iraq Inquiry, offering to give evidence, which I've got to think about.

Wrote a letter to *The Times* supporting John Bercow as Speaker. He rang me about it and I thought about it, checked it with him and sent it to them, telling them it was exclusive. It'll go in on Saturday.

I did a letter in support of Chris Knight, who's been sacked by the University of East London for his activities during the Alternative Summit.

I got a Tube to Tottenham Court Road and walked to the Groucho Club, to a dinner for the award of the Martha Gelhorn Prize to the Best Journalist of the Year. John Pilger had asked me, and I was sitting next to him, between him and Christine Lamb, who is a correspondent who's reported from Afghanistan and Zimbabwe. Alan Rusbridger, the Editor of the *Guardian*, was there; Don Macintyre, now from the *Independent*; and a lot of other people . . . Sandy Matthews and his wife, who said we'd met over the years in the peace group down in Devon, where they live.

At one stage Don Macintyre from the *Independent* said to me, 'If you were Speaker, what would you do?' So I made the point about strengthening the Legislature against the Executive; and simple points, that I was supporting Bercow, and Rusbridger picked that up.

Came home, coughed a lot.

Friday 19 June
I'm feeling my age very much more. I find it a struggle to get upstairs. I'm unsteady on my legs. If I go down the escalator, I have to hold on very tight. I have to have hold of a railing when I go up and down stairs. I doze and am tired all the time. But there you are, I've just got to get used to that. My mind is okay.

Hilary phoned and had a word. He made a statement yesterday about climate change.

Saturday 20 June

The Times printed my letter about the Speakership, supporting John Bercow, and gave it pride of place; and then I bought the *Daily Telegraph*, which had a supplement with all the claims that had been made by every Member of Parliament over the last four years. It reveals a lot of things, one of which is that many people claimed for council tax that was higher than the actual figure. Today it has been indicated the police may come and interview some MPs, and that's an incredible thing to happen but absolutely right.

I did some office jobs and had lunch and a snooze.

Then, after lunch, I caught the Tube to the Embankment and walked for about a mile almost, to Blackfriars Bridge, to speak at the Tamil demonstration. I got there early and lots of people came up and said hello, and they asked me if I'd go on first, so I did. I don't know how many of them understood English, but my speech was the first one I've made about the Tamils – I hope I got it right. I've got it on tape. Then I chatted to a few people.

When I got home I realised I hadn't sent a birthday card to Jean Strutt (née Jean Davidson), with whom I shared a pram in the late '20s. She's been a widow for twenty-eight years, I think she said. Her husband, the Reverend Charles Strutt, died in 1981.

Just as I was going to bed I had a phone call saying: would I stay up for an hour to do an interview with George Galloway about the Speakership? He'd seen my letter in *The Times* calling for support for John Bercow. I said I would, and then worried that if he – George – endorsed Bercow, that would ruin his chances. Anyway, he did ring and we had a discussion on the Speakership, we had a discussion about Iran and the coverage, about Israel and the Middle East.

Sunday 21 June

Radio Wales phoned at seven o'clock in the morning about the Speakership, and then I did another interview with LBC.

Tony Byrne was in this morning, scrubbing the steps and the front pathway, getting rid of all the green slime and moss. He said to me, 'If the BBC man slipped down the stairs, he'd take you to the cleaner's!' He's very thoughtful and kind.

Then, at 2.15, John Grice picked me up and drove me to Leeds – a beautiful day! Went to the Grand Theatre in Leeds, 600 people there. It's a beautiful theatre, built in 1878. I sat out in the front, smoked my pipe, signed books, just outside the theatre, so that I could smoke, and lots of people came up. It was such fun! Then did the lecture, and very, very warm indeed – lots of warm references to Hilary, which was lovely.

Home about twenty-five past one because there were roadworks on the M1, which delayed everything.

Monday 22 June

Was picked up to do a programme for the BBC on the day the war broke out, and actually it was a long interview about what life was like in the war – what was the food like, what were the clothes like? I'd taken my Air Raid Precaution book, photographs of me in the Home Guard uniform, and I talked about the war and rationing.

I was driven straight from there to the *World at One*, to do an interview on the Speakership election, which is today.

John Bercow came first, led in the first round, and then that knocked a few votes off Margaret Beckett and other people; and later, by quite a clear majority, he defeated Sir George Young and was taken to the chair. He's the first Jew ever to be elected Speaker of the House of Commons. He made a good little speech.

I did another couple of interviews, and the point I'm making now is the real issue of reasserting the Legislature against the Executive, the Commons against the Government, holding the Government to account, and how you can't go on having MPs as sort of elected civil servants, told what to do; and about the role of the Select Committees, and so on.

Tuesday 23 June

Jan Henriksson, this Norwegian film producer, arrived nearly two hours late to do this interview on NHS privatisation. We sat in the back garden. He brought with him Dr Julian Tudor Hart, who has written many, many books on the Health Service. He's a GP himself, very, very committed to the Welsh miners. And also Allyson Pollock, who's written so much about privatisation and the folly of private financing of the NHS. I liked her very much. I had met her before.

I think I mentioned – I hope I did – at the beginning, that Dave had put a little note about Mike's death sixty-five years ago in *The Times* this morning, and actually the *Telegraph* rang up to ask about it, so there may be a little bit in the *Telegraph* tomorrow. It's nice to remember Mike. He was only twenty-two. God, younger than my grandchildren, and he was killed at that age.

I caught the bus, went to Portcullis House, had a cup of tea and went up to the Royal Society of Chemistry Parliamentary Links Day. Steve had managed to get John Bercow to speak and he arrived, with his secretary and somebody else, and gave me a huge hug! It was very sweet of him. And then he made a very sensible speech about science and politics, paid a warm tribute to Stephen for organising it, to Hilary and then he said, 'And Tony Benn, one of the greatest Parliamentarians of our lifetime, and I'm going to give him tea – we'll have it on the Terrace so he can smoke his pipe.'

Later, I wanted to see the Speaker's procession, so I stood in the Speaker's Corridor. As Bercow came by, I bowed to him, and he smiled in a nice way.

Later, I wanted particularly to hear Bercow make his statement from the chair, and he said three things. He said, 'I hope Members' contributions, questions, will be brief; I hope Ministers will be brief in reply; and I hope no statements presented to the House are released in advance to the media in the morning' – i.e. if there's a statement, the House is going to hear it first, which is a thing I've long wanted. I thought it was very, very good.

Thursday 25 June
John Rees arrived. John has been shunted out of the leadership of the SWP because they don't like the amount of attention he gives to the Stop the War movement. But now he's got a commission from the Islam Channel, and he brought along a programme he made on fascism, which I thought was excellent, about the BNP.

Saturday 27 June
Train to Castle Cary, where I was met by Chris and driven by car to Glastonbury, to the Green Field. Now, I've been to Glastonbury

many, many years, but I always get so excited! It was a beautiful sunny day and there were all these people, in their tents and walking on both sides of the road, and the pedestrians took precedence over the cars, and everyone was so cheerful. I had an armband which allowed me through.

I got to the Green Field terribly early at about a quarter to one, and I wasn't on till four. So they gave me a cup of tea, put me in a tent and I went to sleep for a couple of hours.

When I woke up there was a woman next to me – I think she'd come from one of the little yurts and I hadn't noticed her.

Then I went and spoke at the Green Field. There were about 500 people there, and it was a question-and-answer session. So I didn't have to say anything; I just answered questions. I gave exactly the same answers as I give, as you'd expect, at all my lectures, at Windsor and Oxford and Salisbury and everywhere. This really interested me, because you get the same reaction to the same comments at a left audience as you do at right-wing and ordinary audiences, so there must be some coming-together.

I was waiting to be taken back and there was a young Zambian called Chile Price, twenty-one, singing. He'd won an award for songs warning against gun crimes, and so on. He was a very sweet boy. I liked him very much! We both shared a lift to the station. He's a Born Again Christian fundamentalist. He kept saying, 'Don't you believe in the Second Coming? Don't you believe in Armageddon? Don't you believe, as it says in the Bible, that Israel will have to conquer the Middle East before the Second Coming?' It was sort of – except that he was such a nice lad – it was sort of frightening nonsense, and I tried to throw a little bit of doubt on it.

On the train, we had a fascinating seminar all the way to Paddington, nearly a couple of hours. There was a retired vicar and his wife, a medical scientist, a Post Office manager of forty-five, and we talked all the way to Paddington.

Sunday 28 June
Got *The Observer*. It is rubbish! Anyway, there was a lot about Michael Jackson; his death has been front-page banner headlines for three days.

I had a meal, and then watched the latest *Bremner, Bird and Fortune* on 'The Recovery', which was quite hilarious.

Monday 29 June

I fed the birds, and the black cat who lives nearby came and sat at the window and tempted me out again, but wouldn't agree to sit on my lap.

I signed and posted the letters Ruth had done.

Then I had a phone call from the Ramadhan Foundation, inviting me to go to Kuala Lumpur in December for a peace conference, which is going to be attended by thirty-six countries. I looked at my diary and I just can't do it.

Incidentally, I spoke at their peace conference recently and I got a cheque from the Malaysian Government for £1,000. Well, I can't take money from foreign governments, so I wrote back and thanked them and said I was giving it to Crisis, which I will do.

Tuesday 30 June

I went to Paddington to collect Jean Corston, who was coming to London for the first time since her husband Peter Townsend's death and was very nervous so I said I'd pick her up, and I took her in a taxi to the House of Lords. She's still in shock from Peter's death. It was the first time I'd ever taken a taxi right to the door of the House of Lords, and a guy in a top hat and a red coat greeted us as we got out.

Stephen and I caught the 4.17 train to Shoreham, for a meeting of Emily's local Labour Party. We walked to Emily's committee room. It's owned by her constituency agent, Ricky, who is a music teacher, I think; and they have this shop which doesn't really sell anything, but apparently, under planning permission, it can't be turned into a committee room.

Pratima was there – that's Nita's mother, and also Emily, and a girl called Charlotte, who is a friend of Emily's from Wadham College in Oxford.

Anyway we sat there, and Stephen took a million pictures, and then we drove to the Labour Hall . . . it was the sixtieth anniversary of it having been built, after the old one was bombed in the war.

Ricky's wife, Sally, was there, a very friendly woman, and Ricky and Sally really keep Emily going.

Joy Hurcombe was there. She'd sent me a lot of background about that hall. It has a rich history. It also accommodated miners' wives and children during the miners' strike.

I was a little bit careful in the meeting because Emily's views are quite different from mine, but I explained what I thought as best I could, and answered questions. There were about eighty people there.

Then we left, and Stephen – with Emily, Pratima and Charlotte in the car, and me in the front – drove me to East Croydon, and I got home about quarter past twelve. I was absolutely whacked!

Wednesday 1 July
I was very tired. Very hot day – thirty-two degrees, I think.

The Al Jazeera TV channel is doing a half-hour profile. They're doing it of a number of people, under a heading called 'Voices of Truth'. We sat in the garden and I did a long interview with them, and then they photographed me, typing away in the office, and so on.

At 3.30 John Grice collected me and drove me to Lichfield to give a lecture in the Garrick Theatre, a beautiful theatre, built six years ago. Al Jazeera arrived – they'd had permission to film – and I sat and chatted to people, and then I gave my lecture, and it was okay. It was an older audience, friendly.

John drove me home. I slept for an hour each way in the car, which I desperately needed.

Michael Jackson's death is still echoing along. And, oh, Mandelson announced today that he was postponing the part-privatisation of the Post Office.

National Express, which owned the East England rail-line from London to Edinburgh, has failed to deliver, and so their franchise is being withdrawn, so we've nationalised one rail-line, and the whole privatisation of the railways is now seen as a totally crazy thing to have done.

Cameron is just so negative and juvenile in his criticism.

So, on the whole, I can see a possibility that Labour might win. I don't entirely rule it out. Public opinion is very volatile. Cameron and Clegg are so ineffective, and if Brown – having taken this huge hammering – survives, that will be proof of his strength. But when I look at people like John Reid and Patricia Hewitt and others, who held office in Government and are now working for companies engaged in Government contracts and privatisation, it's very revolting.

Thursday 2 July
Al Jazeera turned up again, after lunch, from 2.15 to 5.30, and it was just endless! I was an instrument for their performance. I suppose, to get a half-hour friendly profile on Al Jazeera, which reaches about seventy million people, is worth it, but by God, it couldn't be more exhausting!

Friday 3 July
I got ten hours in bed, which did help.
   Went off to Trafalgar Square with Al Jazeera to film, and it was an extraordinary experience! The Square was all decked up for a big Gay Pride event.
   There was one woman watching us, sucking a lollipop. So, in a gap in filming, I said to her, 'What do you do?' and she said, 'Oh, I'm a lady of the street.' So I said, 'Are you a prostitute?' and she said, 'Yes.' Perhaps she came up thinking I was a possible customer . . . She said, 'I know nothing about politics – are you Labour or Conservative?' So I said, 'Labour' and she wandered off.
   Then we moved further down after that, to the southern corner of Trafalgar Square, to get a picture of South Africa House, and two black police community-support officers came out: 'You can't film here because of security and you can't film the police.' So I said, 'We're not trying to film you.' One of them recognised me and she said okay, so we did get it.

Saturday 4 July
I have been invited tonight to Shami Chakrabarti's . . . to what's called her eightieth birthday. She and her husband are both forty. It's in the Soho Hotel, said 'Dress smart', so I've got to put on a smart suit and get a bus to Oxford Circus. I had to walk down Dean Street, which

was closed and absolutely packed with people who'd been attending the gay and lesbian celebrations in Trafalgar Square.

I went to this hotel, a frightfully fancy hotel – it must have cost the earth to have a huge party there. It was packed, and I didn't recognise anybody! Then Peter Kellner of YouGov came up to me, and we sat on a couch and talked for a bit. He said that he had written a book about democracy and included the speech I wanted to make when I was kept out of the House of Commons in 1961 after winning the Bristol by-election. We had a friendly talk. I've always been rather suspicious about Peter Kellner, but he runs YouGov, this public-opinion organisation, which is very effective.

I gave Shami a hug. I didn't see anybody else actually that I knew, so I wandered round and came back out into the street, which was packed still, and I walked down Dean Street towards Piccadilly Circus. One middle-aged woman, early fifties, with her friend, wanted to be photographed with me. She said she looked after old people, so I said, 'Well, I'm a candidate for that' and then I wandered on. I stood at Piccadilly Circus, trying to catch a 94 bus – it was so hot on the bus I actually did think I was going to collapse. Anyway, I got safely home to Notting Hill Gate and walked back and went to bed.

Sunday 5 July
I had a lovely email from a guy called Mark Taylor, which I will read – I've put it in my archives:

> Tony,
>
> You probably don't remember me. I am one of thousands you have helped over the years. I came to see you, as a constituent (in Chesterfield). I was seeking a place in medical school and was having problems with funding, as I had already earned one degree. You supported my application for a discretionary award with the Derbyshire County Council. I'm eternally in your debt as, with your help, I received a grant and became a doctor – thank you.

So I sent him an immediate reply:

Dear Mark,

I was very touched to get your email and delighted to hear you've completed your medical degree and are now a doctor. What an achievement! Congratulations and thanks for all you're going to do to keep us all fit!

All the best for the future,

Tony

That's the sort of letter that does make life worthwhile.

Monday 6 July

There are twelve birds now coming into the garden because I'm feeding them so generously.

I had to go off to the hospital, and as I was walking through Notting Hill Gate a man of about thirty-five, rather well dressed, said, 'I was very pleased to see the article in the *Financial Times* by Lord Browne about you.' So I bought it, and it was an article, on page three of the *Financial Times*, saying Lord Browne recommends that we follow the advice of Benn – on my industrial policy. You could have knocked me down with a feather actually! Anyway, it was very amusing that somebody should now be recognising that an industrial policy that actually supports manufacturing industry is relevant.

I caught the Tube to London Bridge, walked to the hospital and I got there very early, and a twenty-six-year-old Jamaican nurse took particulars. She said she had a little baby of five, and she said she was a Jehovah's Witness. I said, 'Of course, you don't celebrate Christmas or Easter.' 'No!' she said. 'They were pagan events. But as you will remember,' she said, 'in the eighteenth century the Jehovah's Witnesses came into existence', as if somehow I was old enough to remember the eighteenth century.

Then I went to the waiting room and there was a man there with tattoos, a plumpish guy of about forty-five, I think, with tattoos all over his arm. So I said, 'What do you do?' 'Well,' he said, 'I'm a window cleaner. I only do window-cleaning in pubs.' He said, 'I used to be a drummer – I used to play in a band with Kylie Minogue, and she was such a lovely woman.' Then he said his wife was the manager of a dress shop at Westfield Shopping Centre. You know, in hospitals, it's like trains and boats, you sort of meet people quickly.

I got lost, and I asked a guy, 'How do you get out?' 'Oh,' he said, 'are you Mr Benn?' 'Yes.' I thought he was a cleaner. I said, 'What do you do?' 'Well,' he said, 'I'm a surgeon', and he took me all the way to show me out.

Tuesday 7 July

There was a massive thunderstorm – I mean, the water was pouring – the streets were full of pools of water. Water was pouring through the ceiling in the back corridor again, predictably.

Wednesday 8 July

Somebody from the BBC came to do an interview with me about the Moon landing in 1969. I remembered that there had been somebody who'd been round the Moon who came to see us, and I rang up Josh. It was Frank Borman – I'd forgotten his name.

I went to the Earls Court Literary Festival to a beautiful house, owned by a very wealthy Palestinian, who makes it available free to the festival organised by Keith Clancy, who is blind, with a dog called Oscar, and a partner called Sharon.

So I went in and there were about eighty people there, in this little room, and I gave my talk about *Letters to my Grandchildren*. There were a lot of good questions, and at the end I was asked to unveil a picture on the wall, which was a portrait of me, by artist Joy Thomson.

There's a G8 Summit in Italy. There was a statement made about the control of the banking system. It seems that they're doing even less than was done in 1946 when we nationalised the Bank of England and gave the Treasury control of the Bank of England, and the Bank of England control of every other bank and the right to decide what was a bank – pretty comprehensive. That was, of course, Hugh Dalton's achievement.

I begin to mark the days now, in terms of how many days left before I've got to stop smoking for my operation.

Thursday 9 July

Another bad night with dreams, and all my business about thinking

I'm going to die. I'm worried about my operation. I have to admit it to myself, that could be the reason.

Anyway, Ruth was in, and as soon as she arrived the whole place lit up! She was fantastic. She typed articles to which I was committed, forewords to books, letters, and oh, just wiped away my backlog almost completely!

The news today is all about the tapping of the telephones of famous people by the *News of the World*. The guy who was editor while some of this happened now works for David Cameron as his Press Officer. The thing could have some political impact.

Tuesday 14 July
Drove by car to the House of Commons to meet Mary Ratcliffe. Now, Mary has written to me over many, many years. She has the most beautiful handwriting. I met her in the Central Lobby and took her down to the Terrace for a cup of tea, with her granddaughter, Laura, who is twenty-two and is a singer.

Mary is eighty-four, I think about a month older than I am, and she was in the Wrens, the woman's naval service, during the war, working on the sort of decoding that was done at Bletchley Park. She writes poetry, and is very active in the hospice movement and helping old people, and acupuncture. I had tea with her, and later (after a meeting which we both attended) I took her to Paddington. I bought her ticket for thirty-nine quid and gave it to her and got her on a train that was leaving two or three minutes later. A very nice lady and she was so friendly and affectionate.

But a couple of things I realised . . . First of all, I realised that, at eighty-four – she's just had a new hip and new knee, which is something I haven't had – she's very frail, and she was very grateful that I had looked after her and taken her to the station and done everything. I sort of saw my own condition through her eyes. Here was I, a man of eighty-four, with a pacemaker, just about to have an operation, helping a woman of similar age and condition. I think she enjoyed it.

Wednesday 15 July
A lot of pigeons come into the garden: I go out and say 'Birdies!'

and they descend as soon as I've thrown the seed. There's a black cat who used to run away from me but now comes and scratches on the window till I go out and stroke him. So I have got pets without any responsibility for them. I watch the birds carefully, there's a robin that comes, a couple of jays, but mainly wood pigeons. It is like a scaled down version of humanity: food is the most important thing; security is the next most important thing.

Friday 24 July
Up at 4.30 and Josh, who stayed overnight, woke a bit later, and we set off just after six, by taxi, to Guy's Hospital. Met Mr Glass, the consultant urologist, and I had the prostate operation, called a TURP, from nine to ten. Taken to Room 25, in Florence Ward.

Josh looked in, as did Lissie. She's off on holiday tomorrow.

Saturday 25 July
Poor night. Mr Glass came in the morning.

Then, in the afternoon, Ruth arrived, with Dave, Barbara Campbell, Emma Mitchell, Andrew, her friend, and it was very sweet of them. They arrived with cards and presents.

They wheeled me down in a wheelchair, to the entrance of the hospital, where I could puff my pipe, which was very nice.

Then, after they'd gone, Josh and Liss came to visit.

Sunday 26 July
A better night.

Talking to the staff – I'll come to that, because I'm going to put my conclusions about all this in a moment, at the end of this section.

I watched TV on the machine that's over my bed.

Josh came in, and he took me down and we had another puff – I had another puff, outside the hospital.

There is a problem with my potassium and high blood pressure, for some reason.

Lissie looked in, in the evening, late, and she's going off on her holiday tomorrow morning, bless her heart.

Monday 27 July

Three young doctors looked in this morning for a talk, and then Mr Glass said I might be out tomorrow.

In the afternoon I had the catheter removed. I thought this was an absolute dream, but, to my amazement, I couldn't wee, and I had what I can only describe as an absolutely shattering pain because, every time I felt I wanted to wee, I'd go into the bathroom and I couldn't, and the pain got to the point where, at eleven o'clock at night, I had to press my buzzer and a very nice nurse called Marie came in, from a good socialist family, and she found a doctor, so at one o'clock in the morning, I had another catheter installed. The sense of relief was unbelievable!

Tuesday 28 July

The new catheter is working well. Glass looked in. I put the phone right to him so that he could talk to Josh.

Ruth was in, and we were planning the next few days. She's going to stay in London till the end of the week; they want me at St Thomas's on Monday.

Josh arrived to take me home. Ruth had everything beautifully set up. She'd turned the sofa in the living room into a bed for me, although actually, tonight, she slept on it, and I slept in my bed upstairs.

Then Josh went off, and I'll see him, no doubt, every day.

Dave rang, and his really big news is that Frances has been accepted for ordination as a minister in the Church of England. Oh, that's such wonderful news! My mum would be overjoyed, over the moon – well, she is over the moon – having campaigned all her life for the ordination of women, that her own granddaughter should be ordained. It's just unbelievable! Piers has also got some contract signed for a book he's writing.

I was very, very tired. I went to bed at about ten. Ruth was absolutely fabulous, just looking after me like a permanent ward sister.

Wednesday 29 July

Lissie phoned in the morning. I told her about Frances.

Ruth brought breakfast to me, in my bedroom.

I'm feeling very, very tired, but I was determined to bring this diary up-to-date, even though it's scribbled from notes and my memory is very shaky, but at least there is an account of what happened every day.

Hilary rang, from holiday, which was lovely.

Josh is due in at six. Ruth will be in before then.

My computer is on the blink at the moment, so I don't know how I'll cope with all that.

So, it's now a quarter-past five on the afternoon of Wednesday 29 July. Now, these are my thoughts about the operation. First of all, my personal feeling about it . . . I don't like to admit it but I was very worried about having a general anaesthetic and a prostate – I didn't know what they'd find – and I gradually accommodated myself to the idea that, if I did die, that was an appropriate thing to do at my age. People do die! When I was in Oxford recently, I went to the place where I met Caroline in 1948. And so I got that straight.

When I got into hospital I was very relaxed, but the experience in the hospital was quite extraordinary really. After all, I'm one of the few people who knew Aneurin Bevan – well, sat in Parliament with Aneurin – who set up the Health Service, and to see it in action is unbelievable. Absolutely perfect care for patients! I asked Mr Glass, the prostate surgeon, what it would have cost to have had it done privately and he said, 'Oh well, four or five thousand pounds.' They ought to tell everybody when they leave the hospital what it would have cost, or could have cost privately, so they realise what a privilege it is! What makes me so furious is that the BBC has an attack on the NHS every week, and the people they talk about it with, not one of them would use the NHS – they'd all be on private health insurance, BUPA, or something. That makes me so cross!

The other thing I noticed was how very young everybody was. My mother had such a respect for the doctor – 'The doctor will tell you' – and now the doctors who come in to see me are . . . well, only a little bit older than my grandchildren, in their twenties and thirties. They're so clean and so keen about everything, and so helpful and friendly. And the nurses were wonderful! There was an Indian woman called Menagai Rethinasamy, I said to her, 'I must thank you.' 'Oh no, no, you mustn't thank me – you must thank everybody!'

So I'm going to send a letter of thanks to Patricia Moberly, who visited me twice in the hospital and is the Chairman of Guy's and St Thomas's Trust and who is really responsible.

The other thing I noticed was, of course, I think 80 per cent of the staff at Guy's and St Thomas's are non-white – Indian, African, Chinese, Malaysian, and so on. It is a world community, and I like that, and that's another great change.

Of course the technology has changed because, with the help of the computer, any doctor would find my entire medical history, and that is something which you would never have been able to do in the past.

And then, thinking about death, I decided: Well, if I did die there, how appropriate! I'm eighty-four, I've had my life, and people would be sad, but it would be . . . it would be natural. The family would be very sad, but death at my age is not a tragedy. It's just something that happens.

Anyway, these are my thoughts on Wednesday afternoon, at twenty past five, about my time in hospital. I don't know how long I will last because, at the moment, I'm terribly tired, and the thought of going back to the sort of programme I had – have had for the last eight or nine years – is just terrifying. If I was told I had to go and do a meeting in Liverpool this afternoon, I just don't think I could do it. But maybe, if I have a break for the next two or three weeks, I could. We'll just have to see.

All right! Well, there you are! Ruth has been absolutely fabulous. She's such a kind friend, such a sweet person . . .

All the children have been supportive. Josh has all the strength of character that Caroline had, and Melissa has all her warmth. So, I'm enjoying life now. I'm living in the afterglow of . . . of my time with Caroline.

That's all there is, for my diary, unless something sensational happens tonight.

Chapter Seven

2009–2013: Life after diaries

The final entry by Tony Benn in his diaries was made on 29 July 2009 when what he thought was a routine operation was followed by a collapse from which recovery was slow, punctuated by a series of hospital stays. More importantly, the entry marked the end of diary-keeping since the fifteen-year-old schoolboy began to write a journal in earnest in 1940. From this remarkable record of British political life, amounting to tens of millions of words, nine edited volumes have been shaped.

In this last chapter of A Blaze of Autumn Sunshine, *the events and dramas of the four years from 2009 to 2013 are recalled and reflected upon by Tony Benn, now in his ninetieth year, in the form of a memoir: the Brown premiership, the Cameron–Clegg Coalition Government of 2010; the election of Edward Miliband as Labour Leader; the consequences of, and reaction to, the crisis of international capitalism in America and Europe; the 'Arab spring' in Libya; the rise of UKIP and disillusionment across Europe with the EU – not to mention the personal challenges of poor health, widowerhood, moving home and ageing.*

Politicians are never allowed to be ill and so as older age and poor health beset me, it was a salutary time. I was described as frail, which I don't like. If your frailty is disclosed, it does weaken your capacity to bc thought of in tcrms of what you're saying, if people are thinking 'How's he coping?' instead of listening to what you're saying. Maybe in ten years' time, when I'm 100, I might feel it is justified!

In August 2009 I had a collapse of some kind; after I had been released from hospital following a routine operation, complications set in and I was readmitted for a second spell, when they diagnosed a stroke, and I was really paralysed – mentally – for a few weeks. During that time I ceased to keep the diary, and never took it up again.

The amount of work involved in keeping the diary had been enormous – it was a heavy responsibility to reproduce the day's events; secondly, no longer being a Member of Parliament and influential in the daily political round, the ongoing flow of what you might call 'parliamentary gossip' was denied me, so I wasn't able to say anything that people couldn't find out from reading the newspapers. Released from the burden of being an archivist and Labour historian, I felt a great sense of freedom.

But I have mixed feelings about it now, because this final diary has missed some very important years on the world stage, and in my own life. So here are some of my thoughts on the major events between July 2009 and the present.

While I was recuperating from my stay in hospital, in the autumn of 2009, the Labour Government was faced with the aftermath of the banking crisis. Brown handled the financial crisis that began in 2008 very well, I thought. He intervened decisively, he took over RBS, and I got the feeling that the Labour Party was being reawakened by the crisis, to deal with the situation in a direct, positive way. That crisis has continued all the way through and is still, today, used as an excuse by the present Government for all the problems it has – that Labour mishandled the crisis. The response the Coalition has pursued is a very negative one.

Should *we* have entered a coalition with the Liberal Democrats in 2010? I was a bit torn about that, because a lot of the unhappiness and difficulty in the Labour Party arose from overtures to the Liberal Democrats, when Tony Blair offered a job in a Labour Cabinet to Paddy Ashdown. 'Lib-Labbery' in the Labour Party was one of the factors that contributed towards the birth of the SDP after 1979, and to New Labour and all the rest of it. On the other hand, I think that if the Liberals (for whom I have some respect) went along and supported a government, it would strengthen that government; and it has sustained and strengthened the Conservatives.

A society where your economy is based simply upon the analysis of wealth and who makes money does put the interests of working people second, and that creates discontent; the discontent leads to protest all over the world. I think people see the present system in Britain as being very undemocratic, dictated entirely by the FTSE 100 and what's happened to shares and so on. The interests of ordinary people tend to be disregarded. There was rioting a year after the general election, in the early August of 2011. I think what happened was that there was a rising sense of frustration, and where you get frustration that is not accompanied by campaigning to put it right, then it takes that form. That is frightening and disturbing, and also has the effect of building up the right, who make it an issue of law and order. But they were very short incidents.

What the Coalition has succeeded in doing is shifting the blame for the crisis from the banks and from the huge disparities of wealth that have opened up in the twenty-first century onto the people who are, for whatever reasons, the poorest: welfare recipients. The Coalition Government has been very clever at doing this without any loss to themselves or the wealthy whom they represent. Welfare cuts could only make this situation worse.

When the leadership of the Labour Party was open to candidates, I supported Ed Miliband from the beginning of his campaign to succeed Gordon Brown. He had worked in my office for a time, doing work experience as a fifteen-year-old when I was looking for a bit of help. He then went to America and became an economics expert, and his judgement was very good. He was a brilliant boy and he is a brilliant man.

I knew his parents well, of course. I can't say I ever became very friendly with the boys, but I used to go for meals with Marion and Ralph Miliband, and I got to know the family. Ralph was a riveting academic and his books are enormously worth reading; Marion I like very much, and I trust her judgement; so I feel some familiarity with Ed and David.

It would be presumptuous to try and predict what Ralph

Miliband's analysis of the current crisis would be, but he would have had a profound understanding of it as a crisis of capitalism, and his contribution would have been academic and also very practical. He had a broad vision. He didn't just look at the day-to-day hotchpotch of argument between the political parties. Ralph said to me once, towards the end of his life: 'My boys say to me, "Dad, if we did what you recommend, would it work?" What would your answer be to that, Tony?'

I said to Ralph, 'Well, my children ask me the same question!'

My children don't really cross-examine me, but they don't see things in quite the way I do because, obviously, I had to go through the experiences that I had to pick up the ideas I have; and I can't really blame my children for not following me, and I wouldn't want them to follow me in that way.

Ralph's death was a great loss to me. And another close friend died in 2009 – Jack Jones, one of the great trade-union leaders of the twentieth century. I did have a huge regard for Jack. I thought he was an absolute model of what a trade-union leader should be. Listening to him was riveting. He was a solid socialist trade unionist, very loyal to the Labour Party. Jack moved a motion at a TUC conference to abolish the House of Lords. On the anniversary of my fortieth year in the Commons my friends made a cake in the shape of Parliament. So Jack, who came – he was very sociable and liked parties – was given the honour of cutting up the Lords' slice of the cake.

Jack was, I think, in a category of his own. His personal qualities were very strong and supportive. He knew exactly what he wanted to do and he went along with it, and ambition never entered into any consideration of what he wanted – he was a very modest man.

Margaret Thatcher, who died this year, was another principled figure, and undoubtedly a courageous Prime Minister. I disagreed with almost everything she stood for, but she was a political signpost, not a weathervane, and she never changed direction – unlike many politicians, who blow in all directions. She knew what she wanted and she refused to budge. She and her Cabinet took on the miners, as the strongest workers in the Labour movement, but whereas the NUM stood by Arthur Scargill, her Cabinet colleagues got rid of her.

David Cameron is, I think, a Conservative of the Thatcher variety and, like Thatcher, has some socially liberal views. He has his own ideas tucked away, such as support for gay marriage. I am in favour of gay marriage. I think if people want to live together and have their relationship blessed in the form of a marriage service, you have to respect that. It is something that's a matter of choice for them. I think that the prohibition on the Church of England marrying gay couples will change in time.

Since the election of the Coalition Government in 2010, UKIP has been on the rise, especially at local elections, where they have gained control of a few councils. I think UKIP is a right-wing force. When things get really desperate and people ought to move to the left, there is a reaction of pessimism, which leads people to be attracted by arguments on the right – about immigration and welfare, and all the rest of it. You find the hard-right developing in other countries similarly, and you have to watch out for that: the hard-right has an appeal to cynical people, and its roots grow in the political process.

As a response, Cameron has announced more measures on limiting immigration and cutting back the numbers of people who will be allowed to come to Britain. Actually, the National Health Service is run by immigrants; and the dislike of foreigners is a very right-wing idea. We have got to be careful of that argument becoming a central one as opposed to a peripheral one. It is an issue you have to deal with sensitively, because it does arouse anxiety, but at the same time you owe it to people to speak truthfully about it and to recognise that immigration has been beneficial to this country – and still is.

During most of 2010, the WikiLeaks story dominated the papers. WikiLeaks is very important because information about government is the essence of democracy. If you don't know what's happening, you can't reach a sensible judgement on it: the publication of Hansard is one example, and the Freedom of Information Act is another.

In the case of WikiLeaks there was a group working with Julian Assange who got hold of a mass of US classified documents, including State Department cables, and published them on the Internet between April and November 2010. Assange was subjected to a European arrest warrant at the end of 2010 (unrelated to the WikiLeaks) and, had he been arrested, I think the Americans would probably have got him to the United States, where he would have received a long sentence. In June 2012 he moved into the Ecuadorean Embassy (where he has political asylum). It must be miserable being holed up like that, but I think he really is at risk, because Bradley Manning, who passed classified material on to WikiLeaks in America, is in prison and is facing a very long sentence.

I think Assange's role, as a symbol of the whole WikiLeaks story, makes him right and that he is to be supported; it is a direct challenge to the secrecy of politics. You just don't know what the Government, which you're supposed to support, is really doing and why, and WikiLeaks brought that out.

The 'Occupy' phenomenon swept America and Europe in 2011 – as a response, I think, to the financial crisis: some very thoughtful people said during the crisis: 'We do the work and we don't run the country, we are slaves of a system, and if you're really going to change anything, you've got to open up a discussion about that system', and so the Occupy movement came about. They were not political, in a narrow sense, but they were looking at society in a general way, which was helpful to the left. They were trying to re-create in the public mind an idea of where power really was in society, and how they represented a majority who were unrepresented. It started in Wall Street and then it came over to London. 'Occupy London' were moved on from outside the Stock Exchange after a month, so they set up in the courtyard in front of St Paul's Cathedral. The Church of England's response seemed ambiguous, and the Canon of St Paul's (Giles Fraser) resigned after disagreements in St Paul's about it. How the present establishment of the Church will respond to similar challenges to the power of capitalism will be interesting. The signs from Justin Welby are encouraging.

2011 also saw the NATO intervention in Libya in March of that year. I was not in favour of intervention in Libya, and Stop the War – of which I am President – opposed the policy. There is a strong peace movement in Britain, there always has been, and to keep that flame alive whenever it's necessary is both relevant and helpful.

I'm not in favour of Western powers intervening in domestic issues in order, allegedly, to deal with a crisis, but in the process re-creating the old imperial pattern whereby the West runs the world. The arguments for going in are credible, and justified on the grounds that they're working for peace, but it leads to great resentment on the part of the countries being occupied.

What is happening in Syria and Iraq can't be separated from the Israel/Palestine conflict. I think Barak Obama has come out very clearly now on the two-state solution, which will not be acceptable to the Israeli Government. In the end there will have to be a two-state solution in Palestine, so I welcome Obama's statement very much. I thought what he said to the Palestinians was positive and constructive and indicated to them that they had not been deserted by the Americans, which many Palestinians thought had happened; also, it warned Benjamin Netanyahu that he couldn't go beyond a certain point. Obama is now a President in his last term, which gives him a certain freedom.

The one occasion when I'm strongly in favour of national flags is when they're limited to teams rather than wars! I enjoyed the Olympics very much, and then the Paralympics; it gave people a great boost. The whole event was carried out with enormous imagination and was a genuine international occasion whereby the human race celebrated its talents. I thought it did Britain a lot of good internationally, and it built up the Paralympic movement and made sport a very important issue in schools. Anyone looking back on the Olympics will do so with affection, and will want to thank those who organised it so brilliantly.

Along with the Olympics, much of 2012 was dominated by the revelations coming out of the Leveson Inquiry into the press. In January 2007 Clive Goodman, the royal editor of the *News of the World*, had been jailed for hacking into the royals' phones – intercepting phone messages from Clarence House. Then followed the allegations about systematic phone-hacking by Murdoch journalists. It became an issue of civil liberties and the abuse of power. There are various centres of power: political parties are centres of power; money is a centre of power; and the media is a centre of power. And the Murdoch Press used the power that he had acquired to abuse civil liberties by phone-hacking.

But Murdoch's real influence is in shaping public opinion on issues that will be decided in general elections. The press is free in the sense that the *Government* doesn't interfere in it, but it is pursuing its own political policies without any sort of check. Murdoch has a view, and he will play it as hard as he can in his newspapers, and it will go direct to his readers; this is seen as the free press operating, but it is an abuse of power.

It would appear that the police were involved in the phone-hacking, or some of it, and human beings – being what they are – will be subject to temptation. If a very powerful man offers you a position that gives you power in society, you will be tempted to take it; and I imagine those journalists who were tempted by Murdoch's money saw this as a way to develop their own careers.

The Leveson Inquiry did a very thorough job, over the course of a year, and recommended in November 2012 that the press system should be underpinned by supportive legislation. Then a body of opinion emerged from Parliament, influenced by the media, saying that this is interfering with the freedom of the press. I think that if you do have a complaints system, it's not unreasonable to ask Parliament to enforce it, that wouldn't involve the papers being told what to print, but it would involve underpinning their responsibility for what they do print and how they do behave. So I am in favour of legislation.

There is a case for saying that one man/one corporation can only own one national newspaper, and that you can't have one man owning a whole series of newspapers in one country. That is nothing to do with restricting the freedom of the press – it is about the role of the press, and press proprietors in our society. My friend Chris Mullin was very much in favour of limiting the Murdoch Empire which, he argued, had contaminated all the organisations that it was involved with: the press, sport, the police – it had its tentacles everywhere and was a corrupting influence.

The breadth of Leveson's Inquiry was demonstrated by the number of casualties: Sir Paul Stephenson, the Metropolitan Police Commissioner, had to resign; John Yates, the Assistant Commissioner, had to resign; Rebekah Brooks resigned; Baroness Buscombe of the Press Complaints Commission resigned; Andy Coulson resigned. It was the first time anyone had ever touched the subject in such a general way, and they were forced to resign because what they were doing had been brought out into the open. Press intrusion is nothing new, although the means have changed. I was subjected to journalists rummaging through my rubbish bins, and my children were ambushed going to school by reporters trying to discredit me or the Labour Government in the 1970s.

Ever since becoming a widower (in 2000) I was aware that my house was too much for me. But the prospect of moving out of the family home in Notting Hill Gate, where I had lived since 1951, was difficult to contemplate. Caroline and I moved in that year, over sixty years ago; all my children were brought up there. But the roof leaked, the electricity was a fire hazard, there were three flights of stairs; I had my office in the basement. It really was too big for me, too much for me on my own, and so my children helped me to find the flat around the corner where I now live. I did finally manage to move all my archives and most of my belongings into storage, and in April 2011 I packed up my remaining stuff and walked round the corner to my present flat. To move out was something I was really quite scared of, but in the event it went very smoothly. I had planned it all. It was a relief, in the end.

My eldest son, Stephen, can't bear to go by the old family home now; it's all boarded up and being radically restructured by the new owners. My youngest son, Joshua, has negotiated to buy the front door and he's going to move it to Stansgate and re-create the entrance and front steps! The plaque that I had put up in memory of Caroline is going to remain on the front wall of the house. If there was ever a plaque to me, I hope it would say 'Socialist, diarist, campaigner', or something of that kind.

I am very happy in my flat. I kept some of my books in London (the reference ones and essential books). I also brought mementoes that were given to me at various stages of my life, for example, during the miners' strike and Wapping: mugs and plates and things of that kind, given to me by the trade unions.

I brought with me some little ceramic figures of five Labour Leaders: Attlee, Wilson, Callaghan, Brown and Blair. I also have a series of Russian dolls – given to me by someone, because I wouldn't have bought a Yeltsin doll myself! If you look inside Yeltsin you find

Gorbachev; inside Gorbachev is Khrushchev; inside Khrushchev is Stalin; inside Stalin is Lenin; and inside Lenin the Tsar. There's also a model pillar box and a post office, probably acquired when I was Postmaster General.

There is a commemorative plate done by the Kent miners, and it's got a picture of Arthur Scargill and miners and their wives and families. In 1984–5 there was a classic battle for the future of the mining industry. Margaret Thatcher decided that trade-union power had to be destroyed, and the most powerful trade union was the miners', because the nature of mining breeds solidarity. If you're a miner you have to depend entirely on the people working with you in the pit. So when she made war on the miners and described them as the enemy it produced this most powerful reaction, and the miners' strike lasted for a year, from March 1984 to March 1985.

I also have a vial of my own blood in a case. When my father died and I inherited his title, the House of Lords said my blood had turned blue and I was therefore disqualified from being an MP. I took the opportunity of going to hospital and asking them to take out some of my blood, and the actual blood is still in the vial. It was taken out by an African doctor called Harry Poku, from Ghana. I took it to court, and the court said that the peerage is an 'incorporeal hereditament' – a piece of real property in my body affixed in the blood. That was the law, and that was the battle I had to fight.

I have a container of some of the first oil to be brought up from the North Sea. I was appointed Energy Minister in the summer of 1975 and within a few weeks the oil had been discovered. At the time, it was a sensational development, lifting for ever the problems with energy shortages. My aim was to develop that and get control of it, because when oil companies come to a country they can take over. But by negotiating very hard with the oil companies I got them to agree that, if they came, they had to give a share of the ownership of their companies to the British Government. When I left office in 1979, 25 per cent of all the North Sea oil belonged to the Treasury, and Margaret Thatcher sold it all off. This offered us a real opportunity and we wasted it, because the oil money could have gone on unemployment pay and on funding the austerity programme.

I have a wooden chair given to me by a man called Hedley Dennis, who told me it belonged to Keir Hardie; I went to Wales and picked it up in my car. It's really a chapel seat, and reminds one of Hardie's commitment to radical socialism and Christianity. I'm very fond of that and I'm proud to have been made President of the Keir Hardie Society.

In the fireplace, behind the chair, there's a replica bust of me (by Ian Walters); the original is in Bristol City Hall and there is another copy in the House of Commons. Ian Walters also did the huge head of Nelson Mandela that sits by the Royal Festival Hall. So, you see, every memento I have in the flat has a story or a history to it. Because the flat is so much smaller than the house, most of my working papers had to go into storage with the rest of the archives. My father's books are all in storage, as are my mother's papers and all of Caroline's work. We recently had to buy lots of containers to take the extra stuff – we are a family of hoarders.

I have had a lot of fairly minor illnesses, which cumulatively have set me back a bit. I can't remember them all now, but I'm aware of the fact that old age has set up handicaps, which limit what I can do. In February this year I fell at home, and Ruth called an ambulance on the 111 system. The ambulance staff were marvellous and, because I was on a blood-thinner, I ended up in Chelsea and Westminster Hospital. Hospital is an institution and, when you're there, you're really imprisoned. There are lots of doctors and staff who come and ask you endless questions; they're very friendly and kind and so on, but I did long to get out. You have to do what you're told in hospital, and I find that a bit oppressive.

I only expected to be there for twenty-four hours, but I ended up being in for over two weeks. My consultant was Dr Michael Pelly, who came to see me several times, and I liked him very much and had confidence in him.

There were so many people coming in – there were nurses; there were care assistants; there were people who bathed me; there were people who took me to the loo. I was friendly to everybody and gradually got to know them as best I could, but I was part of an institution, I fitted into their institution, and they knew what they wanted to do. I just had to go along with it. I can't remember what the meals were like – I've never been interested in food. I did make it clear that I was a vegetarian.

Sanjay Kumar, who is making a film about me, came to visit regularly; he got into trouble with Dr Pelly, because we left the hospital so that I could smoke my pipe in the street and have a cup of tea in Starbuck's next door. Apparently I missed a couple of tests, and that's why the consultant was cross.

I spent most of my time there waiting – waiting to get out! I did eventually, and that was when it was decided that I needed an intensive programme of care at home. I have been very well looked after by my family, but professional care was needed. I have people here a lot of the time, seeing that I have a meal and a bath, and so on. I can't do everything I'd like to do. Being in a flat with people coming in around the clock means that you feel directed, to some extent; on the other hand, it does meet your needs – you get food, your clothes are washed and you're helped to have a bath. So it is also rather nice. You don't have to worry when the phone rings – somebody answers it and passes the message on to Ruth, who deals with it, or to me if it is family or friends. Ruth organised the carers: she looks after all my arrangements now and I couldn't carry on without her.

Pearl will start by getting me breakfast and cleaning the kitchen and bathroom, things that normally I would have done myself, but which I now find difficult. She prepares lunch, and then Kathleen comes in the afternoon and cooks a meal for the evening; sometimes she goes out shopping with me to Tesco's or Marks & Spencer, or for a walk around the park. Henry arrives later in the evening. I wake up about 5.30 in the morning and set the bath going, and he waits to help me out of the bath and sometimes helps me get dressed.

I hope I can cope on my own again one day, because although they're very friendly people and it's a comforting feeling having carers, I would like to be independent. I can see why care is such a big issue for older people, because when I was an MP I would have lots of older people coming to me in my constituency surgeries with needs that weren't being met, but which could and should have been met. My view of social care for the elderly has developed out of my own experience both as an MP and as an old person. So I am very lucky to be in a situation where I have my own needs met. But one of the things about old age is that everything is less certain. You don't know what to expect from day to day and what you can plan, and that creates anxiety – you're not sure what you can cope with. If I have to go to the shops, I have to be sure that I have a coat and a bag or a trolley; I now find shopping quite difficult, and I've slipped and fallen many times.

My driver, John Grice, takes me to long-distance meetings. He's totally reliable, very charming, strong and amazingly good at technology. He always gets me to a meeting on time and has all the details of the venues, the people, the times at his fingertips (literally), so I don't have to worry about anything. It's a fantastic service.

He's a modest, highly intelligent guy, and his comments about current affairs are perceptive and informed. We talk about things generally, but I don't try to persuade him – we spend hours together in his car talking. He knows my views quite clearly because he hears them every time he takes me to a meeting!

At this stage of my life I am lucky enough to find myself buoyed up by several capable women: there's my daughter Melissa, Ruth Winstone (my editor) and Emma Mitchell (my publisher at Hutchinson) and Jean Corston; they are the people who sustain me really on a regular basis. And now Pearl and Kathleen, whom I have already mentioned.

Melissa is a remarkable woman. She wrote a book on education last year, and she's just finished another book, called *What We Should Tell Our Daughters*. We're very close. She's my only daughter, and she comes to see me regularly.

Jean Corston was the Labour Party's organiser in the South-West and, when I was the MP in Bristol, we travelled a great deal together. She's a respected member of the House of Lords now, very busy. She pops in for an hour in the mornings occasionally and often rings me. I did visit her in the West Country, and stayed with her after the hospital operation.

Then there is Ann Henderson. I met her in Scotland. She was a train driver – the only woman train driver I've ever met – and she got into the trade-union movement and was involved in campaigns that I was involved in, so I got to meet her then. Now she works for the

Scottish TUC. If she's in London she'll pop in every few months, and if I go to Scotland I will see her.

For the past two years I have been the subject of a film by Sanjay Kumar, which has kept me busy and is really my premature obituary! He came to see me two or three years ago and talked and talked. Then said he wanted to make a film. He's put an enormous amount of effort into it. By early next year he hopes to have released it. It's a very interesting way of sort of reliving your life – as if you were an actor, only you're living your own life. Whether it'll work out at the end I don't know, because to end a film of that kind is quite tricky. I don't know how you do end it! It covers all my political life. When Enoch Powell said, 'Every political career ends in failure', my argument is that my failure came much earlier than the end of my political life!

The film is called *Will and Testament*, not *Last Will and Testament*. He's a very clever man, Sanjay . . . a very colourful guy. He made his money working in computers and then moved into film. He has put an enormous amount of time and effort and his own money into the film, and it's the first attempt, really, to present my life as I would see it, and so I'm pleased to have the opportunity of doing that. He has set up a Facebook page, and he says that the largest number of people – the group of people who give it the biggest response – are the eighteen- to twenty-four-year-olds.

Sometime after I left Parliament I was approached to take part in a series of talks in theatres, with an audience. That started a long run called *An Audience with Tony Benn*; these are really public meetings. I loved doing them, and particularly the question-and-answer sessions after the first half. I still do the occasional show – I did one not long ago on the Isle of Man.

You get a broad cross-section of people in the audience. They do remind me, every time, of how we underestimate the intelligence of the public. They have shrewd questions and are very perceptive, and they really make me think. I have a kind interviewer called Sam Norman, who chairs it extremely well. She interviews me for about half an hour and then there's an interval, and then she opens it up to audience questions. I think meeting and working with other people is what keeps you going. The theatre shows are the nearest thing to a public constituency meeting that I do. Meetings where people agree with you have a slightly artificial feeling. I want to be active, and when the time comes to stop them completely I will be very depressed.

Throughout my life I have been an amateur 'improver', and a few years ago while travelling around the country I cobbled together a seat attached to a backpack, and another one attached to a small suitcase, to enable me to sit down at railway stations, on busy trains and even at airports. My legs had started to pack up by this time, so it was immensely useful, and I was often asked about it. As discussed in my diary, somehow the *Richard & Judy* show got to hear about it and invited me on. They also invited James Caan of *Dragons' Den,* who thought it was a good idea.

I was then introduced in 2008 to, Grahame Herbert, who had invented the Airframe folding bicycle. Grahame came to see me and, over mugs of tea, we sat in the garden and talked over the idea. He agreed to go away and produce a working model that could be integrated into a cabin-sized suitcase. It was like having Einstein to help me with my maths homework – he was so imaginative and clever. We eventually settled on calling it the 'Seat-case', although we toyed with the idea of 'Benn's safe seat' or the 'Back-bencher'. An engaging, eccentric patent lawyer called Michael Deans – who had once wanted to be an MP – advised us on protecting the idea.

There was another flurry of media coverage in 2010 and it seemed as though it might be taken up by a major luggage manufacturer, but then came the European economic collapse and it was difficult for companies to find investment. At this point the project was put into storage, but I hope one day it will help a lot of other people to travel painlessly.

I never imagined I'd live to ninety. I don't have the energy I had before. I get tired. My engagements involve quite a lot of organisation, but I've found it a very satisfying period. On the other hand, it's also frustrating, because although I'm still in the Labour Party and active in the ordinary sense, I'm not a key player in policy-making. But people can pick up what I'm talking about and discuss it, and that is the role that I suppose I play, to encourage others.

One of the nice things about becoming an institution is that I am asked to celebrate unusual events. Like when the Marquis of Bath sent me a message by racing pigeon to celebrate the Festival of Stamps in 2010. An old East Ender called Ted Hendrie, of the Royal Racing Pigeon Association, came along and I took the message from the pigeon outside my house. That was a first! Originally the pigeon was to have arrived at the House of Commons, but it was forbidden on health and safety grounds. So it came to my front garden instead.

In October 2012 the old Transport & General Workers' Union office in Bristol, where I had worked when I was the MP for Bristol South-East, was taken over by UNITE and they renamed it 'Tony Benn House'. I was very proud of that, and I went down to Bristol for a little celebration. I'm sure there's as much warmth in Chesterfield, which I represented for seventeen years, as there was in Bristol, but I haven't been back to Chesterfield as much. It's difficult going back to a seat you've represented; once you were the Member and you were the centre of things, and when you go back you are just a figure from the past.

At Easter we – the four children and some of their partners, the grandchildren and my brother David and his children and grandson – all spent a few days at Stansgate.

Stansgate has been the family holiday home for a hundred years. It was bought by my grandfather from a catalogue for £600, and it was a prefabricated house, put together on the edge of the Essex coast.

It is pretty crowded when we are all together and not everybody in the extended family has a room, but Stephen, Hilary, Joshua and Melissa each have their own room; there are lots of bunk beds, and other rooms where the grandchildren scatter when they're there. I've got a big room in the corner of the house, overlooking the river. It can be very cold in winter, especially when the wind is blowing. There is night-storage heating in some rooms, but it hasn't got central heating.

We mainly do a lot of talking, but we do watch a little television and films. We've got videos and DVDs . . . it's just holiday time really. My brother, David, has got a house nearby and he comes over and we talk, and I walk over and see him and his family. I like to go for a few days at a time, throughout the year.

It's very hard to predict the future, because you don't know how people's minds are moving, but I think there is a lot of dissatisfaction with the cuts, a lot of discontent within the Coalition, and I think the Labour Party is looking more confident and secure; and, in the normal course of events, that should produce a Labour Government. But a Labour Government would be struggling with the same problems that the present one is struggling with, and how it would cope we would just have to see. I don't think there'll be any desire to go back to New Labour and all those policies, Thatcherite policies, so I think the Labour Party would be more radical and could be critically attacked for that. But I think there's a lot of public support to be picked up if you do say the right things. You have to have hope, or you won't put the effort in. But if you say, 'Will it come right in the end?', then I'm not sure.

I'm now waiting for the great-grandchildren to come along, as I think every younger generation brings fresh ideas into the world.

Index

Aaronovitch, David 66, 167
Abbas, Mahmoud 69, 137
Abbott, Diane 36, 58
Adam (driver) 53
Adams, Gerry 145
Adamson, Joy 231
Addington, Jim 64
Adie, Kate 154
Adonis, Andrew 219
Ahmadinejad, President Mahmoud 261
Alawi, Ali 75
Aldington, Toby 214, 214n
Alexander, Douglas 48, 210
Alexander, Wendy 48
Ali, Tariq 84, 179
Alibhai-Brown, Yasmin 256
Amos, Valerie 127
Ancram, Michael 39
Aldrin, Buzz 159
Allaun, Mrs 208
Altikriti, Anas 261
Andrews, Julie 202
Andrews, Simeon 58
Andropov, Yuri 96
Annan, Kofi vii, xii, 1, 3, 6, 8, 13, 118, 141, 153
Antoinette, Sister 42
Arno, Rose 171
Arno, Tom 171
Ashdown, Paddy 16, 19
Assad (Bladerunners hairdresser) 87
Assange, Julian 282-3
Attenborough, Richard 36-7
Attlee 150, on crises 171, *Let Us Face the Future*
    172, 243, ceramic figure of 286

Baden-Powell, Robert 96-7
Bailey, Roy, xi, 24, 33, 58, 144
Balls, Ed 169
Bannister, Sir Roger 159
Barber, Frances 138
Barenboim, Daniel 92
Barker, Harley Granville 161
Barker, Rodney 138
Barnett, Anthony 129
Bath, Marquess of see Thynn, Alexander

Beckett, Margaret 264
Benn, Caroline (Carrie) x, 43, 51, 224
Benn, Caroline Wedgwood (Pixie) x, 14,
    29, 57, 64, day of Hilary's birth 65-6, 68,
    74, 76, 79, 80, 81, 82, 128, 138, 143, 145,
    anniversary of meeting 157, 178, 215, TB
    nightmare about 225, 276-7, family home
    286, 288
Benn, Claire 70
Benn, Daniel x, 166, 224
Benn, David Wedgwood x, 18, 34, 35, 89, and
    Russia 96, 135, 144, 156, 166, 224, 226,
    274, family at Stansgate 293
Benn, Emily x, 35, 41, speech to 2007
    Conference 47-48, 64, 166, with
    grandfather in Oxford 186 and 214,
    Channel 4 awards 219, constituency
    meeting 267
Benn, Sir Ernest 62
Benn, Hilary x, 10, 20-21, floods 30-31, foot
    and mouth disease 32-3, 34, 41, 44, 48, 55,
    day of birth 65, 68, 77, 85, 89, and badger
    cull 101, 105, 122, 136, 143, refuses
    badger cull 147, 166, 169-70, 175, 183-4,
    189, 191, 193, 200, at Davos 214, and
    Lisbon Treaty 217-8, 219, 224, 247, 248-9,
    259, 261, 263, 276, Stansgate 293
Benn, James x, 29, 166, 175, 188, 224
Benn, James (cousin) 70
Benn, Jonathan x, 13, 95, 186, 224, 245, 257,
    obtains First 261
Benn, Joshua x, 1, 2, 4, 7, 9, 13, 14, 19, 20,
    28, 33, 34, 35, and Orange 38-9, 40, 43,
    51, 52, 68, 71, 80, and TB archives 83,
    95, 104, and leaking roof 112, future of
    family home 114, 117, 127, computer
    expert 131 and 133, and National
    Trust 134, 135, 136, 145, upgrading
    BT technology 151, job with Crisis 156,
    graduation 165, 183, 186, 200, 203, and
    'Sak' 208, 217, and father's driving 221,
    father's internet problems 222, 224,
    anxiety over TB operation 230, and TB
    blog 232 and 236, TB's operation 274-7,
    family home 286, Stansgate 293

Benn, Melissa (Lissie) x, 14, 19, 34, 35, 59, 69, 81, and *One of Us* 105-06, 117, 125, 128, lecture 137, 147, 156, 165-6, 178, 182, photograph in NPG 185, and *Richard and Judy Show* 192, relationship with father 199-200 and 201, 204, filming with Richard and Judy 212, 217, with Mariella Frostrup 219, 52nd birthday 221, and Marion Miliband 223, 224, 226, 229, British Book Awards 237, 274, 275, 277, support to father 290, *What we should tell our daughters* 290, Stansgate 293

Benn, Michael x, 166

Benn Michael (d 1944) 17-18, 39, 144, 235, 265

Benn, Piers x, book 275

Benn, Stephen x, 10, 14, 34, 35, 48, and Bill Clinton 52, 60, 77, 80, 106, 112, 115, 116, 127, and David Davis 139, 166, 200, 213, 219, and father's driving 221, 224, 238, 253, RSC 265, in daughter's constituency 267, and family home 286, Stansgate 293

Benn, William x, 166

Benn, William Wedgwood (*see* Stansgate)

Benn Gordon, Hannah x, 125, 137, 156, US election 182, 200, thank-you note 204

Benn Gordon, Sarah x, 125, 137, 156, US election 182, 200, 201, 204, on China 204, 224

Bennett, Jamie 135

Bennett-Jones, Owen 127

Bercow, John (Speaker from 2009) 261, TB letter to *The Times* 263, elected Speaker 264, statement from Chair 265

Berezovsky, Boris 11

Berry, Halle 61

Bevan, Aneurin 121, 243, 276

Bhutto, Benazir 80

Bickerstaffe, Rodney xi, 36, 57, 84, 114, 183, and Jack Jones 241, Jack Jones's funeral 245

Billington, Rachel 105

Bingham, Thomas (Lord Chief Justice) 256

Bin Laden, Osama 138

Bird, John 138, 197

Birt, John 67

Blackburn, Robin 84

Blackmore, Lorna 188

Blair, Cherie 23, 99, 127, 128

Blair, Sir Ian 50, 51, 174

Blair, Tony xii, xiv, 3, 12, 17, war crimes 18, last PMQs and resignation19-20, 22-3, 34, Campbell *Diaries* 24-5, 40, 44, 55, on Iran 60, *The Blair Years* 66-7, the Quartet 69,

and God 71, 73, Catholicism 79, 81, 85, 91, 98, 104, 127, 129, 130, 137, Miners' Gala 150, 182, Hamas 205, at Davos 214, and Cabinet/Iraq war 203, 257, and Paddy Ashdown 279, ceramic figure of 286

Blake, Sister 65

Blears, Hazel 221, MPs' expenses 245-6 and 249, resignation from Cabinet 253, apologises 259

Blix, Hans 152-3

Blunkett, David 245-6

Blunt, Crispin 84, 85

Boaden, Helen 153

Bolton, John 182

Bonnin, Claire 202

Booth, Lauren 48, 128

Boothroyd, Betty 83

Borman, Frank 272

Bose, Pratima 267

Boulton, Adam 46, 84-5

Bower, Hetty 100, 102

Bragg, Billy xi, 27, 43, 47, 63, 129

Bragg, Melvyn 14

Brandreth, Gyles 83

Branson, Richard vii, 1, 2, 5, 7, 8, 13, 37, and Northern Rock 66, and Brown 86

Bremner, Rory 99-100, *Silly Money* 197

Brett, Lady Marion 65-6

Brigstocke, Marcus 70

Brill, Tim 231

Broadbent, Ed 245

Brockway, Fenner 185

Brookes, Rebekah 285

Bromley, Anita 233

Broomfield, Nick 90

Brown, Gordon xii, xiv, 8-9, 16-17, 19, 20, constitutional reform 21-3, 24, 25, chairs COBRA 30, 37, 39, 40, and Thatcherism 41, 44, 45, speech to 2007 Conference 47, General Election 51-4, 55, 56, 66-7, 73, 74, Lisbon Treaty 77, 81, 83, 85, and Northern Rock 86, 97-8, 99 and 101, 108-09, and income tax 115-17, 119, 122, 125, 127, 129, and Nantwich by-election 130, lorry drivers' protest 133, Labour Party bankruptcy 134, detention 136, 137, Bush's visit 142-3, assessment of premiership 145-6, Miners' Gala 150, and Obama 157, and succession 157-8, Beijing Olympics 160, 163, the crisis 164, 167, 2008 Conference 169, Coalition 170, and Mandelson 180, and American protectionism 183, 194, terrorism 199, and nuclear deterrent 200, 2nd bank bailout 208, at Davos 215, 216, leadership bids 221, Bank of England 232, and royal family 234, and G20 Summit London 237, MPs' expenses 245-6 and 248, 250, peerages 252, and Miliband/Mandelson 253 and 256, future 254-7, at PLP 257, 269, handling of crisis 279, 280, ceramic figure of 286

Brown, Sarah 19, 48, 194

Brown, Tina 14

Browne, John (Lord Browne of Madingley) 271

Brownsmith, Eric 243-4

Bruce, Fiona 23

Brunel, Isambard Kingdom 241

Bruni, Carla 112

Bryant, Jayne 261

Bullock, Sir Steve 227

Burrows, Saffron xi, 2, 24, 30, 35, 52, 87, 98, 117, 130, 219, 242-3, with TB to Cuban embassy 248

Burrows, Susie 52

Buscombe, Janet 285

Bush, President George W. 3, 15, 35, 61, and Palestine 69, and Iran 71, 73, presidential election 81, 86, post-war Iraq 136, visit to London 141, 160, 161, Russia 162, financial bailout 170 and 172-3, 2008 US Election, in Iraq 199, 200

Butler, Bill 110,

Butler, David xi, 105, 128, 247

Butler, Gareth 105, 128

Butler, Marilyn 128

Butler, Professor Peter 28

Butler, Robin 15, 31-2,

'Button, Lord' 32

Byrne, Tony xi, 39, 59, 200, 252, 263

Caan, James 292

Cable, Vincent 70, Post Bank 229

Callaghan, James 15, 74, 91, 93, 150, 1979 Election 247, ceramic figure of 286

Cameron, David xii, 36, 39, 40, 41, 44, 45, General Election 51, 56, 77, 145, Coalition 170, 2008 Conference 173, decentralisation 220, and MPs' expenses 248, 268-9, press officer 273, Clegg Coalition 278, TB assessment of 281-2, immigration policy 282

Campbell, Alastair xii, Diaries 24-5, 45, 67, 69, 88, 219

Campbell, Barbara xi, 124, 165, 185, 274

Campbell, Fraser 15

Campbell, Menzies 16-17, 36, 45, 51

Cannadine, Sir David 93

Carmichael, Michael 15

Carnegie, Charlotte 267

Carter, President Jimmy vii, 1, 2, 3, 5- 9, 13, honorary doctorate14-15, 32, nuclear power 73-4, Hamas 118, 141, Iran 152-3

Carter, Rosalynn 16

Carter, Peter (PC) xi, 117, 166

Cassen, Bernard 148

Castro, Raul 248

Cavan, Michael 98

Chakrabarti, Shami 2, 63, 110, 246, 269-70

Chambers, Ray 6

Charles, Prince of Wales 90

Charlton, Sir Bobby 159

Chavez, Hugo 16, 60, 86, 102, 148-9, 182

Cheney, Liz 73

Cheney, Dick 182

Chomsky, Noam 10-11, 153

Christian (the lion) 231

Christian, Louise 100, 109

Christie, Julie 70

Church, Caroline 231

Churchill, Caryl 141

Churchill, Sir Winston 20, 95, 114

Clancy, Keith 272

Clapham, Michael (Mick) 219

Clare, Dr Anthony 63

Clark, Sally x, 166, 201, 224

Clarke, Charles 67, 130-31, 169, 193, MPs' expenses 245-6, at PLP 257

Clarke, Kenneth 209

Clarke, Nita x, 35, 219

Clegg, Nick xii, 106, 112, Coalition 170, 269

Clinton, President Bill 6, 7, 52

Clinton, Hillary 50, presidential candidate 81-2 and 84, 90, 95, 106, backs Obama 137, in China 222

Clooney, George 112

Cocker, Jarvis 186

Collins, Joan 127

Conway, Derek 89

Conway, Clive 95, 98

Cooklin, Dr Michael 112, 197

Cooper, Stephen 129

Corbett, Robin 161

Corbyn, Jeremy 48, 55, 58, 100, 202, 203, 243

Corston, Jean xi, 143, husband dies 257, 267, support to TB 290

Coulson, Andy 273, 285

Cox, Geoffrey 231

Cripps, Stafford 243

Crookall-Greening, Grace 193

Crosland, Anthony 190
Crow, Bob 27, 165, No2EU campaign 216-7, No2EU broadcast 251, European elections 254-5
Cruddas, John 88, and Post Bank 229
Crystal, David 10

Dacre, Paul 93
Dalton, Hugh 272
Dalyell, Tam 192
Daniel, Sally 267
Daniel, Ricky 267
Darling, Alistair 44, and Northern Rock 67 and101, 109, liquidity measures 117, lorry drivers' protest 133, 154-5, extent of crisis 164-176 *passim*, 189, MPs allowances 241-2
Darwin, Charles 162
Davies, Quentin 47
Davis, David 83, 93, 139-140, 143, fights by-election 144, 147, 178
Davis, Evan 153, 160
Dawkins, Richard 162
Day, Robin 247
Dell, David 72
Deans, Michael 292
Denham, John 158
Dennis, Hedley 288
Denny, Brian 216, 218
Deripaska, Oleg 180 and 180n
Desai, Meghnad 131
Diamond, Anne 173-4
Diamond, Dr 65
Diana, Princess 14, 113
Dimbleby, David 11, 247
Dimbleby, Jonathan 167
Donaldson, Jeffrey 116
Downham, John 208
Driscoll, Margarette 50
Dromey, Jack 88
Dunwoody, Gwyneth 116, 131
Dunwoody, Tamsin 131

Easton, Frances 43
Eavis, Michael 18
Edwards, John 82, 90
Elliott, Mike 26
Elworthy, Scilla 7
Enfield, Edward 126-7
Enfield, Harry 126
Eno, Brian 55, 90, 163, 203
Esler, Gavin 35
Etemad, Dr Akbar 152-3
Evans, David 146
Evans, Faith 106

Fainlight, Ruth 70
Fedotov, Yuri 168
Felix, Julie 237
Fergusson, Alex (Scottish Parliament) 110
Ferry, Bryan 90
Field, Roger 13-14
Finnegan, Judy *see* Richard and Judy
Firmin, Pete 19
Flint, Caroline 255
Fletcher, Mary 62
Fletcher, Simon 36, 214
Flowers, Professor Brian 74, 76
Flynn, Paul 261
Follett, Ken 36
Foot, Michael 243
Fortune, John 138, 197
Foster, Norman (architect) 218
Fowler, Norman 173
Fraser, Giles 129, 283
Freedland, Jonathan 261
French, Colin 230
Frost, David 72, 153
Frostrup, Mariella 10, 219

Gabriel, Peter, vii, xi, 2, 5, 13
Gaitskell, Hugh 150
Gallimore, Patricia 250
Gale, Roger 229
Galloway, George 40, 42, 59, 73, 109, 141, 169, 203, Gaza convoy 219-20, 263
Gapes, Mike 35
Gardiner, Barry 169
Garland, Judy 98
Gary (Midpoint Services) 243
Gavan, Michael 98
Gaynor, Mitzi 201
Gentleman, David 72, 90, 100, 163
German, Lindsey xi, 34, 55, 65, 68, 87, 90, 109, 141, 147, 163, Left Convention167, 195, 203, and SWP 217, 220
Gibson, Ian 67, and 'Star Chamber' 253
Gill, Ken 36, 38, 57, 114
Gillius, Daniel 33
Giuliani, Rudy 81, 90
Gladstone, William 51, 182
Glass, Mr Jonathan 199, 230, 274-5, 276
Goldsworthy, Julia 11
Goodman, Clive 284
Goodman, Geoffrey 114, 245
Goodman, Margit 114
Goodwin, Fred 223
Gorbachev, Mikhail 16, Russian doll 287
Gordon, Paul x, 125, 185, 200
Gore, Al 7, 15

Grayling, Anthony 179
Grayson, Richard 29
Green, Damian 167, parliamentary privilege
    191-4, 196-7, 240
Green, Pauline 171
Greenfield, Mandy vii
Gregson, John 102
Grice, John xi, 104, 135, 180, 207, 218,
    222, 238, 250, 253, 263, 268, work and
    character 290,
Grieve, Dominic 194, Liberty's 75th anniversary
    256
Griffin, Nick 107
Guinness, Sabrina 90
Gurney, Sam 53

Hague, Wiliam 51, 88
Hain, Peter 16, 36, 85, 88
Hall, Sir Peter 92
Halliday, Denis 141
Hancock, Audrey 73
Hardie, Keir 115, 150, 246, 288
Hardy, Alfredo Toro 34, 60, 143, Madrid
    conference 148-9
Hardy, Gabriella 149
Harman, Harriet 88, Labour Party bankruptcy
    134, 140, 196, Jack Jones's funeral 244
Hardy, Jane 195
Harris, Charlie 91
Harris, Gill (Gill Hornby) 91
Harris, Holly 91
Harris, Matilda 91
Harris, Robert 90-91, view of Blair 92
Harris, Sam 91
Harrison, Alastair 190
Haw, Brian 141, 226
Hayes, Billy xii, 169, and Post Bank 229
Haylett, John 102
Hayman, Helene 51
Heal, Sylvia 43
Healy, Denis 196
Heather, Gary 189
Heffer, Doris 62, 133
Heffer, Eric 62, 133
Henderson, Ann 33, 110, 111, 290
Hendrie, Ted 293
Hendy, John 165
Henriksson, Jan 264
Hennessy, Peter 193, and nuclear deterrent 196
Herbert, Grahame xi, 161, the 'seat-case' 163,
    174, 228, 240-41, 258, 292
Heseltine, Michael 232, 254
Hewitt, Patricia 269
Hicks, Alan 3

Hicks, Hazel 3
Hill, Harry 10
Hill, Dr Sarah 206
Hislop, Ian 53, 147
Hitler, Adolf 171
Hobsbawm, Eric 84
Hodge, Margaret 107
Hoey, Kate 120-21
Hoggart, Simon 153
Holloway, Richard 33
Hoon, Geoff 207, 255
Hopkins, Kelvin 90, 99
Hopper, Davy 150
Horovitz, Michael 63
Howard, John 33, 69
Howe, Sharon 186
Hudson, Kate 55, 109, 163, 202
Hughes, Sylvia 135
Huhne, Chris 61, Lib-Dem leadership 62
Hume, John 132
Hunt, David (Lord Hunt of Wirral) 60
Hunt, Philip (Lord Hunt of King's Heath) 47
Hunt, Tristram 63
Hurcombe, Joy 268
Hurd, Douglas 54
Hussein of Jordan, King 2
Hussein, Saddam 72, 118
Hutton, John 25, 109, 169
Hutton, Lord (Brian Hutton) 32
Huzzard, Ron 159

Ingrams, Richard 127, 144, 147

Jackson, Jesse 36
Jackson, General Sir Michael 75
Jackson, Michael (singer) death of 266-7
Jackson, Tom 247
Jagger, Bianca 100, 141, 203
Jagger, Mick 90
Jameson, Lee 52, 54
Jarvis, Kate 215
Jay, Mary 187
Jenkins, Roy 15
Johnson, Alan 131, 251-3
Johnson, Boris 73, mayoral debate 119-
    122, 124, Henley by-election 145, and
    Metropolitan Commissioner 174
Johnson, Joy 36
Johnson, Rachel 167
Johnston, Alan 23, leadership 252
Jones, Digby 25
Jones, Fred 145
Jones, Jack 114, death 241, funeral 244-5, TB
    assessment of 281

Jones, Jack (son) 245
Jones, Matthew 244
Jones, Mick 241, father's funeral 245
Jones, Nicholas 227
Jones, Sylvia 145
Judd, Frank 261

Kaplinsky, Natasha xi, 35, 50, 85, 100-101, 113,
    baby 175, 239
Karadzic, Radovan 155
Karlin, Miriam 258
Karzai, President Hamid 220
Kaufman, Gerald 100, MPs' expenses 250
Keaton, Diane 86
Kellner, Peter 95, 270
Kelly, Jude 92
Kelly, Ruth 170
Kelly, Stephen 231
Kendall, Kay 102
Kennedy, Senator Edward 89
Kennedy, Helena 92, 248, 252
Kenny, Paul 26, 59, 165
Kent, Bruce 109
Kenyatta, Jomo 71
Keynes, John Maynard 130
Khairoldin, Zohreh 95, 186
Khan, Imran (solicitor) 228
Khan, Sadiq 92, 97
Khama, Ian 190-91
Khama, Ruth 190
Khama, Seretse 190
Khrushchev, Nikita 96, Russian doll 287
Kiang, Professor 6, 8
King, Mervyn 183, 232
King, Oona 53
Kinnock, Neil 102, 114, Miners' Gala 150,
    169, Jack Jones's funeral 244
Kirkbride, Julie 252
Kissinger, Henry 8
Klopacz, John 155
Knight, Chris 262
Knightley, Keira 165
Krizman, Zdenka 206
Kucinich, Dennis 15, 16
Kumar, Sanjay 289, making of Will and
    Testament 291
Kustow, Michael 84
Kyi, Aung San Suu 6, 8

Lamb, Christine 262
Lammy, David 36
Lamont, Norman 67, financial crisis 222
Lansbury, George 150
Lavery, Ian 26

Lawson, Neil 140
Learmonth, Will 10
Lee, Hermione 186
Lee, Jin Young 164
Lee, Pearl 289-90
Lenin, Vladimir 287
Lennox, Annie 203
Lever, Harold 91
Leveson, Sir Brian 284, Leveson Inquiry 284-5,
    TB support of 285
Levy Andrea 10
Leys, Colin 184
Lindsay, John 233
Liria, Carlos 148
Littlewood, Tony 44-5
Litvinenko, Alexander 28
Livingstone, Ken 34, 36, 73, 113, mayoral
    debate 119, 121-2, 214
Lloyd George, David 61-2
Loach, Ken 248
Logan, Davy 51
Lowe, Kathleen 289-90
Lumley, Joanna 242
Lynch, Jack 254
Lyons, Sir Michael 221-2

MacDonald, Ken 256
MacIntosh, Maureen (Mrs Mac) 260
MacIntyre, Colin 89
Macintyre, Donald (Don) 262
MacKay, Andrew 249, 252
MacKenzie, Kelvin 140
Mactaggart, Fiona 257
McAndrew, Patrick 89
McCain, John 81, 90, and Republican
    nomination 95, 106, 177
McCann, Dr Gerry 29-30
McCann, Dr Kate 29-30
McCartney, Sir Paul 90, divorce 98
McDonnell, John xi, 12, 55, 58, 165, 177, 203,
    and Mace 207, People's Charter 228, 243,
    246
McDougall, Linda 89
McGee, Brian 187
McKenzie, Bob 247
McKinnon, Gary 164
McLennan, Gordon 84
McNally, Tom 87
McPherson, Alison vii, 113, 259-60
McPherson, Jade 259-60
McPherson, Ross 259-60
Machel, Graca 8, 34
Machover, Moshe 202
Madeleine (Sage Theatre, Gateshead) 218

Madeley, Richard *see* Richard and Judy
Maguire, Kevin 256
Mahon, Alice 238
Maitlis, Emily 153
Major, Sir John xii, 77, 222
Malloch Brown, Mark 190
Mandela, Nelson 1, 2, 5, 7, 9, 13, 16, 33, 34, 37, 108, Ian Walters' bust of 288,
Mandelson, Peter xii, 67, 99, 126, 174, 178, 179-80 and 180n, 209, 216, 219, and mammon 223, 226, and David Miliband 253 and 256, 259, Post Office 268
Manel, John 75
Manley, Georgina viii
Manning, Bradley 283
Mansfield, Michael 2, 248
Maria (New Wimbledon Theatre) 105
Mark (Charleston House gardener) 130
Marshall, Walter 74, and nuclear power 76, 152
Marshall-Andrews, Robert 195, 214
Martell, Yan 10
Martin, Diana (Di) 230, 231
Martin, Geoff 18
Martin, Mary (Lady) 103
Martin, Mary (actress) 103
Martin, Matthew 171
Martin, Michael (Speaker till 2009) 51, 60, 103, Damian Green case 191-4, 250, resignation 251, 261, 262
Martin, Nancy 171
Matthews, Sandy 262
Maude, Francis 11
Mayo, Marj 84
Medvedev, Dmitry 162, 168
Menezes, Jean Charles de 63
Meyer, Sir Christopher 75
Milburn, Alan 67, 131, 169
Miliband, David xi, 36, 48, 65, and 'rendition' 101, as successor to Brown 130-31, and Lisbon Treaty 140, 153, Brown succession 157-8, 161, and Russia 162-4 and 168, 221, 223, and Peter Mandelson 253 and 256, 259, 278, 280
Miliband, Edward (Ed) xi, 2, 21, 36, 46, 56, 132-3, 137-8, 140, 163, at 2008 Conference 169, 183, Energy Secretary 194, 223, 251, Brown leadership 252, TB supports 280
Miliband, Justine (Justine Thornton) 138
Miliband, Marion (Marion Kozak) xi, 21, 132, 137-8, 163, friendship with TB 223, 245, 280
Miliband, Ralph 132, 184, TB assessment of 280-1

Millar, Fiona 88
Miller, Professor 261
Miller, Jonathan 72
Miller, Sienna 165
Mills, John 47
Milne, Seamus 153
Minnelli 98
Minogue. Kylie 271
Mitchell, Austin 47
Mitchell, Ellie 57
Mitchell, Emma viii, 53, TB visits family 57, 91-2, 106, 240, 274, support to TB 290
Mitchell, George (Senator) 210
Mitchell, Heather 57
Mitchell, Jean 57
Mitchell, Simon 57
Mitchell, Stanley 57
Mitchell, Tony 57
Moberly, Patricia 178, 277
Monbiot, George 238
Montague, Sarah 211
Moran, Margaret 251, 252
More, Thomas 102
Morley, Elliot 249
Morgan, Piers 24, 99, 112
Morris family 171
Morris, Lucy 171
Morris, Norman 171
Mortimer, Jim 243
Moore, Michael 16, 23, 61, 84, 163
Morogo, Raul 148
Mosley, Max 156
Mosley, Oswald 107
Moses, Lord Justice (Alan) 100
Mugabe, President Robert 6
Mullin, Chris xi, 48, *Diaries* 223-4 and 226-7, and Diaries 251, MPs' expenses 251, and Murdoch empire 285
Murdoch, Rupert 140, 156, 284, and Leveson Inquiry 284-5
Murray, Andrew 220
Musharraf, President 89
Mussolini, 171

Naughtie, James 53, 106
Neave, Airey 91
Neeson, Liam 229
Neil, Andrew 27, 74
Nellist, Dave 230
Nestor, Frances x, xi, accepted for ordination 275
Nestor, Michael x
Nestor, Michael (Little Michael) x
Netanyahu, Benjamin 284

Nicholson, John 169
Nicolson, Jack 86
Niebuhr, Reinhold 8, 10
Nineham, Chris 163
Norman, Sam 291
Nunn, Sam 8
Nyree (of Virgin) 4

Obama, President Barack 28, presidential
    candidate 81-2 and 84, 89, 90, 95, 106,
    118, 136, and Israel 137, backed by
    Clinton 137, in London 157, financial
    bailout 170, 177, backed by Colin Powell
    179, 182-4 passim, 192, Afghanistan 200,
    inauguration 209, 231, 232, at G20 in
    London 237, and Texas 241, Israel/
    Palestine 284
Oborne, Peter 173
Oelwang, Jean 7, 37
O'Grady, Frances 18, 26, 27
Ollis, John 154
Ollis, Julie 154
Olmert, Ehud 69
O'Riordan, Manus 245
Orr, Judith 34
Oscar (guide dog) 272

Osborne, George 179-80
Owen, Tim 106, 229

Paddick, Brian 119
Page, Derek 255
Paine, Thomas 8, 120
Paisley, Ian 51, 131-2, 139
Palin, Michael 90
Palmer, Nick 100
Panitch, Leo 184
Park, Sir Keith 208
Parker, Nurse 201
Parris, Matthew 53, 77, 153
Parry, Maya 138
Partridge, Frances 215
Patten, Chris 15
Paul, Henri 114
Paxman, Jeremy 249
Pelly, Dr Michael 288
Perks, Robert 83
Peterkin, Sir Peter 64
Pettifer, Dr Jane 13, 195
Phillips, Melanie 11
Phillips, Morgan 171
Phillips, Trevor 96
Pietragnoli, Lazzaro 120
Pilger, John 61, 141, 262

Pilling, Sir Joe 93
Pinkney, Larry 182
Pinter, Sir Harold 141, 200
Poku, Dr Harry 287
Polar, Hernando de Soto 1
Pollock, Dr Allyson 264
Pond, Chris 83
Pope, Vicky 219
Powell, General Colin 179
Powell, Enoch 116, 255, 291
Powell, Jonathan 110
Prentis, Dave 59
Prescott, John 127, 219, Jack Jones's funeral
    244
Price, Adam 51
Price, Chile 266
Primarolo, Dawn 1, 36, 197
Prince, Rosa 177
Pritchard, Dr Blake 29, 166, 175, 188, 224
Prodi, Romano 120
Purchase, Ken 43
Purnell James 130-31, 198
Purves, Libby 53
Putin, Vladimir 11, 96

Quinn, Lucy vii

Ramsbotham, General Sir David 212
Ramsbotham, Lady 212
Rankin, Ian 179
Rantzen, Esther 251
Ratcliffe, Mary 273
Reagan, Carol 90
Reagan, President Ronald 102
Rebuck, Gail (Lady Gould) 88, 153
Redwood, John 15
Redgrave, Jemma 106, 229
Redgrave, Vanessa 229
Rees, John xi, 40, 42, 65, 68, Left Convention
    169, 195, 203, and SWP 217 and 265
Rees, Merlyn 92
Rees-Mogg, William 14
Regan, Bernard 165
Reid, John xii, 102, 190, 269
Rethinasamy, Menagai 276
Rice, Condoleezza 161
Richard and Judy (Richard Madeley and Judy
    Finnegan) 161, 192, 212, 217, 219, the
    'seat-case'292
Richards, Henry 289
Richards, Steve 70
Richardson, Natasha 229,
Ridley, Yvonne 71, 204, Gaza convoy 219
Rifkind, Sir Malcolm 51

Rimington, Dame Stella 24
Roberts, Cynthia 184-5, 186
Robertson, Geoffrey 63
Robeson, Paul 98
Robinson, Gene 151
Robinson, Geoffrey 88, TB meeting for 230
Robinson, Mary vii, 1, 2, 5, 7, 8
Robinson, Nick 139
Roddick, Anita 212
Rohde, Laura viii
Romney, Mitt 90
Ross, Jonathan 98
Rousseau, Jean-Jacques 8
Rowson, Martin 223
Rudd, Kevin 69, 178
Rumsfeld, Donald 73, US election 182
Rusbridger, Alan 262
Russell, Heidi 149
Rutherford, Margaret 59, 188

Sackur, Stephen 145
Saklatvala, Ceri 208
Salmond, Alex 48, 51, 110
Sarkozy, President Nicholas 112
Sanders, Bernard 183
Sanders, Glennys 238
Sanders, Larry 183
Saunders, Red 88
Scales, Prunella 70, 161
Scargill, Arthur 59, 227, 281, miners' strike 287
Schmidt, Helmut 32
Schwarzenegger, Arnold 251
Scott, Selina 86-7, 175, and Channel 5 News 239
Sergeant, John 247
Shah, Sanjiv 23
Shallice, Jane xi, 88, 90
Sharon (Earl's Court Festival) 272
Shawcross, William 73-4
Sheen, Maria 151
Sheridan, Tommy 43, 59
Shepherd, Alison 27
Shepherd, Richard 25
Sheridan, Colonel 91
Sheridan, Dinah 102
Short, Clare xii, 141, and Cabinet /Iraq war 203
Sidaway, Marlene 245
Sillitoe, Alan 70
Silverton, Kate xi, 18, 21, 236
Simpson, Alan xi, 46, 85, People's Charter 228, and Ian Gibson 253
Simpson, Derek 36, 59, 165, 245, 246

Sinclair, Angus 64, 193
Sissons, Peter 33
Skidelsky, Robert 130
Skinner, Dennis 26
Smith, Gayle 6
Smith, Jacqui 50, detention 136, 158, Terrorism Act 210, 221, 236, and Damian Green 240
Smith, John 70
Smith, Lyn 159
Smith, Rachel 199
Snow, Jon 138, 176, and Damian Green case 192, 219, 254
Snow, Tom 138
Soper, Donald 148
Southcott, Mary 129
Spicer, Sir Michael 25, 78
Stalin, Josef 96, Russian doll 287
Stansgate, Viscount (William Wedgwood Benn, TB's father) 34, 126
Starkey, David 80
Steel, David 38
Steele, Polly 184, video portraits 235
Stephenson, Paul 34, 238
Stephenson, Sir Paul (Metropolitan Commissioner) 285
Stewart, Rod 90
Stewart, Rory 75
Stourton, Edward 211
Stowe, Ken 76
Straw, Jack xii, 22, 47, 50, 51, and bugging 93, 95, 130, 157, 254, Liberty party 256
Strutt, Charles 263
Strutt, Jean 263
Swantee, Olaf 39

Tatchell, Peter 214
Taylor, Mark 270-71
Thatcher, Margaret xii, 15, 28, 39, 41, 62, 87, 102, 137, 1979 Election 247, TB assessment of 281, miners' strike 287, North Sea oil 287
Thomas, Dylan 165
Thomas, George 60
Thomson, Joy 272
Thomson, Mr 101
Thomson, Caroline 212
Thomson, George 212
Thompson, Emma 212
Thompson, Phil 116
Thornton, Andrew 274
Thynn, Alexander (Marquess of Bath) 293
Tolstoy, Nikolai 214
Tomlinson, Ian 238

Townsend, Peter 257, 267
Toynbee, Polly 153
Toynbee, Arnold 32
Trebell, Henry 161
Triesman, David 190-91
Trimble, David 132
Trusty, Phillip 233-4, released on parole 245
Tudor-Hart, Dr Julian 264
Tung, Mao Tse 222
Turnbull, Richard 40
Tutu, Archbishop Desmond vii, 1, 2, 5, 7, 8, 9, 13

Uddin, Pola 248
Updale, Eleanor 106

Vanson, Yvette 248
Vanunu, Mordechai 8
Vaz, Keith 37
Vidal, Gore 209

Waldegrave, William 15
Walden, Celia 99, *Telegraph* article 114
Wales, Sir Robin 98
Walker, Linda 171
Walker, Air Marshal Peter 171
Walters, Ian 185, bust of TB 288
Wark, Kirsty 107
Warner, Canon (St Paul's) 137
Watkins, Susan 85
Weatherill, Bernard (Jack) 60
Weatherill, Lady 60-61
Weatherhead, Leslie 225
Wedderburn, Bill 114
Weinstock, Arnold 76
Wells, Hannah 171
Wells, Mimi 171
Wells, Ray 171
West, Admiral Lord 66, 161
West, Sam 161, 178, 217
West, Timothy 161
Whelan, Charlie 246
Whittome, Tony xi, 239-40, *Letters to my Grandchildren* 249 and 258
Wilkinson, Emily 96
Williams, Marcia 171
Williams, Peter 83
Williams, Rowan (Archbishop of Canterbury) 96-7

Williams, Shirley 19, 242
Williams, Susan 190
Willsmer, Basil xi, 64, funeral 67-8, 162
Willsmer, Heather 68, 162
Wilson, Harold 31-2, 116, 150, ceramic figure of 286
Wilson, Mary 116
Wilson, Robin 116
Wilson, Merv 46
Winfrey, Oprah 7
Winstone, Joan Marigold 171, accident 199, 201, 231
Winstone, Mercedes 148
Winstone, Michael 148
Winstone, Miro 148
Winstone, Ruth viii, xi, 1, 9, 25, 39, 41, 42, 45, 46, 53, 66, 68, 70, 72, 73, 80, 83, 87, 89, 99, 105-6, 109, and TB's birthday 113, TB funeral plans 117, 121, 127, at Charleston House 130, 131, 135, 143, the 'seat-case' 144, Madrid Conference 148-9, 152, 155, 157, 165, TB visits Devon home 171, 179, plan for new book 181, 191, novel 193, 198, 201, 202, 208, and *Letters to my Grandchildren* 213, Channel 4 Awards 219, TB's driving 221, and Mandelson 223, 224, 227, TB's 84th birthday 230, 231, 'seat-case' development 241, 249, and *The Archers* 250, editing 258, 259, 272, TB operation 275-7, TB fall at home 288, and TB home care 289, 290
Winstone, Victor (HVF) 171, 231
Wolfgang, Walter 100, Labour Party bankruptcy 134, 141-2
Wood, Ellen 245
Woodley, Tony xii, 26, 46, 48, 59, 165, 245, 246
Woodward, Shaun 25, 47
Woolaway, Bruce 230
Woolaway, James 230
Wrack, Matt 98
Wright, Steve (Radio 2) 98

Yaqoob, Salma 12
Yates, John 285
Yeltsin, Boris 11, 96, Russian doll 287
Young, George 264

Zephaniah, Benjamin 36, 164, 248